The Gam

MORE SONGS THE WHALEMEN SANG

Illustration from the log of the Charles W. Morgan's first voyage, Log 143

The Gam

MORE SONGS THE WHALEMEN SANG

by Gale Huntington

LOOMIS HOUSE PRESS
CAMSCO MUSIC
2014

© 2014 Loomis House Press

CAMSCO Music
www.camscomusic.com

Loomis House Press
www.loomishousepress.com

ISBN 978-1-935243-96-0

Cover illustration: "The Gam," 1926 oil on canvas by Clifford W. Ashley, courtesy of the New Bedford Whaling Museum

Back cover author's photo courtesy of Larry Kaplan.

PREFACE

The publication of this volume of collected songs by E. Gale Huntington represents the second time Gale was wrong about not ever being able to publish his life's work. The first was when *Songs the Whalemen Sang* was republished by The Mystic Seaport Museum in 2012, proudly re-introducing a critically important yet under-recognized collection of songs sung by sailors and whalemen to an eager public of singers, collectors and fellow scholars.

While he never lived to see either volume appear together, those who knew Gale always had the sense that he lived his later years on Martha's Vineyard with the same urgent awareness of their importance to share as readers will find in these works today.

But *The Gam* meant a great deal more to Gale. It marked his own realization that he had matured as a meticulous collector and scholar, admittedly self-taught, and awkwardly proud of that fact. He refers to *The Gam* in this introduction, as "essentially a continuation — a sequel to *Songs the Whalemen Sang*." Yet the primary sources were different, as was the geographic reach of the songs themselves. To assemble *Songs the Whalemen Sang*, Gale drew largely from the single 1879 journal of Sam Mingo, a Vineyard native and blue water sailor who kept a "log" of songs he learned while at sea.

To prepare *The Gam*, however, Gale turned to multiple sailors' logs and journals, and also to sources from his and his wife Mildred Tilton's own families and from others in his own community. He had come to recognize the need to seek, better understand, and render the most accurate sources of these songs as well; so during the years that he spent writing this volume — and even after, while waiting to see it published — he had many substantive exchanges with individuals who in different settings devoted their time to history and musicology.

THE GAM

After settling permanently on the Vineyard in the 1930's, it was often said of Gale that the majority of his excursions off-island were trips to Providence, Sharon, New Bedford, Salem, and Cambridge, Massachusetts, where he spent hours of study for this book, "getting it right," bringing his catch back to the Vineyard on the ferry from Wood's Hole, and loving every minute of the work.

Elon (Gale) Huntington was born in 1902 in New York City, the son of a Navy surgeon whose career brought the family to many parts of the US before Gale left for Stetson University in 1921. His connection to Martha's Vineyard began through his family's summer travels, but after graduating college he returned to the Island where he soon met and married Mildred Tilton, whose seagoing family was regarded on the Vineyard as great singers of the old songs.

Gale sang and performed locally too, and while he lived on the Island for sixty-seven years, he refused to refer to himself as a native Islander. Nonetheless, he grew naturally into a role as a respected historian, collector, researcher, and writer. I doubt many cared about what training he had then. He was the person who knew where songs came from and could also sing them the way neighbors remembered them.

So here in Gale's final work is a collection of over 200 songs (plus a couple of fiddle tunes), that have been to sea, traveled around the world, and found their way to the hands of a sailor, fisherman, teacher, scalloper, quahogger, editor, author, and self-made scholar who wished nothing more than to share his love of music with others. This volume also carries forward a tradition to which Gale truly still had connections, through the whale men and merchant seamen he saw daily on an island that once saw more maritime traffic pass its shores than any place else on earth.

Larry Kaplan
Essex, Connecticut
February 25, 2014

ACKNOWLEDGEMENT

This acknowledgement is difficult because so many individuals have helped me in the preparation of the book. Without exception those in the libraries and museums where Mil and I worked were not only helpful, but interested. In particular I want to thank Edouard A. Stackpole; Richard C. Kugler, Kenneth R. Martin, and Stuart Frank; Raya Elevich and Jennine Ayotte were both very helpful in locating melodies that were needed for the songs. There are many others whose help and encouragement made this work possible.

But more than any, my wife, Mildred Tilton Huntington is responsible for this book. Mil helped me in the search for songs, in transcribing the songs and in putting the bibliography together. I wanted to call this *The Gam*, by Mil and Gale Huntington. That she would not let me do. But at least I can say here that the book is quite as much hers as it is mine.

INTRODUCTION

This book is essentially a continuation — a sequel — to *Songs the Whalemen Sang*. The songs here, most of them, are from journals kept by whalemen on those so long voyages. I say most, for some are from whalemen's logbooks, some are directly from whalemen, themselves, and a few are from books contemporary with the great days of whaling, the period between about 1830 and 1860.

The journals are personal records kept by any member of the whaleship, and some are very interesting. Pamela Miller in *The Whale is Ours* has given us some beautiful examples of creative writing from the journals. The logbooks, on the other hand, are almost universally dull except perhaps for geographers, ethnographers, and meteorologists. The logs give a day-to-day record of the voyage — wind, weather, position of the vessel, whales sighted, whales killed and whales lost, vessels sighted, spoken, or gammed, and usually not much else. The log was usually kept by the first mate or, if he could get out of it for one reason or another, by one of the other mates.

The songs in the journals, with almost no exceptions, do not include the melodies to which they were sung. That could be because most of the singers were musically illiterate. In a few instances the name of the melody to which the song was sung is given and where the melody could be found it is used.

But because a song without a melody is really not a song at all, melodies have been provided for almost all of the songs in the book. Where it could be found, the melody, or a melody, to which the song was originally sung, has been used. Where the original melody could not be found a melody that seemed to fit and is more or less contemporary with the period of the voyage has been used. For quite a few songs, melodies have been supplied. We hope that is not a mistake, it was done because a song should be sung. In all cases, the source of the melody is noted.

THE GAM

As in *Songs the Whalemen Sang*, no punctuation has been used. That is because in the journals almost no punctuation is used and where it is found it usually does not help. In some cases spelling and capitalization have been improved slightly, but is hoped not enough to hurt.

Songs were sung in fo'c'sle, cabin, and in the steerage, almost always entirely unaccompanied; however, sometimes a fiddler would play the melody with the singer, but not too loudly, for the words of the song were the important thing. The fiddle was the seagoing instrument of the Yankee whalers. In later years when Portuguese seamen began to play such an important part in Yankee whaling, the Portuguese viola began to be heard. The viola is slightly smaller than the guitar and the bass E string is missing. The three upper strings are multiple like those of a mandolin. It is a very sweet-toned instrument. Undoubtedly, Portuguese songs were sung but we have never found any in the few Portuguese journals and logbooks that we have studied. The concertina, so popular with British seamen, seems seldom to have gone on Yankee whalers.

Song was important on those very long voyages — often three and four years. Often there would be weeks and even months when no whales were sighted and when most of the men would have little work to do. Of course there were always men aloft in the daylight hours, looking and hoping for whales, and there was always a man at the wheel and a mate on duty. But those must have been times of awful boredom for the rest of the crew. On most whalers there were few or almost no books. The decks could be scrubbed only so often and that also went for painting the vessel. The cook and the steward and the cooper had work to do, but for the rest of the men it was not so. What did they do? They sang and they told stories and they did scrimshaw. Also, unfortunately, there were a good many fights.

When I was a boy growing up summers on Martha's Vineyard — later we became year-round residents — there were many retired whalemen on the Island and even a few still active ones. I used to love to listen to their stories and ask questions about whaling. But it was only after I came to know my future wife's grandfather, Welcome Tilton, and her great uncles, Bill and Zeb Tilton, that I began to learn and sing some of the old songs. Welcome had gone whaling for one voyage when he was thirteen years old, not as a cabin boy but as a foremasthand. When he got home four years later he said that he was never going whaling again, it wasn't exciting enough.

INTRODUCTION

By that he must have meant that being cooped up on a whaler with thirty-five or thirty-six other men was not his idea of a happy life. After that the whaleman went on the big coasting schooners that carried coal, lumber, ice, and other cargoes all up and down the coast. All those years on the water he learned and sang songs. When he was about thirty-three years old he married Hattie Butler of Nomansland and went codfishing from there, and later pound fishing on the north shore of the Vineyard. I learned quite a few of his songs and should have learned a lot more, but I was not collecting songs then, but only learning those that I liked to sing.

I learned even fewer of Bill Tilton's enormous repertory of songs. Bill had gone whaling three or four voyages and then went in deepwater merchant vessels both British and American. Because of his tremendous voice it wasn't long before he was a chanteyman. When he left deepwater he became a fisherman, first on Nomansland and then from Menemsha. Once I asked him to sing me a chantey. "I wull not," he said. "Why not?" I asked him. "Because they ain't songs," he told me. I did learn "Blow The Man Down" from Bill but he claimed that wasn't really a chantey.

Zeb had never gone whaling but he sang and I learned a few of his songs. He was always a coaster and I made a few trips with him on his beautiful little schooner, the *Alice S. Wentworth*. There were four more of the Tilton brothers, George Fred, Willard, Edward, and John R. They all sang. George Fred was the only Tilton who had master's papers for deepwater ships. He sang, but as he couldn't carry a tune his singing was often more than slightly painful. Most of his whaling was for bowheads in the Arctic. Willard was a whaleman but I never learned any of his songs. John R. was a great singer but I never learned any of his songs. I did learn a few of Edward's songs. His repertory consisted entirely of gospel songs and some are in this book. Some of the songs of the singing Tilton will be found in "Folksongs From Martha's Vineyard," No. VIII of *Northeast Folklore*.

Such, in addition to quite a few years as a commercial fisherman, was my background in whaling songs, songs the whalemen sang, and nautical lore. Then in 1954 something happened that started Mil and me on a long, long search. I was then teaching history at Tisbury High School in Vineyard Haven. I always tried to bring as much local history as possible into my teaching and that time it was Vineyard whaling from Edgartown and Holmes Hole, which was the old name for Vineyard Haven, and the class was interested. One of my pupils, Joni Merry, said, "Mr. Huntington, my father found a whaleman's logbook in the dump. Would you like me to bring it to class?" I said that I most certainly would, and the next day she did.

Actually, it was not a logbook but a journal kept by Sam Mingo on a voyage of the bark *Andrew Hicks* begun in 1879. Sam Mingo was an Indian from Christiantown, a small village on the north shore of the Vineyard. Most Indian boys from the Vineyard had made at least one voyage whaling, and some got pretty well up the ladder of command. Sam Mingo was fourth mate that voyage. The journal Joni Merry let me take home was interesting in spots but in the back pages of the book were some twenty-five songs and more fragments of songs. Those songs fascinated me, for they showed the same catholicity of taste as did the songs that I had learned from Welcome and Bill Tilton. Before I took the journal back to school, I copied all of the songs, and it was a good thing that I did for almost certainly the book has been lost. This is what happened. Joni's father gave the book to Addie Smalley, who was Sam Mingo's daughter and who had married another Indian whaleman, Amos Smalley, of Gay Head. Amos and Addie had no children, and after their death everything in the house, except the furniture, was taken to the Gay Head dump. If by some miracle the journal did survive I have no idea where it is.

It was that lost journal, then, that sparked Mil's and my long search. I thought that perhaps if Sam Mingo had put songs that he liked in the back of his book perhaps other whalemen had done the same thing and indeed they had. Or some of them had, for songs are found perhaps in only some of the books.

Over the years Mil and I have searched the logbooks and journals in all the important repositories: the Nicholson collection in the Providence Public Library, and collections in all of the following: the Kendall Whaling Museum in Sharon, Massachusetts, the Peter Folger Museum of the Nantucket Historical Association, the Houghton Library of Harvard University, The Whaling Museum of the Old Dartmouth Historical Society, in New Bedford, The New Bedford Free Public Library, the G.W. Blunt White Library at Mystic Seaport, the Peabody Museum in Salem, The Essex Institute in Salem, the Dukes County Historical Society in Edgartown.

There are many whalemen's books in private collections and in small historical societies, but Mil and I have looked through most of the major

INTRODUCTION

collections and have undoubtedly seen a good percentage of all the logbooks and journals extant.

We found over the years of our search that the songs sung by the whalemen were almost universally like those of the singing Tiltons and those found in Sam Mingo's journal; they most certainly did not consist only of songs of whales and the sea. The whalemen sang everything that was sung at home about the hearth and beside the pump organ in the parlor. Remember that singing a hundred or two hundred years ago without radio, television, record players, or tape cassettes, was very much more important than it is today. The songs recorded in the journals seem mostly to be those learned from other singers. Perhaps some of those songs were exchanged during gams.

The more common songs learned in childhood and which everyone knew, like "Barbara Allen" and "Mr. Frog Did A-Wooing Go," were almost surely sung but did not need to be recorded. But in any case, the variety of the recorded songs is striking. Stephen Foster songs, minstrel show songs, Scottish and Irish ballads, and some songs that the whalemen themselves had written.

Interestingly, only two Child Ballads were found for this book, "The Suffolk Miracle" and "Our Goodman," and only one, "The Shepherd's Daughter" from *Songs the Whalemen Sang*. That would seem to bear out Dr. Edward Ives' suggestion about Child Ballads in the male tradition, which is that men were continually learning new songs to update and enlarge their repertory while women, who seldom sang in public, were the ones who kept the older traditional songs alive.

However, one category of songs is missing in this book — that is the bawdy songs. Mil and I never found a complete bawdy song in any of those logbooks and journals that we searched. We did find fragments of such and then the page or pages would have been torn out or cut out with a knife. Who did that? Was it the whaleman's wife after the book was brought home, or was it another singer who wanted the song but couldn't be bothered to copy the words? But the bawdy songs were sung. William Histed who made a voyage in the ship *Cortes* out of New Bedford in 1854 compiled a big manuscript book of songs during the voyage. That book is now in the New Bedford Free Public Library. Histed left us a page-numbered index of all the songs in the book so we know exactly which ones are missing and they are all bawdy.

One interesting aspect of Mil's and my search is that there was a tremendous continuity in the musical tradition of the whalemen. From the earliest songs found, those in the sloop *Nellie* journal of 1769, to the songs in one of the latest, that of the bark *Andrew Hicks* journal of 1879, the variety of the songs is almost identical. Perhaps a corollary to that is the fact that over a period of more than a century Yankee whaling itself changed very little. The bomb gun was introduced in mid-nineteenth century but its use was very limited. Until the very end of Yankee whaling, whales were mostly all killed with a lance. There were changes but they were amazingly few.

Also, and this too is amazing, except for the steam whalers out of San Francisco, which fished for bowheads in the Arctic, sail was the sole motive power. The last whaler left New Bedford in 1925 and she was under sail. And as a boy in the early years of this century I can well remember the whaling barks and schooners at anchor in New Bedford's Acushnet River, and tied up at the wharves.

    Gale Huntington
    Chilmark, Massachusetts

CONTENTS

PREFACE	v
ACKNOWLEDGEMENT	vii
INTRODUCTION	ix
LIST OF ILLUSTRATIONS	xxi
SONGS OF WHALES AND WHALING	1
A Brand Fire New Whaling Song Right from the Pacific Ocean	2
A Whaling Song	15
Brave Boys (The Greenland Whale)	18
Diego's Bold Shores	20
The Sperm Whale Song (The Wounded Whale)	21
The Sperm Whaling Song (Second Version)	23
Blow Ye Winds	24
Blow Ye Winds (Second Version)	25
Captain Bunker	27
Sweet America	28
Whaler's Song	30
Soon Thy Bark Must Leave Our Harbor	31
Song of the Nantucket Mariner	32
A Song of Whaling	33
A Stove Boat	36
Come All That Sail From Edgartown	40
The Tin Swankey Pot	43
Heave Away	44
There She Blows	45
The Nassau Homeward Bound	47
The Lass of Maui	48
The Pretty Maid of Mohe (Second Version)	51
Rolling Down To Old Maui	53

THE GAM

Calm	55
A Hardtack and A Half	56
The Whaling Voyage	58
Song of the Ship Vineyard	62
Barque *Ohio* Outward Bound 1850	64
Bark *Roscius* Outward Bound (Second Version)	65
Song to Captain S.D. Oliver	67
Outward Bound	69
The Old Oaken Bucket	71
The Wonderful Whalers	72
The Sea Girt Isle	75
A Voyage On New Holland	76

SONGS OF THE SEA AND SHIPS — 87

Shipwreck Near Gay Head, January 14, 1782	87
The Loss of the Albion	91
A New Song Maide	94
The Wreck of the City of Columbus I	96
The Wreck of the City of Columbus II (The Ill-Fated Steamer)	97
The Wreck of the City of Columbus III (The City of Columbus)	98
Shipwreck on Long Island Shore	101
The Ocean King	103
Nauticle Filosophy (Barney Buntline)	105
Nautical Philosophy (Second Version)	106
The Boatswain's Call (Unmooring....)	108
The Sailor	110
Ben Backstay's Warning	111
Bering Sea	113
Ships In the Ocean	115
Up Anchor For Home Boys	117
Bury the Dead	118
The White Squall	120
The Sailor's Grave	121
The Sailor's Grave (Second Version)	122
The Bold Privateer	123
The Sailor's Farewell	125
The Deep Deep Sea	126
The Mariner's Grave	127

CONTENTS

The Drownded Miner	128
Pity the Poor Seaman	131
Serenade Song or Hurrah For the Rover and His Beautiful Lass	132
The Buccaneer's Bride	133
Second Version	134
Rolling Home	134
Sailing Home from England (Second Version)	135
The Pirate Lover	136
The Pirate of the Isle	138
Ned Bolton	139
Under Way	142
Spanish Ladies	144
A Floating Home	146
Tarpaulin Jacket	148
The Mariner's Life	150
Marm Haucket's Garden (The Nantucket Skipper)	151
William Taylor	153
William Taylor (Second Version)	155
Bold William Taylor (Third Version)	156
Caroline and Young Sailor Bold	159
A Song Concerning Love (The Captain Calls All Hands)	162
The Chile Girls	163
Black-Eyed Susan	165
Second version	167
Pretty Polly (The Tarry Trousers)	168
The Sailor's Return (Green Beds)	170
Oh Captain, Captain Tell Me True (The Sailor Boy)	172
My Willie's on the Dark Blue Sea	173
The Female Cabin Boy	174
The Female Sailor	176
Lady Franklin's Lament for her Husband	178
The Flying Dutchman	180
Sweet William (William and Nancy)	182
Constant Lovers (The Silk Merchant's Daughter)	184
TRADITIONAL SONGS AND BALLADS	**191**
A Song of Love (High Germany)	192
Ten Thousand Miles Away	194

THE GAM

The Drunken Fool (Our Goodman)	195
The Suffolk Miracle	198
Willie Brennan (Brennan on the Moor)	202
Uncle Sam and Johnny Bull	205
We Met 'Twas in a Crowd	207
The Weaver	210
Little Brown Jug	212
The Raging Canal	214
New Song	216
Ellen the Fair	218
The Lily of the West	219
On the Green Mossy Banks of the Lea	221
Second Version: No Title	222
Never Change the Old Love for the New	224
The Highwayman	225
Cruiskeen Lawn	227
Across The Fields of Barley (Bill Grimes)	228
The Butcher Boy	230
The Nightingale	233
An Old Song	235
Lord Lovel	236
The Maid of Erin	238
The Winds That Blew 'Cross the Wild Moor (Mary on the Wild Moor)	239
A Fisherman's Girl	241
Poor Little Joe	243
The Flower Girl	244
The Stepmother	246
Norah O'Neal	248
The Old Bog Hole	249
The Lament of the Irish Emigrant	250
Kathleen Mavourneen	252
Little Nell of Narragansett Bay	253
Golden Slippers	255
The Eastbound Train	256
A Lady's Answer	258
The Letter Edged In Black	260
Highland Mary	262
Bonnie Annie Laurie	263
Rob Roy McGregor-O	264

CONTENTS

My Highland Home	265
Jessie the Flower of Dunblane	266
Bruce's Address to His Army	268
POPULAR SONGS OF OR NEAR THE PERIOD OF THE VOYAGE	**271**
Ben Bolt — The Answer to Ben Bolt	272
The Grave of Ben Bolt	273
Parody on Ben Bolt	274
Jingle Bells	276
Second Version: Dashing Through the Snow	277
The Lone Starry Flower	278
The Rose That All are Praising	279
My Love	280
Maggy by my Side	282
Maggie by my Side (Second Version)	283
Why Art Thou Not Here	284
Sweet Nellie Brown	285
Wind of the Winter's Night	286
Nellie	287
All's Well	288
Home Again	289
Her Bright Smile Haunts Me Still	290
Lily Dale	291
Long Long Ago	293
Do They Miss Me At Home	294
Meet Me by Moonlight	296
When the Roses Were in Bloom	297
The Watcher	299
Annie of the Vale	300
Gentle Annie	301
Ella Rhee	302
Darling Nellie Gray	303
Good Old Jeff	305
The Belle of Baltimore	306
The Vacant Chair	308
The Belle of the Mohawk Vale	309
Columbia the Gem of the Ocean	310
Lines to Delia	312

MISCELLANEOUS SONGS — 315

- A Psalm of Life — 315
- Free Thinkers Reasons for Refusing to Preach — 317
- The Virgin Nineteen Years Old — 318
- Woman's Rights I — 320
- Woman's Rights II — 321
- A Song for a Wedding — 323
- Wedlock — 325
- The Lily of Lake Champlain — 328
- Song of Old — 330
- The Speaking Flower — 333
- Murphy Delany — 334
- Chicago — 336
- I'll Taste No More the Poisonous Cup — 338
- Water Lue — 340
- The Noble Ship *Catalpa* — 341
- Drinking Gin — 343
- The Virtuous Wife: A New Song — 345

GOSPEL SONGS AND SONGS WITH A RELIGIOUS FLAVOR — 353

- The Cleansing Fountain — 354
- The Mariner's Hymn — 355
- Sabbath Morning Nov. 13th 1852 — 356
- Revive Us Again — 357
- Hallelujah I'm a Bum — 358
- Men Are Like Ships — 359
- When the Roll is Called up Yonder — 360
- Work for Jesus — 361
- Will You Be Found Among the Wheat — 362
- A Sinner Saved — 363

TWO FIDDLE TUNES — 367

- Piscataquag and The Edinburgh — 367

GLOSSARY — 369

REPOSITORIES — 382

BIBLIOGRAPHY — 386

INDEX OF SONG TITLES — 401

LIST OF ILLUSTRATIONS

Illustration from the log of the Charles W. Morgan's
first voyage, Log 143; © Mystic Seaport, G. W. Blunt White Library   ii

Photograph of wharf scene with four whaleships, including
Helen Mar of New Bedford, and two Fish Markets;
© Mystic Seaport, #1973.899.112   xxiv

Albumen print; starboard view of whaling vessel
Charles W. Morgan; © Mystic Seaport, #1956.1633   86

Platinum print photograph of coopers at Merrill's Wharf,
New Bedford; © Mystic Seaport, #1973.899.272   190

Captain and Mrs. James A.M. Earle and son Jamie on deck
of *Charles W. Morgan;* © Mystic Seaport, #1973.899.231   270

"Abandonment of the Whalers in The Arctic Ocean September 1871"
lithograph by J.H. Bufford; publisher Benjamin Russell;
© Mystic Seaport, #1942.3   314

"Whale-oil Pete" Photograph of a man who is most likely a crew member
of the *Charles W. Morgan;* © Mystic Seaport, #2009.22.84   352

Advertising booklet, circa 1869; © Mystic Seaport, #1970.240.85   366

THE GAM:
MORE SONGS THE WHALEMEN SANG

Photograph of wharf scene with four whaleships, including *Helen Mar* of New Bedford, and two Fish Markets

Songs of Whales and Whaling

'Twas a love of adventure a longing for gold
And a hardened desire to roam
Tempted me far o'er the watery world
Far away from my kindred and home
                            (Diego's Bold Shores)

THERE'S NO doubt that excitement, wanderlust and the hope of a rich financial reward were important enticements to induce Yankee lads to join the whaling fleet. Not that any great enticements were needed; Whaling, for over two centuries, was one of the greatest industries New England boasted, and going out whaling was an accepted rite of passage for many of the young men. This area produced some of the finest seamen and some of the finest ships in the world, and pride of seamanship and love of the sea helped convince many to undertake the long voyages — often of four years or more — that were required to reach the north Pacific whaling grounds, fill their holds with oil, and return.

Danger, privation, loneliness and boredom were the counterpoises to the glamour of whaling, and the whalemen's songs told of all the aspects of this unique life that is no more. Here are some — I wish there were more, but many have been lost.

THE GAM

A BRAND FIRE NEW WHALING SONG
RIGHT FROM THE PACIFIC OCEAN

But where it lies why blast my eyes
You've often heard I'll pledge my word
Of what they call Japan boys
I'll let them tell who can boys
I've been that way but still can say
I've only formed the notion
Japan is found somewhere around
The North Pacific ocean

But never mind 'twas on the wind
In almost unknown seas lads
We stood which blew if logs were true
A four or five-knot breeze lads
Our mast heads manned and every hand
In genuine train for whaling
While for a bit we feasted it
On cold salt junk regaling

When from the main was heard the strain
With joy to whalemen fraught sirs
Sung out as loud as common cloud
Would thunder there's white water
And quick as thought the sound is caught
On decks springs up the captain
And where away is heard to say
While silence all are wrapt in

SONGS OF WHALES AND WHALING

Upon our lee two points or three
Abaft our larboard beam sir
Cried he aloft in voice so soft
You'd think 'twas penguin's scream sir
And how far off in voice so rough
Is what you've had your eyes on
The captain cries the man replies
Quite sir on the horizon

You worsted head the captain said
Up helm hard up you jackass
Flames take it here you steward clear
Sail sail and bring my spy-glass
I'll up and see what it may be
While you the yards may square in
He tells the mate with joy elate
The noise to have a share in

Now forward there jump up and square
The yards the mate is bawling
My men men I wonder when
You'll answer to my calling
We up and haul meantime they bawl
Aloft there keep her steady
And down below again we go
To be for lowering ready

Across the tide we gaily glide
A fine breeze on our quarter
We're not deceived for now relieved
Aloft sings out white water
And hark the strain from fore and main
Is heard of there she breaches
Aloft some run to see the fun
Some stay to hear the speeches

THE GAM

Now there they blow and there they go
And there she blows they're bawling
Get ready boats in alto notes
Meantime the mate is calling
There blackskins it lop tails it
And Kippler humps they bellow
A landsman there would surely swear
That half the crew was mellow

And there go flukes with eager looks
We mark the way they head sir
We've neared them half and one would laugh
To hear the odd things said sir
Some dreamed last night and dreamed aright
Of whales and blood and corses
Old bungs with glee declares that he
Dreamed too about truck horses

And round the boats you'll hear the notes
Of all the mainhatch gentry
And old nick n'er was busier
When typhoons are most plenty
Their craft they view their tubs they slew
'Twould set the whales a-quaking
The half to know of what a row
The boatsteerers are making

And lo again the whales are seen
Port helm the captain sings out
Port helm all cry till the reply
Port helm the helmsman sings out
How lead you now he answers how
And there is bid to keep her
And not to stray to flames away
Like some old bothering sleeper

SONGS OF WHALES AND WHALING

But fair and soft he's home aloft
Who'll give it out in style o
Why captain see that whale can be
Scarce off the ship a mile o
See there she blows and there she goes
Ahead too like vexation
The captain says and pray where is
This running botheration

Why here sir here why can't you see
Just on the larboard bow sir
Why that one is the captain says
A bothering little cow sir
But look out there these soldiers are
Much better worth our taking
By jove I see their humps he says
They're scarce a ripple making

That's right old sogs lie lie like logs
I'm thinking you'll not far get
Ah blow it out I'll change that spout
To blood as thick as tar yet
Thus threatens he till bid to see
All things got clear for lowering
And then the call of mainsail haul
Snug up he gives out roaring

All hands on deck now for God's sake
Move briskly men if ever
The whales in sight are slow as night
A better chance ye'd never
Stand by once more brace up the fore
And mizzen yards and luff there
Well well I say belay belay
You're braced up sharp enough there

THE GAM

Your cranes all swung aye aye each tongue
On board the ship replying
Then lower all each davit fall
Through glowing hands is plying
Let go all gone haul up down down
Out oars and spring together
Give us fair play and we'll today
At least one soldier weather

Four boats our pride together glide
Along the sunny main sir
Where'er they roam the sparkling foam
Bedecks the watery plain sir
In generous strife like things of life
They're bounding o'er the billows
And beauty bright would own the sight
Worth all her flowers and willows

And new the power of every ear
Is felt more swift propelling
Each gallant boat and see the spout
Is just beyond them swelling
The sparkling spray points out the way
The humps gleam o'er the ocean
While every view new nerves each crew
And gives each boat new motion

Pull men for lo see there they blow
They're going slow as night too
Pull pull you dogs they lie like logs
Praise be they're headed right too
Then each who steers his crew off cheer
While with judicious glance sir
Each marks his way upon his prey
To unperceived advance sir

SONGS OF WHALES AND WHALING

The chance is ours the mate now roars
Spring spring nor have it said men
That we could miss a chance like this
To take them head and head men
There's that old sog lies like a log
Spring spring and show your mettle
Strain every oar Let's strike before
He'll gally mill or settle

And so it is the chance is his
The others peak their oars now
From his strained eyes the lightning flies
And like a lion he roars now
Pull pull my lads why don't you pull
For God's sake pull away men
Hell's blazes pull but three strokes more
And we have won the day men

Stand up there forward pull the rest
Hold water give it to her
Stern all stern all God damn it heave
Your other iron through her
We're fast we're fast stern all give way
Here let me come ahead men
There peak your oars wet line wet line
Why bloody zounds you're dead men

The monster struck with fin and fluke
High high o'er their heads sends flying
The foaming brine while out the line
Yet slack springs stop defying
A turn is caught and now the boat
With force resistless sped sir
Ever humming while each flake drawn out
Spins round the loggerhead sir

THE GAM

But still in vain he cleaves the main
In vain the ocean lashes
Still in his wake his struggles make
Onward impetuous dashes
His fearless foe prepared to throw
The lance and quench its gleaming
In the warm tides that from his side
In crimson currents streaming

Next he rounds to and makes as though
Both hope and life had failed him
But no that spout comes roaring out
Clear as though nothing ailed him
And more observe with graceful curve
He now from out the ocean
Rounds his huge length renews his strength
And with majestic motion

High o'er their heads his huge flukes spreads
And though in blood now reeking
Down headlong goes from his fierce foes
In flight a refuge seeking
Deep neath the waves where pearly caves
Resplendent as the morn sir
With echoes ring his mermaids sing
And Triton winds his horn sir

For aid for aid a sign is made
Hands wave and hats are shaking
For now their spoil is coil on coil
Their line like lightning taking
Vain all their force to check his course
Deep deep and deeper sounding
Til scarce can float that joyous boat
Late o'er the billows bounding

SONGS OF WHALES AND WHALING

Nor vainly made that sign for aid
One boat their danger heeding
Across the deep the rowers sweep
And every sail is speeding
And now longside is seen to glide
And now her line to heave them
And it they take while their last flake
Is menacing to leave them

Their trusty line forced to resign
The second's boat has taken
Her line in turn begins to burn
Though seen their hopes awaken
For lighter now she heaves her bow
From out the waves around her
And less the strain that to the main
As if fast anchored bound her

He's gone his length he's spent his strength
He'll soon be up to spout men
Then cheerily your energy
In unison lay out men
Haul one haul all together haul
See see he's giving back line
Stick overboard now chance afford
Of getting foul your slack line

The boat moves slow for far below
Where deep sea lead ne'er sounded
Though immense that line tense
With its own weight is rounded
Untired they toil till coil on coil
Their own line all on board sir
The first is to its own boat's crew
The crew made fast restored sir

THE GAM

With joy again they heave the main
As now with rapid motion
Their unseen prey pursues his way
Beneath the face of ocean
And hauling still their practiced skill
Soon marks the course he's steering
And from the line detects each sign
He gives of reappearing

Till from the deep with mighty leap
High and high he breaches
So strongly sped his scarred grey head
High as the topmast reaches
And like a rock with mighty shock
From mountain top descending
Loud thunders he upon the sea
Ocean with ether blending

And hark once more that lengthened roar
From out his spout hole gushing
His breath long spent now finds a vent
Like steam from boiler rushing
And see his blood the azure flood
Again with crimson dyeing
While on the wave as if he'd brave
His foe he now is lying

His struggles cease but short the peace
That to him now is given
For see ahead like arrow sped
A boat toward him is driven
His die is cast she too is fast
Two more harpoons now gore him
And following fast that last harpoon
The lance is gleaming o'er him

SONGS OF WHALES AND WHALING

No feeble force directs its course
No careless aim is taken
The fatal shaft sinks to its haft
And his vast frame is shaken
Again he cleaves the the foaming waves
Again the billow lashes
But short his flight for now in fight
Fierce on his foe he dashes

Hard on he drives pull for your lives
And o'er the billows leaping
The boat swift sped just clears his head
As on resistless sweeping
With flukes well plied the foaming tide
He heaves in wild commotion
While far around the blows resound
And roars the troubled ocean

Writhing with pain he mills again
And now the turmoil ended
Prone on his back the mad attack
Renews with jaws extended
His tusks he shows two horrid rows
Like harrow's teeth projecting
Once brought to bear no chance was there
Of that light boat protecting

So wide the space that one might place
Between those jaws extended
Boat oars and men scarce even then
Were the whole space demanded
A moving cave a living grave
Terrific yawns to seize them
Nor skill nor strength a half boat's length
From that dread danger frees them

THE GAM

Unequal fight his matchless might
Unwielding naught avails him
Against his foes in combat close
And the keen lance assails him
And now his blood a purple flood
From out his spout hole gushes
And far and wide the foaming tide
Encrimsoned round him blushes

A savage sight though with delight
And boisterous shoutings greeted
And now close on him passive grown
Both boats with thrusts repeated
Unsated yet more fiercely set
Deep in his heart their lances
While shivering he upon the sea
Scarce his own length advances

The combat's o'er for see the gore
A torrent each breath doubles
Fresh from his heart with fitful start
From out his spout hole bubbles
A crimson flood a sea of blood
Unmingled frothy reeking
Bathes his vast sides as on he glides
Some spot of refuge seeking

To end his woes for now the throes
Of death his frame are shaking
And mad with pain he scours the plain
His dying circle taking
His rapid way the blood stained spray
In cloudless sunshine gleaming
Marks far and wide high o'er the tide
A crimson radiance streaming

SONGS OF WHALES AND WHALING

One boat alone within that zone
Of blood impetuous dashes
Half hid her head as o'er it spread
The sundered billow splashes
While by her sides the foaming tides
Above her gunwales curling
Rush to her wake convolve and break
In countless eddies whirling

With giant force his spiral course
In lessening circles winding
Like serpent's folds their prey still holds
From death no refuge finding
Till spent at length with his last strength
From out the wave he breaches
And falls fin out while many a shout
From out the billow reaches

With deafening din as falls that fin
And death that jaw relaxes
The glad huzza a wild hurrah
More loud and louder waxes
Dead dead they cry as to the eye
The lance applied discloses
Of life no spark the unerring mark
That he in death reposes

O'er his vast bulk as o'er a hulk
Upon the waves extended
The billows play and fling their spray
With oozing blood still blended
The black flag flies the ship decries
From far the well known sign sir
And toward their prey fast ploughs her way
Across the foaming brine sir

THE GAM

And soon she lies longside her prize
With headyards back while gliding
Fast down its tall mast
The topsail fast is sliding
The headline's thrown the buoy has shown
Its place and round the small sir
The ponderous chain clanks till its strain
Clenches securing all sir

If old George Fox knew half the knocks
We get in getting oil sirs
The scanty fare the sleepless care
The danger and the toil sirs
And knew too what his friends have got
To be where all are freemen
I'm thinking he would start to see
A Quaker cheat a seaman

A foremast hand 1831

This long whaling ballad was published in New Bedford in 1831 in a small paperbound booklet, and the authorship is credited to "a foremast hand." There is the information that the melody is "Maggy Lauder," and that is what we have here.

In *Studies In Folk-Song and Popular Poetry*, Alfred M. Williams devotes almost four pages to a discussion of the song. He notes particularly the power of the song, and thought that as poetry it was as good or better than anything that had been published in this country up to that time. We wonder how many would agree with that opinion.

The whole story of sperm whaling is here. The excitement when white water was seen, meaning breaching whales, the orders to get the boats ready for launching. Then the approach to the whales, the harpooning and the long "Nantucket sleigh ride" until the whale decided to dive. Then the near loss of the whale when the line in the first mate's boat was gone in that long dive almost to the last flake in the tub. But the second mate bends on his line in the very nick of time. And then the kill. That is a bloody and brutal business surely, but powerful.

"Maggy Lauder" gets a little tiresome after 20 or 25 stanzas. But remember, in folksong, melody was the vehicle.

SONGS OF WHALES AND WHALING

A WHALING SONG

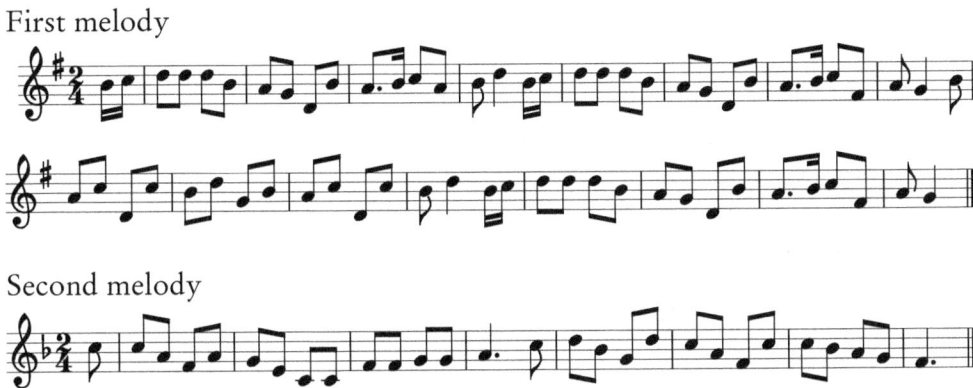

When spring returns with western gales
And gentle breezes sweep
The ruffling seas, we spread our sails
To plough the wat'ry deep.

For killing northern whales prepared
Our nimble boats on board,
Our craft with rum, our chief regard,
And good provisions stored

We view the monsters of the deep
Grest whales in numerous swarms
And creatures there that play and leap
Of strange unusual forms

Cape Cod our dearest native land
We leave astern and lose
Its sinking cliffs and lessening sands
While Zephyr gently blows

Bold hardy men with blooming age
Our sandy shores produce
With monstrous fish they dare engage
And dangerous callings choose

THE GAM

Now towards the early dawning east
We speed our course away
With eager minds and joyful hearts
To meet the rising day

Then as we turn our wandering eyes
We view one constant show
Above around the circling skies
The rolling seas below

When eastward clear of Newfoundland
We stem the frozen pole
We see the icy islands stand
The northern billows roll

As to the north we make our way
Surprising scenes we find
We lengthen out the tedious day
And leave the night behind

Now see the northern regions where
Eternal winter reigns
One day and night fills up the year
And endless cold maintains

When in our stations we are placed
And whales around us play
We launch our boats into the main
And swiftly chase our prey

In haste we ply our nimble oars
For an assault designed
The sea beneath us foams and roars
And leaves a wake behind

A mighty whale we rush upon
And in our irons throw
She sinks her monstrous body down
Among the waves below

SONGS OF WHALES AND WHALING

And when she rises out again
We soon renew the fight
Thrust our sharp lances in amain
And all her rage excite

Enraged she makes a mighty bound
Thick foams the whitened sea
The waves in circles rise around
And widening roll away

She thrashes with her tail around
And blows her reddning breath
She breaks the air a deafening sound
While ocean groans beneath

From numerous wounds with crimson flood
She stains the frothy sea
She gasps and blows her latest blood
While crimson life decays

With joyful hearts we see her die
And on the surface lay
While all with eager haste apply
To save our deathful prey

Ricketson, *History of New Bedford* 1858

Daniel Ricketson in his *History of New Bedford* (p. 68–69) called this just "A Whaling." He said that it is probably the oldest whaling song extant. Perhaps. But also, perhaps "The Greenland Whale," called "Brave Boys" in this book is as old or older. Ricketson says that the author of the song was Dr. John Osborn who was born in Sandwich on Cape Cod in the year 1713.

The first melody is a play-party version of "Barbara Allen" that was traditional on Martha's Vineyard. The first line of music for the first stanza, the second line for the second stanza and so on. The second melody is supplied, repeated for each stanza.

THE GAM

BRAVE BOYS
(THE GREENLAND WHALE)

It was eighteen hundred and thirty-nine
On the fourteenth day of May
When weighed our anchor and set our sail
And for Greenland bore away brave boys
And for Greenland bore away

Now our captain's name it was William Moore
And the mate's name was the same
And our ship she was called the Lion so bold
As she ploughed the raging main brave boys
As she ploughed the raging main

Now the captain he stood in the top crosstree
And a fine looking man was he
A-searching the horizon with a spyglass in his hand
It's a whale, a whale, a fish brave boys
It's a whale a fish cried he.

And the mate he stood on the quarter deck
And a fine looking man was he
Overhaul, overhaul at your davit tackle falls
And it's lower your boats to the sea brave boys
And it's launch your boats to the sea

SONGS OF WHALES AND WHALING

Now the boats being lowered and the whale being struck
It give one flurry with its tail
And down went the boat and those six jolly tars
And they never come up no more brave boys
And they never come up no more

When the captain heard of the loss of his men
It grieved his heart full sore
But when he heard of the loss of that whale
Why it grieved him ten times more brave boys
Yes it grieved him ten times more

But the summer months are past and gone
Cold winter's a-coming on
So we'll steer our course back to New Bedford
And the pretty girls standing on the shore brave boys
And the pretty girls standing on the shore

Welcome Tilton

This is a very old song. Perhaps it goes back to the very early years of the seventeenth century, and its proper title is "The Greenland Whale Fishery." However this Yankee version probably only goes back some 200 years. It was one of the very most popular of all the whaling songs.

Both Welcome and Bill Tilton sang "Brave Boys" but to different melodies. The first is Welcome's melody, Bill's will be found in "Folksongs from Martha's Vineyard." The second melody here is one that Willard Marden used.

Baring-Gould, *A Garland of Country Song*, p. 56; Baring Gould and Hitchcock, *Folk Songs of the West Country*, p. 50; Belden, *Ballads and Songs*, p. 104; *The Book of Navy Songs*, p. 76 and p. 120; Cohen, *101 Plus 5 Folk Songs for Camp*, p. 132; Colcord, *Songs of American Sailormen*, p. 151; Eckstorm and Smythe, *Minstrelsy of Maine*, p. 226; Harlow, *Chanteying Aboard American Ships*, p. 223; Huntington, *Songs the Whalemen Sang*, p. 9; Huntington, "Folksongs from Martha's Vineyard," *Northeast Folklore*, VIII; Karpeles, *Folk Songs From Newfoundland*, p. 157; Laws, *American Balladry From British Broadsides*, p. 150; Lomax and Lomax, *Our Singing Country*, p. 214; Mackenzie, *Ballads and Sea Songs from Nova Scotia*, p. 155;

THE GAM

Peacock, *Songs of the Newfoundland Outports*, p. 147; Purslow, *The Foggy Dew*, p. 37; Reeves, *The Everlasting Circle*, p. 134; Vaughan Williams and Lloyd, *The Penguin Book of English Folk Songs*, p. 50. Whall, *Sea Songs and Shanties*, p. 69; Winn, *Some Less Known Folk Songs*, Vol. II, p. 17.

DIEGO'S BOLD SHORES

'Twas a love of adventure a longing for gold
And a hardened desire to roam
Tempted me far o'er the watery world
Far away from my kindred and home

With a storm-beaten captain so fearless and bold
And a score of brave fellows or two
Far away to the hardships of hunger and cold
Sailed this fearless and jovial crew

Have you ever cruised on Diego's bold shores
That are washed by the Antarctic wave
Where the white-plumed albatross merrily soars
O'er many a poor whaler's grave?

Did you ever hear tell of that mighty sperm whale
That when boldly attacked in his lair
With one sweep of his mighty and ponderous tail
Sends the whaleboat so high in the air?

Did you ever join in with those heart-ringing cheers
With your face turned to Heaven's blue dome
As laden with riches you purchased so dear
You hoisted your topsails bound home?

Reynolds Leaflet

SONGS OF WHALES AND WHALING

"Diego's Bold Shores," was a quite popular whaling song. There is a five-double stanza version in Huntington's *Songs the Whalemen Sang* and a four-double stanza version, so what we have here is actually only a fragment, but a fragment that tells the story in brief. In the *Reynolds Leaflet* it is specified that the song sings to the tune of "In The Shade of the Old Apple Tree," so as well as we could fit it to the words that is the melody we have here.

Colcord, *Songs of American Sailormen*, p. 196; Harlow, *Chanteying Aboard American Ships*, p. 213; Huntington, *Songs the Whalemen Sang*, p. 30.

THE SPERM WHALE SONG (THE WOUNDED WHALE)

Lo as the sun from its ocean bed springing
Bright o'er the water its glistening beams glow
When from the mast head come the joyful cry ringing
A whale off the Lea beam a whale there she blows

Call up your sleepers then larboard and starboard men
Your main yard aback and your boats clear away
Hard off the lea beam see the white water gleam
Making the foam into garlands of spray

Lo! The leviathan in vastness is lying
Making the deep his voluptuous bed
Waryly around him the sea birds are flying
And foaming billows dash over his head

THE GAM

Broad high and sinewy there goes his black Flukes
As slowly and stately he sinks in the main
Now peak your oars awhile rest from your weary toil
Waiting and watching his rising again

Now row hardies row for the pride of your nation
Row hardies row give way all you know
Now if you've blood give it free circulation
Give way my lads give way all you know

Now see each boat advance gaily as to a dance
Flitting like shadows across the blue main
Stand up and give him some send both your irons home
Cheerily stern all trim the boat give him line

Fins and flukes are now in commotion
Black skin and boats too are clearing the spray
Loud now and shrill sounds his pipe o'er the ocean
Wounded and sore he brings to in dismay

Haul line every man gather in all you can
Your lance and your spade from the thwarts clear away
Now take your oars again each now and every man
Safely and surely we'll hold him in play

Wounded and sore yet with strength undiminished
Madly he lashes the sea in his ire
Till a lance in his life and his struggle is finished
Slowly he sinks with his spout-hole on fire

Now hear the joyful shout free from each seaman stout
Awaking the deep in its turbulent war
Now from his spout-hole high see the red signal fly
Slowly he sinks and the struggle is o'er

Bark Josephine 1891

SONGS OF WHALES AND WHALING

SECOND VERSION: THE SPERM WHALING SONG

Bright as the sun from its ocean bed springing
Broad o'er the waters glistening beams throws
????
Hark on our lea beam a whale there she blows

Call up the sleepers the larboard and starboard men
Main yard aback! Man the boats lower away
Hard on our lea beam see the white water gleam
Wreathing her form in a garland of spray

Now the leviathan in vastness is lying
A making the seas a voluptuous bed
Whilst reeling o'er her the sea birds are flying
A watching the billows that break o'er his head

Broad high and close too there she goes flukes in air
So stately and slowly she sank in the main
Peak all your oars awhile rest from your weary toil
Waiting and watching her rising again

Row Hearties pull if you love your ambition
Spring to your thwarts let the reeking sweat flow
Now if you've got blood let it have demonstration
Bend to your oars and give way all you know

See every boat advance as gaily as to a dance
A gliding like shadows acrost the blue sea
Stand up and give him some send both your irons home
Stern all trim the boat see the line all free

Surrounded with foes yet with strength undiminished
So wildly she lashes the sea in her ire
A lance in her life and the struggle is finished
So slowly she sinks with her chimney on fire

Loud rings the joyful sound from every seaman stout
Watching the sea in its turbulent roar

THE GAM

Look from her spout hole the red signal flying
So slowly she dies and her struggle is o'er

Ship Leonidas 1854

There seems to be no set title for this song. It is called variously, "The Wounded Whale," "There She Blows," "The Sperm Whale Song," and "The Sperm Whaling Song." Also the whale is variously he and she. But one thing is certain, the song was very popular with whalemen and for a long time. There are two versions in *Songs the Whalemen Sang* dated 1836 and 1843 and the two versions here are 1854 and 1891.

There is a version in the *Reynolds Leaflet* that we are not including here because it is almost identical with the version in Joanna Colcord's *Songs of American Sailormen*. The melody seems always to have been "Hail to the Chief," which is what we have here, and both versions sing pretty well to it.

Colcord, *Songs of American Sailormen*, p. 189; Huntington, *Songs the Whalemen Sang*, p. 23; *The Reynolds Leaflet*.

BLOW YE WINDS

'Tis advertised in Boston
New York and Buffalo
Five hundred of Americans
A-whaling for to go

SONGS OF WHALES AND WHALING

Chorus

So blow ye winds in the morning
Blow ye winds high-ho
Clear away your running gear
And blow boys blow

They ship you to New Bedford
That famous whaling port
Where shark-shops sell you boots and clothes
Of every size and sort

For this will be a pleasant cruise
The brand-new hand is told
Of course when we are down on whales
You get your mince pie cold

The green hand fears the swaying masts
Because they look so tall
I'm scared to death of climbing sir
For fear that I might fall

The mate is standing in the waist
Says he When I say so
'Tis lay aloft you son-of-a-gun
Or overboard you'll go

Last night we had a whale 'longside
'twas Haul you lubbers haul
The captain in the riggin'
So loudly did he bawl

Joseph Chase Allen

BLOW YE WINDS (Second Version)

Its advertise in Boston
Likewise in Bristol
Five hundred bold Americans
A whaling voyage to go

THE GAM

Chorus

Cheer up my hearty lads
In spite of winds and weather
Cheer up my hearty lads
We'll all go a shore together

They'll take you to New Bedford
That famous whaling port
And send you to some damned rascal
And he will fit you out

They will tell you that there ships
They are so big and stout
That you can earn 500 dollars
Before you are 9 months out

Then there is that cursed compass
That will grieve your heart full sore
It has just two and thirty points
But you will have thirty more

Ship *Hillman* 1854

"Blow Ye Winds" was one of the most popular of all whaling songs. Both versions given here are fragments. Undoubtedly it was so popular not only because of the first melody which Colcord says is "The Baffled Knight," Child 112, but also because it describes so vividly the trials and tribulations of a green hand on a whaling voyage. The green hands came from the city slums and also from back country farms.

That business about the "Cursed compass" has never been explained. For complete or at least more complete versions of the song check the references. The second melody is supplied.

The Book of Navy Songs, p. 96; Colcord, *Songs of American Sailormen*, p. 191; Cohen, *101 Plus 5 Folk Songs for Camp*, p. 191; Harlow, *Chanteying Aboard American Ships*, p. 130; Huntington, *Songs the Whalemen Sang*, p. 42; Hugill, *Shanties from the Seven Seas*, p. 223.

SONGS OF WHALES AND WHALING

CAPTAIN BUNKER

Our captain stood upon the deck
A spyglass in his head
A viewing of those gallant whales
That blowed in every strand
Get your tubs in your boats my boys
And by your braces stand
We'll have one of those gallant whales
Hand boys over hand

Chorus

So be cherry my lads
Let your hearts never fail
While the bold harpooner
Is a striking the whale

Overhaul overhaul
Your davit tackles fall
Till you land your boats in the sea
One and all
Our waist boat got down
And of course she got the start
Lay me on Captain Bunker
I'm hell for to dart

Our first mate he struck
And the whale he went down
The captain he stood by
All ready to bend on

THE GAM

Which caused the whale for to vomick
And the blood for to spout
In less that ten minutes
He rolled both fins out

    Ross, *Etchings of a Whaling Cruise* 1846

This version of "Captain Bunker" is also found in the *Bulletin of the Folksong Society of the Northeast*, No. 6, p. 14, and it too is taken from *Etchings of a Whaling Cruise*. The melody used here is adapted from the one in the *Bulletin*.

The first stanza and chorus of "Captain Bunker" are also found in Melville's *Moby Dick*, p. 189. There it is essentially the same as in *Etchings* except that in the fourth line Melville has "That blew at every strand," instead of "That blowed in every strand."

SWEET AMERICA

Come all you jovial sailors
That love your native home
Among strong winds and rushing seas
Some foreign climes to roam
Your echoing voices raised with ours
To cheer us on our way
Our ship is full and homeward bound
To sweet America

SONGS OF WHALES AND WHALING

It is eight and ten so tedious months
Our voyage we did pursue
From north to south we scoured the coast
Of Chile and Peru
At length those happy days arrived
No longer we will delay
Our ship is full and homeward bound
To sweet America

It's you and I on the briny deep
Our voyage we did pursue
And we'll spread our canvass to the gale
And bid you all adieu
Our swelling sails will catch the breeze
Our ship she gathers way
So cheer us to that happy place
Called sweet America

And when we are safe landed
All on our native shore
We'll bid adieu to troubles past
And think of them no more
We'll roam about with pretty girls
Each happy night and day
Enjoying love and sweet liberty
In sweet America

Bark *Catalpa* 1856

Sweet America has not been located and it should have been for surely it must have had some currency. It is a homeward bound song and also a whalemen's song. Note that America must have been pronounced Americay, and that is the pronunciation that is found in any old songs and ballads.

THE GAM

WHALER'S SONG

>There she lies there she lies
>Like an isle on ocean's breast
>Where away west souwest
>Where the billows meets the skys
>Port the helm trim the sail
>We must chase this mighty whale
>
>Spout spout spout
>The waves are purling all about
>Every billow on its head
>Strangely wears a crest of red
>See her lash the foaming main
>In her flurry and her pain
>
>Take good heed my hearts of oak
>Lest her flukes as she lies
>Swiftly hurl you to the skys
>But lo her giant strength is broke
>Slow she turns a mass of lead
>The mighty mountain whale is dead
>
>Row row row
>In our vessel she must go
>Over the broad Pacific swell
>Round Cape Horn where tempests dwell
>Many a night and many a day
>Hence with us she must away
>Till we joyful hail once more
>Old Nantucket's treeless shore
>
>Cheever, *The Whale and his Captors* 1850

There is a much longer version of "Whaler's Song" in *Songs the Whalemen Sang* from the Ship *Lexington* journal for a voyage made in 1853.

SONGS OF WHALES AND WHALING

The melody for that version is a setting of "Hearts of Oak," and a portion of it is used here. However, it would be difficult to find any melody that would fit the whole song because the lines are so uneven, not to mention that last line in the last stanza. However, that last line almost makes the song because it is so descriptive of Nantucket as it was in the 1850s when almost all of the island was sheep pasture.

Huntington, *Songs the Whalemen Sang*, 17.

SOON THY BARK MUST LEAVE OUR HARBOR

Soon thy bark must leave our harbor
Soon thy sails must be unfurled
Soon the last fond look be taken
Soon the last adieu be heard

Loved forms will gather round thee
Each to say a few kind words
They will give their parting blessing
Their good wishes and their aid

Good success we trust thou'll have
Where so'er they bark may go
Many joys to mark thy pathway
Many hopes to cheer thee too

If misfortune should attend thee
Something cause the tears to flow
Think of those at home who love thee
Take hope courage faith renew

Parents, brothers sisters and others
Friends relations all will miss thee
Yet the hope our hearts will cheer
That again we soon shall meet thee

THE GAM

We with letters oft will greet thee
All the news to thee we'll send
Thou shalt know when we are parted
Thou art remembered by thy friends

Ship Walter Scott 1844

Ship *Walter Scott* sailed from Nantucket for the Pacific Ocean August 31, 1844 and returned with a good voyage, almost all sperm oil, March 10, 1849 when she was sold in Edgartown. She sailed from Edgartown not on a whaling voyage, but bound for California with a large company of gold prospectors on board, on June 7, 1849.

This little song is interesting for the use throughout of the Quaker pronouns. Nantucket had a large Quaker population until about 1860, when Nantucket whaling came to an end because of the shoaling of the harbor. Then many of the Quaker families moved to New Bedford and Dartmouth. Melody supplied.

SONG OF THE NANTUCKET MARINER

In all of life's wanderings wherever I stray
O'er old ocean's waves or by lands far away
Of all the dear spots that my heart can beguile
There's no place so dear as my own native isle

Thou dear Island home where our forefathers sleep
I shall never forget thee though far on the deep
I will oft in my dreams as I rest on the main
I return in my visions and greet thee again

SONGS OF WHALES AND WHALING

Loved loved native isle there is no place so dear as my
    Own native isle

The light house that shines on the tumultuous wave
A guide through the storm full of hope for the brave
These visions are with me wherever I roam
Reminding me oft of my own native home
Loved loved Island home There's no place so dear as my
    own native isle

With thee are fond memories still cherished and dear
That are often revived and bedewed with a tear
Of loved ones that rest in the slumbering grave
While I have been tossed on the billowing wave
Loved loved native Isle there's no place so dear as my
    Own native Isle

Ship Lexington 1853

This song shows the thoughts of home and the longing for home that must have been in the minds of so many whalemen during the long months and years at sea. A note below the title of this song in the journal says that it is sung to the tune of "Home Sweet Home." So that is what we have here. It pretty well fits all the stanzas except the first and fifth, in both of which there is a line missing. The one missing in the first stanza is the "Loved, loved native isle" line. For the fifth stanza perhaps the third line could be repeated.

A SONG OF WHALING

September last the Point we past
With Westly Breeze so fair
We went over the shoals like jovel Soles
A whaling cruise to steer
We past the great rip in Leo (?) Ship
And so jovel rocks along

THE GAM

At 8 o Clock we went Nine Nots
With a westly gail so Strong
The wind at East it did in crease
And Blew so verry Strong

Our jovel Crew hove our Ship to
And sent down the topgallant yard
The weather was fine twas our Desine
To stop at the Cape Devards

We trimmed our Sails unto the Gails
Got up topgallant yards
We run our Reckoning out We saw a Spout
We hove our Top Sails to the mast

Then we swong our crains and Lowered a main
And after them so fast
We struck them both so hearty Struck
And killed them Both at last

As soon as they died we got them a long side
And our cables well made fast
By the day Light all hands was piped
We cut them boath that day

When the last peace come in the Sails we Trimmed
And then we bore a way
We had a pleasant traid the Land we maid
We stopt at the ile of May

We loward our Boats got hogs and gots
And then we bore a way
We had a pleasant time and Crost the Line
We run our Reckning all most

We saw lively ground the whails all Round
The spouts they lined the Cost
For to begin they took
To the Southward they all Past

SONGS OF WHALES AND WHALING

Then for 40 we maid our waik Straight
Where we arrived at Last
We Croust the Spanish Shore 3 months or more
Before our vige would obtain

The Southwards Blew Hard We Squared our yards
& Left the Spanish Main
And now at last the Season is Past
To the Northward we will Stear

It being Late when Past the Cape
Whair the Traids Blows fair and Clear
As we sail along we will Pack Sail on
To Nantucket we are Bound

Threw the otian wide our Ship doth Slide
Till we arrivd in the Sound
Att Sirwhy (?) Bite we lay that night
Till day light did appear

When the Eastern tide made our ankers waid
& for the Bar did Steer
We got there that day and there we lay
Till the Lighter come along side

Then off our jackets Streight and Lightnd our Ship
To get over the next high tide
We took the wind which against us maid
I soon tell to you

I heard the Sound we are hard a ground
All on the flats of Carling
We got from their without Cair
& got to the wharf next day

And now at last She is well maid fast
And their the Ship doth Last
When She is well moord we will jump on shore
And there we will work a while

Ship *Polly* 1794

THE GAM

The name of the vessel in this song was undoubtedly *Leo*. The Brig *Leo* left Nantucket in 1792 on a whaling voyage to the Brazil ground. The question is, would the man who made the song have called a brig "Leo Ship?" Perhaps. A man going out to his vessel anchored in the harbor would have said, "I'm going out to my ship" although his ship was actually, perhaps, a brig or a bark.

The "Cape Devards" were the Cape Verde Islands. And the "ile of May" is one of those islands but in *Creole* Portuguese it is pronounced "May." That "We loward our Boats got hogs and gots" is nice phonetic spelling. Those hogs and goats, penned on deck, would provide fresh meat for some time to come.

Notice that when they sighted whales they swung their "crains." A little later those cranes were always called davits.

The melody used here, adapted to fit the words, is the fiddle tune "Over Young to Marry" as found in Huntington's *William Litten's Fiddle Tunes, 1800–1802*. The last two lines of the first stanza can be sung by repeating the second half of the tune.

A STOVE BOAT

Your Stought young men who go a whaling
And who cross the rageing Sea
Little thinking while your Sailing
That grim Death may near you be

SONGS OF WHALES AND WHALING

I hope these lines will move your Patty
And a warning Be to all
I am sure it is a mournfull Ditty
Unto youth it loud Doth Call

Twas on the twenty fifth of August
It was in the afternoon
Then a youth Both Strought and Brawn
Snatched away while in his Bloom

A noble Schools of whales appeared
And for us they straight did Come
With Eager hearts for them we steared
And we soon made fast to one

Our other Boats with speed they hastened
And they rowed up to one
This youth with Courage to him hastened
But he sent him to his tomb

He stove their Boat in Rage and madness
On the waves he struck them all
It filled our hearts with fear and Sadness
They for help aloud did Call

We made great haste them to deliver
And from danger Set them free
But all the Best of mens endevoors
Will not alter Gods decree

We did save but five in number
One was Banished from our Sight
In Death Cold Shade ly Down to Slumber
Out a Dark and lonesome night

A lass Poor youth now we Llement thee
We bewail thy awfull Doom
Cruel Death he Quickly Sent thee
To that cold and watry tomb

THE GAM

We little thought grim Death so nigh the
When the mourning Sun did rise
But Eve it let Pale Death Past By the
And did close thy Lightless Eyes

May each of us whose Lives were Spared
Now Gods goodness Loud Proclaime
Who when in Danger for us Carred
Blest and Praised Be his name

And may all youth now take warning
We thus Seen this awful Sight
Weve seen a flower fresh at morning
Cropt and gone Before twas night

Death flew in Rage it did not tarry
Made us all to Quake and Fear
But have got this news to Carry
unto aged Parents Dear

methinks I see them full a crying
While this dreadfull news they hear
Methinks See them sot and Sighing
For a Darling Son most Dear

But why my friends will Set weeping
You to hom must Surely go
He will not leave his Quiet Sleeping
For hes Bid this world a due

But let me tell his Parents Dear
Brothers and Sisters so nigh
We have no friends that one to near
None that are too Dear to Die

We know his body must ly Sleeping
Until God Bid it Rise
We hope his Soul is now a Reaping
Joy and Blest above the skies

SONGS OF WHALES AND WHALING

What though the waves Do Roar and tumble
Over his body that's below
What though the thunder Loud Doth rumble
Lightning fly Both to and fro

It wont Disturb his Quiet Sleeping
None can hinder his Repose
He don't regard his friends a weeping
feels no trouble fears no foes

But though he is gone to us his cryings
Let us know what he doth Say
You living men Prepare for Dying
You to me must come away

You like the rage of Light are flying
Time Doth Swiftly waft you on
Twill Soon Be said that you are Dying
Soon Be said that you are gone

Ship *Polly* 1974

Here we have a song that combines whaling and death at sea from a stove boat. The melody is adapted from "Dobbin's Flowery Vale," No. 85 in Sam Henry's "Songs of the People." In the journal the title of this is "A Song of Whailling." The second melody is supplied.

THE GAM

COME ALL THAT SAIL FROM EDGARTOWN

Come all you that sail from Edgartown
You very well do know
When around Cape Horn that you are bound
A whaling voyage for to go
With heavy hearts from your girls you part
If in love your hearts unite
With moistened eyes and inward sighs
You leave your heart's delight

Now who can blame that's felt the same
At parting as I do
Or ridicule or call me fool
For he must know 'tis true
When leaving every land and strand
And sailing far from home
There's no peace nor rest within your breast
You're like a bird alone

For love it is a passion
By our parents first impressed
And who can blame that tender flame
From stealing in our breast
No matter who the object be
When Cupid aims his dart
A quick and willing prisoner led
And yet vexing of your heart

SONGS OF WHALES AND WHALING

On February the twenty-seventh
That day I still bewail
On board a south sea whaling ship
From the Vineyard we set sail
To gain an offing from the land
That night in vain we strove
We stretched across the Vineyard Sound
And anchored in the Cove

Next day our good ship under way
Our pilot gave command
And soon we found our goodly ship
Outside of Nomansland
And there our pilot took his leave
And left us under sail
E'er long an old northwester came
A-smoking at our tail

Now lest my song should prove too long
I'll draw it to an end
May health and peace and love increase
With sweethearts wives and friends
As I am only outward bound
I can narrate no more
Nor can one see what destiny
Dame fortune has in store

But with hope and perservance
For dictators we will choose
And cherish them as bosom friends
To win the prize or lose
And for sperm whale we will boldly sail
Across the raging main
And should our voyage auspicious prove
You'll hear from me again

I pray excuse and don't abuse
My rude unpolished rhyme
The thought to gain a poet's name
Ne'er entered in my mind

THE GAM

But to beguile the time awhile
And crown reflections dear
Here for to end I'll recommend
To heaven each absent fair

Now for to leave my lover's theme
Since it is that I'm to mourn
I'll cherish fond that soothing hope
That we may yet return
And hope that on that happy day
To find our girls still true
Till then may heaven be our friend
Sweet nameless girl adieu

Ship *Young Phoenix* 1844

This journal of the voyage of the ship *Young Phoenix* of New Bedford was kept by one J.B. Tomkins. Tomkins says that the song was made by George Wood in 1821 on a voyage of the ship *Equator* of Nantucket. Perhaps Wood was an Edgartown man. In those years many Nantucket vessels fitted out in Edgartown, and many Vineyard whalemen served on Nantucket vessels. That is more background on a whaling song than we usually get.

The "Cove" in the fourth stanza is Tarpaulin Cove on Naushon across the sound from the Vineyard. Until the very last days of sail Tarpaulin Cove was an anchorage for vessels waiting for a favorable wind. The next day the *Equator* got her wind and left the pilot outside of Nomansland.

We could wish that George Wood had told us a little more about the voyage and been a little less lovelorn. The melody is part of the old fiddle tune "Oil of Barley."

SONGS OF WHALES AND WHALING

THE TIN SWANKEY POT

Oh, I am a sailor that plows the salt sea
As quickly I'll show unto you
My home is a whaler a-cruising for grease
Along with a jolly good crew

Chorus
Each morning and night my greatest delight
In fact all the pleasure I've got
Is to sit on my chest crack a joke or a jest
As I eat from my tin swankey pot

Once I was freeman and lived safe on shore
But that was in days long gone by
Now I am a sailor that braves the wild roar
Of the storms as they go sweeping by

Though far we may roam away from our home
I will never forget that dear spot
And each night and morn at twilight and dawn,
I'll eat from my tin swankey pot

We'll laugh and we'll sing the time merrily past
For smiles are far better than tears
And throw cares to leeward and fill up a glass
And drink to our remaining years

Here's a health to the man who first did invent
The best treat a sailor has got

THE GAM

So fill up your can and with real merriment
We'll drink from our tin swankey pot

Final Chorus
Then each watch in the night, be it cloudy or bright
The boys round the deck they do squat
Be they hungry or dry their spoons they let fly
As they eat from their tin swankey pot

Bark Andrew Hicks 1879

Swankey was the name for a cooling drink that the girls of the farm would carry out to the men and boys working in the hot summer fields. It was made of cold spring or well water to which vinegar and molasses were added. The same drink had other names in other parts of New England, one of which was switchel. The swankey pot was the big tin cup or mug or dipper from which the men drank. Actually, mess kid was a more common name for the tin swankey pot on merchant vessels and whalers, too, for it served the double purpose of dish and drinking utensil.

In Ross, *Etchings of a Whaling Cruise,* which was published in 1846, there is the following three stanza "extemporaneous windlass chantey" as Ross calls it. And look at the last line of the first stanza. So swankey as well as the tin swankey pot went to sea on board whale ships.

HEAVE AWAY

Heave him up
O he yo
Butter and cheese for breakfast
Raise the dead
O he yo
The steward he's a making swankey

Heave away
O he yo
Duff for dinner duff for dinner
Now I see it
O he yo
Hurrah for the Cape Cod Girls

SONGS OF WHALES AND WHALING

Now I don't
O he yo
Round the corner Sally
Up she comes
O he yo
Slap jacks for supper

The melody for "The Tin Swankey Pot" is supplied

THERE SHE BLOWS

Of all the venturous breeds of men
In the Vineyard's famous roster
Lives one whose story attracts my pen
In homage these verses foster
So praise the mariner here in rhyme
Is the song of the deep sea sailor
Who clewed his canvas in every clime
By the name of the Old Town Whaler

From the frozen shores of Baffin's Bay
To the far Antarctic stations
Has he vexed the peace of his giant prey
To lance those toothed cetaceans
Nor Arctic berg nor southern flame
Have offered the slightest trammels
To the Old Town whaler chasing his game
In the haunts of those ocean mammals

THE GAM

His good ship skippered by Captain Pease
Was hailed as the staunch Susanna
And had ploughed the combers of western seas
From the north to Dutch Guiana
With a snob-nosed dish-faced apple bow
And the rake of her timbers perky
She swirled like an Indian Ocean dhow
And tacked like a strutting turkey

He thought all lubbers who plowed the soil
On broad ancestral acres
And spent their days in that lazy toil
Were — speaking politely fakers
For life on shore was an irksome bore
And the product was plainly sterile
Without the gale and the ocean's roar
And the thrash of the spouting peril

The mess was stored for months to come
For their hunger's daily rally
With beef and biscuits washed by rum
In the smoke of the fore'ard galley
They had barrels of beef and casks of bread
To answer the call for luncheon
But it must be parenthetically said
Their rum came aboard in puncheons

He had seen Joe Jinkins swallowed up
Like Jonah in a monster's belly
With one titanic gulping sup
And believed him crushed to jelly
But like the Biblical tale of yore
Of the stomach's inward suction
His mate, like Jonah was spewed ashore
Unharmed by his strange eruction

His end he knew by the rule of three
As the cautious ever were crooning
'Twould either be signaled as Lost At Sea
Or killed by a whale harpooning

SONGS OF WHALES AND WHALING

But dying in bed was not for the brave
Why hearken to tinker or tailor
No matter what element furnished his grave
He would die like an Old Town whaler

DCHS archives c. 1880

The author of this semi-satirical whaling song was Samuel Keniston of Edgartown. Edgartown was often called Old Town because it was the first town to be settled on Martha's Vineyard.

Samuel Keniston was long the editor of the *Vineyard Gazette*, and knew personally most of the Island's whalemen and knew the stories of whaling almost as well, perhaps, as the whalemen themselves did. Besides being an outstanding newspaperman he was locally famous for his light verse. Perhaps this was never sung but a melody has been supplied.

THE NASSAU HOMEWARD BOUND

The farmer's heart with joy is filled
When his crops are good and sound
But who can feel the wild delight
Of the sailor homeward bound

THE GAM

Chorus
Where the sky is clear as the maiden's eye
Who waits for our return
To the land where milk and honey flows
And liberty was born

For three long years have passed away
Since we left freedom's shores
Our heartfelt wish has come at last
We're homeward bound once more

So fill our sails with favoring gales
Our shipmates all around
We'll give one cheer to the starry flag
And the Nassau homeward bound

Reynolds Leaflet

So here is still another homeward bound song. It has no title in the *Reynolds Leaflet* so we have given it one. The leaflet says that it is to be sung to "The Wearing of the Green," and that is what we have here. Note that the chorus is sung only after the first and second stanzas and the song ends with the third stanza.

The *Nassau* was an old vessel and had made many successful voyages. But she never made her final homeward bound passage, for she was captured and burned by a Confederate raider in Bering Strait in June, 1865

THE LASS OF MAUI

SONGS OF WHALES AND WHALING

As I was a walking one fine summer day
I loved recreations so far cast away.
As I sat amusing myself on the grass
Who should come there but an Indian lass.

She sat down beside me and squeezed my hand
Saying you are a stranger not of our land
But if you will follow after you are welcome to come
I live by myself in a snug little home.

The sun was setting all in the salt sea
As I wandered along with my little Maui
Together we rambled together we roved
Till we came to her hut in the cocoanut grove.

This pretty little Indian was loving and kind
And all that she done was with a loving delight
For I was a stranger and she took me to her home.
I'll remember the Maui girl as I wander alone.

She stepped up side of me and says unto me
If you'll but consent to live along with me
No more you'll go roving all over the salt sea
For I'll learn you the language of the isle of Maui.

THE GAM

Then I says my pretty fair maid that never can be
For I have a sweetheart in my own country
And I never can forsake her for her poverty
For she has a heart that's as true as the lass of Maui.

'Twas early next morning just at the break of day
I stepped up to this fair maid and these words I did say
My ship lies a waiting so fare you well my dear
We weigh both anchors and homeward we steer.

The last time I saw her she stood on the strand
Adieu she cried and waved her hand
And when you are at home with the girl that you love
Pray think of the maid in the cocoanut grove.

Oh now I am safe landed on my own native shore
My friends and relations flock around me once more
But as I look among them there is none that I see
That I can compare with the lass of Maui.

Bark *Sunbeam* 1863

SONGS OF WHALES AND WHALING

THE PRETTY MAID OF MOHE (Second Version)

As I strolled forth for pleasure one day
For love's recreation in a wild wandering way
I sat myself down on the grass
Who should pass by me but an Indian lass

She sat down beside me and taked my hand
She says You are a stranger not one of this land
And if you are willing you are welcome to come
For I live by myself in a sunny little home

So the sun was past setting all in the salt sea
Together I rambled with my pretty Mohe
Together we rambled together we roamed
Till we came to her hut in a coconut grove.

With fondest expressions she said unto me
"No more you'll go roaming all on the salt sea
If you will come and stay along with me
I will teach you the language of the isle of Mohe

THE GAM

Oh no pretty maiden that never can be
For I have a sweetheart in my own country
I will never forsake her though poor she may be
For her heart is as true as the maid of Mohe

This pretty Indian was honest and kind
She bid me a welcome 'twould be hard to find
Though I being a stranger far far from my home
I will think of this beauty where ever I roam

The last time I saw her she was down by the stream
As the ship passed by she waved me her hand
Saying when you get back to the girl you love well
Oh think of the maid in the coconut grove

Once more I am home on my own native shore
Where friends and relations flock around me once more
I looked all around me but none could I see
That does compare with my pretty Mohe

Bark Andrew Hicks 1879

The usual title of this song is "The Little Mohee," and it has long been popular in the southern mountains, often with an added stanza or two in which the sailor returns to his "Indian maid."

But the two versions here are whalemen's versions as Maui in the title surely indicates. Lahaina on the Island of Maui was long used by American whalemen as a port to refit between voyages.

The melody for the first version is from O'Neill, *Music of Ireland*, p. 1, adapted to fit the words. The second melody is supplied. That for the second version is adapted from "The Lass of Mohee" in Sam Henry's "Songs of the People."

As is seen from the references this was an exceedingly popular song.

Arnold, *Folksongs of Alabama*, p. 72; Barry, *The Maine Woods Songster*, p. 86; Belden, *Ballads and Songs*, p. 144; Colcord, *Songs of American Sailormen*, p. 199; Cox, *Folk-Songs of the South*, p. 372; Cox, *Traditional Ballads and Folk-Songs Mainly From West Virginia*, p. 14; Creighton, *Songs and Ballads From Nova Scotia*, p. 103; Dean, *Flying Cloud*, p. 17; Fuson, *Ballads of the Kentucky Highlands*, p. 84;

SONGS OF WHALES AND WHALING

Henry, *Folk-Songs From the Southern Highlands*; Henry, "Songs of the People," No. 835; Hubbard, *Ballads and Songs From Utah*, p. 96; Hudson, *Folksongs of Mississippi and Their Background*, p. 162; Huntington, *Songs the Whalemen Sang*, p. 148; Kidson, *Traditional Tunes*, p. 110; Kincaid, *My Favorite Mountain Ballads...*, p. 38; Laws, *Native American Balladry*, p. 233; Leach, *Folk Ballads and Songs of the Lower Labrador Coast*, p. 258; Lomax and Lomax, *American Ballads and Folk Songs*, p. 163; Mackenzie, *Ballads and Sea Songs from Nova Scotia*, p. 155; Owens, *Texas Folk Songs*, p. 103; Wetmore, *Mountain Songs of North Carolina*, p. 16; Wyman, *Lonesome Tunes*, p. 52.

ROLLING DOWN TO OLD MAUI

Once more we sail with a favoring gale
A-bounding over the main
And soon the hills of the tropic clime
Will be in view again.
Six sluggish months have passed away
Since from your shores sailed we
But now we're bound from the Arctic ground
Rolling down to old Maui

THE GAM

Chorus
Rolling down to old Maui my boys
Rolling down to old Maui
But now we're bound from the Arctic ground
Rolling down to old Maui

We will heave our lead where old Diamond Head
Looms up on old Oahu
Our masts and rigging are covered with ice
Our decks are filled with snow
The hoary head of the Sea Gull Isles
That decks the Arctic Sea
Are many and many leagues astern
Since we steered for Old Maui

O welcome the seas and the fragrant breeze
Laden with odors rare
And the pretty maids in the sunny glades
Are gentle, kind and fair
And their pretty eyes even now look out
Hoping some day to see
Our snow-white sails before the gales
Rolling down to old Maui

Once more we sail with a favoring gale
Toward our distant home
Our mainmast sprung, we're almost done
Still we ride the ocean's foam
Our stun'sail booms are carried away
What care we for that sound,
A living gale is after us
Hurrah, we're homeward bound.

Reynolds Leaflet

"Rolling Down To Old Maui" or "Mohee" as the whalemen usually pronounced it is a song of the bowhead whalemen who used the port of Lahaina on the island of Maui as a place to refit and transship oil home after six months or so in the Bering Sea and the Arctic. Usually three seasons and sometimes four were spent in the Arctic before heading home. The three weeks or so spent in Lahaina spring and fall were a happy time for the whalemen. They did love those Hawaiian girls. The winter months were spent fishing for sperm and right whales in the Pacific.

The melody used here is the one that Bill Tilton sang the song to, and it is "The Bowery." The Bowery was not written until 1892, so there were earlier melodies. See both Colcord and Harlow. But there was an earlier English song that sang to much the same tune as Bill Tilton's.

Colcord, *Songs of American Sailormen*, p. 197; Harlow, *Chanteying Aboard American Ships*, p. 228; Hugill, *Songs of the Sea*, p. 120; Huntington, *Songs the Whalemen Sang*, p. 27; Spaeth, *A History of Popular Music in America*, p. 262 (for background).

CALM

Had I the downey goney's wings
That hover round our trackless way
Not all the wealth that whaling brings
Should tempt me longer here to stay

The broad Pacific next with storms
Should not appal my heart with fear
But swift I'd fly to meet those forms
That fancy holds forever dear

The wife's embrace and infant's smiles
Should urge me on my rapid way
Till pleased I'd view the beaten shore
Where all my joys and comforts lay

Ship *Pocahontas* 1832

THE GAM

Here is another song of homesickness. The goney's wings would take the sailor where he wanted to be so much faster than the plodding six or seven knots of the homeward bound whaleship. The goney is the bird noted most often in the whaleman's songs. The melody is supplied.

A HARDTACK AND A HALF

Don't talk about your hardships
Don't talk of them to me
For I have had experience
While on the rolling sea
'Twas in the south Pacific
On board a whaling craft
It's there you have to go it
On a hardtack and a half

Chorus

To my boys my humble ditty
From Liverpool we steer
Like every other gay fellow
I like my whiskey clear
Like every other gay fellow
I like to joke and laugh
So away with all your whalers
With a hardtack and a half

'Twas early in the morning
Your scrub brooms in your hand
Get your buckets and draw water
It is the mates command
You will rub and you will scrub
On deck both fore and aft

SONGS OF WHALES AND WHALING

And all of that you have to do
On a hardtack and a half

'Twas early after breakfast
You'll hear the general call
It's turn to the watch
And get up each fall
Old Cromwell walks the deck
And at you he will laugh
To see you hoist away
On a hardtack and a half

Soon the cask is on the deck
And out will come the head
We'll rally from the forecastle
And round it lightly tread
The mate he's a jolly fellow
And well performs his task
He always gives the foremast hands
A good slap at the cask

Soon the work it is all done
And hard has been the toil
We'll all go down the forecastle
And divide the spoil
Each will take his share
And pray that it will last
But there's something very deceiving
About the hardtack cask

Soon the night it does come on
The boys their hunger feel
It's then look out for breakers
For the watch begins to steal
And one will cry and laugh
And he will say at last
The watch on deck has taken
My hardtack and a half

THE GAM

> Come all my jolly seamen
> Who venture on the sea
> Pray give attention
> And listen unto me
> They will surely make a fool of you
> And at you they will laugh
> If the get you aboard a whaler
> On a hardtack and a half
>
> Bark *Pacific* 1870

Hard tack, perhaps better spelled as one word, was officially known as ship's biscuit or pilot bread.

In the days of whaling it was made of whole wheat flour and baked as round flat cakes perhaps six or seven inches across. When fresh it was delicious and very wholesome as the editor of this book can well remember from his boyhood days. It was supposed to last the length of the voyage but it seldom did. After it had been in the casks for many months it lost something of its appeal. Hard tack also often became the home of weevils, but it had to be eaten just the same. It was packed in casks, barrels and boxes that were stowed in the lower hold.

Hard tack, potatoes, salt beef and molasses were the staple foods of the foremast hands. The afterguard — the captain and his mates — usually fared a little better.

The water for scrubbing the decks was drawn from over the side of the vessel, of course, for fresh water was carefully rationed on a whaler. The casks holding the water were also stowed in the lower hold. Sometimes the water went bad, too, but it could still be used as tea or coffee, or with a little rum, as grog. The melody is supplied.

THE WHALING VOYAGE

SONGS OF WHALES AND WHALING

Come all you that have leisure
And list a while to me
And I'll relate the dangers
That wait you on the sea

It was on a pleasant morn
From Fairhaven we set sail
Bound around Cape Horn
To cruise for the giant whale

On board the Adeline Gibbs
Commanded by Captain Baylies
And he was to provide
To guide and to protect us

We first crossed the Atlantic
Six thousand miles or more
And left far far behind us
Our friends and native shore

We soon were off Cape Horn
Midst hail and ice and snow
Where the southwest winds
Incessantly do blow

This is a stormy point
That sailors know full well
For oft they have to reef and furl
Mid squalls of hail and snow

Then down the coast of Chile
For Juan Fernandes we did steer

THE GAM

Robinson Crusoe's well known isle
In ancient tales we hear

We cruised around old Crusoe's isle
About two months or so
And then our captain said
Into port we ought to go

Our noble ship for Callao
We quickly then did steer
And soon the mountainous coast
Of South America did appear

Callao is a famous place
Where whalemen often go
There the destructive earthquakes
Oft lays the town in ruins low

A few miles back of Callao
There is a city of fame
Famed for its pompous churches
And Lima is its name

From Callao to Paita
We with our ship did go
And there it is so barren
Scarce anything will grow

We cruised old Neptune's premises
For more than half a year
Then for the Society Isles
The Adeline Gibbs did steer

We quickly saw the verdant isles
And entered the haven of Emeo
Where the delicious tropical fruits
Spontaneously do grow

SONGS OF WHALES AND WHALING

From Emeo we cruised a while
For the monsters of the sea
But being very unsuccessful
Steered for the isle of Owahee

We passed that lofty isle
Where Captain Cook they slew
And soon the ships at anchor
At Maui came in view

Here lay a fleet of ships
Recruiting to cruise for whales
Bound to Japan or the northwest coast
To encounter typhoons and gales

Sometimes on Japan it is so very warm
Pitch from the seams of ships do flow
Then with our blistered hands
All day we had to row

From Japan we called at many isles
Civilized and savage too
And likewise off New Zealand
Where the cold southwest gales blow

From New Zealand to Talcahuana
For our last port we did steer
And then around Cape Horn
For homes we hold so dear

Then after buffeting the waves
For forty seven months or more
We furled our sails secured our ship
And nimbly jumped on shore

And here's luck to our noble ship
Here's luck to her gallant crew
May they be crowned with loyalty
In passing this world through

THE GAM

Now mothers dear and daughters fair
Oh pity the poor sailor
Who mid storms and tempests
Braves old Boreas blustering railer

B.W.C.

DCHS archives

The initials B.W.C. probably stand for Benjamin W. Collins of Edgartown, who was a whaleman. The song is unusual in that it does not give any of the details of the actual whaling but deals rather with the geography of the voyage. The Yankee whalemen certainly did cover a lot of the globe even on a single voyage.

The *Adeline Gibbs* sailed from Fairhaven September 6, 1841 and returned with a good voyage July 29, 1945, so Collins' "forty seven months or more," is just about right. The melody is adapted from "Courtney's Rando" in Huntington's *William Litten's Fiddle Tunes*, p. 34. The second melody is supplied.

SONG OF THE SHIP VINEYARD

Come my jovial lads let us all bid adieu
To the girls that we love and to whom we'll prove true
Our bark is on the tide with her canvas spreading wide
She waits but our coming to roam the ocean wide

Chorus
Our good old ship the Vineyard is her name
So proudly she goes rolling o'er the main
With her sails of virgin white and her tars of hearts so light
It is merrily they plough the waters bright

SONGS OF WHALES AND WHALING

Our anchor is up and our ship is under weigh
Far out from our native shore our course we will lay
In search of Sperm Whales we will trim our sails
Trusting in Heaven for favoring gales

Two weeks had scarce passed away since we left our native home
O'er this wide world of waters to roam
When the man from our masthead cries out loud and free
There she blows there she blows down under our lee

With a spyglass in his hand our Captain jumps aloft
Tis a sperm whale he cries but one mile off
Get your boats ready boys clear your davit tackle falls
Stand by to lower away and man your boats all

Our boats sped o'er the sea with a speed of light
Spring ahead cries our mate spring boys with your might
Stand up there look out give it to him with a will
Stern all stern all and soon this whale we'll kill

The whale tried out and our oil stored down
Once more for Cape Horn we move steadily on
Its stormy bounds we've passed its winds and howling blasts
On Pacific's trackless waters our craft flies fast

We have swept the Chilian coast at Peru's wild hills we've gazed
On the old off Shore many a time our lights have blased
Now when we speak a ship our answer to her hail
Is the Vineyard Capt Coon with two thousand sperm oil

But one more cruise my lads and then we will away
To our own dear homes in North America
Where the girls with eyes of light and smiles of sparkling bright
Shall welcome us home with joy and delight

Our last cruise is o'er and now we're homeward bound
Again old Cape Horn we've safely passed around
Two hundred more we add in reply to the hail
Then boldly to the breeze we spread our swelling sail

THE GAM

Our native land our native land once more we tread thy soil
No more on the deep blue through rain nor storm we'll toil
Then farewell to our Captain our officers and crew
May long life be theirs where'er they go

Ship Three Brothers 1847

The ship *Vineyard* sailed from Edgartown with Capt. Coon, Master, October 30, 1847 and returned May 7, 1850 with 2,000 bbls. of sperm oil and 150 bbls. of whale oil, so that is surely the voyage recorded in the song. According to a note in the journal the song may have been written by Stephen G. Crawford and given to Charles Coffin. Coffin was a Nantucket name and the *Three Brothers* was a Nantucket vessel.

But Captain Coon probably came from the whaling port of Hudson on the Hudson River which was settled by Nantucket whalemen in the last decade of the 18th century. The name Coon was originally Kuhn. The Kuhns came from the Palatinate and settled on the left bank of the Hudson in the early 1700s near where the town of Hudson was to be. The name was soon Americanized to Coon and of course Coons went whaling.

The melody used here is adapted from "When in War on the Ochen," Huntington's in *William Litten's Fiddle Tunes*. As the meter of the song is pretty uneven the value of the notes will have to be changed in every stanza, as well as for the chorus.

BARQUE *OHIO* OUTWARD BOUND 1850

Brightly the morning sun lit the horizon o'er
When the bark Ohio sailed from the Shore
She was a gallant bark noble and free
Ohio, Ohio success to thee.

Proudly she weared her sails high in the air
Many a manly heart brushed away a tear

SONGS OF WHALES AND WHALING

God speed her on her voyage o'er the dark sea
Ohio Ohio success to thee.

Six ships for a whaling voyage sailed that same day
How many anxious hearts they bore away
Though we wish them all good luck our best wish shall be
Ohio, Ohio success to thee

Three years must roll around ere they can return
How the time will pass away we have yet to learn
But our best our brightest wish ever shall be
Ohio, Ohio success to thee

Three years have rolled around soon they will return
How many anxious hearts now with ardor burn
For sailors love their homes though doomed to roam
Ohio, Ohio success to thee

Now they are homeward bound soon they will be here
May every welcome heart show the welcome tear
For God speed them on their way onward they come
Ohio, Ohio welcome to home.

Ship Lydia 1855

BARK *ROSCIUS* OUTWARD BOUND (Second Version)

Brightly the morning sun
Lit the horizon o'er
When the bark Roscius
Sailed from the shore
She was a noble bark
Noble and free
Roscius Roscius success to thee

THE GAM

Proudly she raised her sails
High in the air
Many a manly heart
Brushed away a tear
God speed her on her voyage
O'er the dark blue sea
Roscius Roscius success to thee

Six ships on a whaling voyage
Left that same day
How many anxious hearts
They bore away
Though we wish them all good luck
Our best wish shall be
Roscius Roscius success to thee

Three years must roll around
Ere she can return
How the time will pass away
We have yet to learn
But our best our brightest wish
Always shall be
Roscius Roscius success to thee

Three years have rolled around
Before they will return
How many anxious hearts now with ardor burn
For sailors love their homes
Though doomed to roam
Roscius Roscius welcome ye home

Now we are homeward bound
Soon we will be there
May every cheerful heart
Share (?) the welcome dear
God speed us on our way
Onward we come
Roscius Roscius welcome ye home

Ship Lydia 1855

SONGS OF WHALES AND WHALING

Bark *Ohio* sailed from New Bedford October 1st, 1850. Five other whalers left New Bedford for the Pacific on that same day, as the song tells us. They were the Ship *Canton*, Ship *City*, Bark *Harvest*, Ship *Leonidas*, and Ship *Monongahela*.

The bark *Ohio* returned with a successful voyage, July 10, 1854. So she was gone almost four years rather than the three years that those waiting for her return had hoped for.

The melody used here is part of "The Miners of Wicklow," from Huntington's *William Litten's Fiddle Tunes*. The second melody is supplied.

SONG TO CAPTAIN S.D. OLIVER

Far, Far to the Arctic Ocean
There the Bow Heads Blow
There's where my mind is turning ever
There's where I want to go
All this ocean am sad and dreary
Every where we stray
O Captain will you go to that ocean
Go to where the Bow Heads lay

Chorus

All these whales are wild and ugly
All those that we see
O Captain will you go to that ocean
O go where the Bow Heads be

THE GAM

All up and down this sea we've wanderd
Since I've been with you
Then Captain let us go to the Northard
There we will see something new
All the whales that are in the ocean
All are wild we see
Then Captain will you go to the Northard
Go where the Bow Heads be

When shall I see the hills and vallyes
Far away on the west shore
O Captain let us leave this ocean
And not cruise here any more
All this ocean am sad and dreary
Every where we stray
O Captain will you go to that ocean
Go where the Bow Heads lay

Ship *Leonidas* 1856

One thing is certain from this song and that is that George E. Mills who wrote it had a very poor opinion of Captain Oliver, and that with good reason for, according to Starbuck's figures in *The History of the American Whale Fishery*, the *Leonidas* had a very poor voyage, which must have been because Captain Oliver wouldn't go where "the bow heads be." Mills changed ships at a port of call and fished and came home in the Ship *Java* of Fairhaven with an exceedingly good voyage.

Starbuck gives Captain Oliver's name as Samuel C. Oliver. Mills says that the song should be sung to "The Ballad of Old Folks at Home," so that is what we have here.

Pamela Miller in *And the Whale is Ours* gives us some beautiful examples of Mills' literary efforts.

Miller, Pamela A. *And the Whale is Ours*, p. 133.

SONGS OF WHALES AND WHALING

OUTWARD BOUND

To Gay Head cliffs we bid adieu
Shook hands with Polly, Kit and Sue
Our anchor weighed our sails unfurled
We're bound to plow the watery world
Hurrah we're outward bound
Hurrah we're outward bound

Away we go with a pleasant breeze
Our ship she scuds nine knots at least
Our captain does our wants supply
And while we've luck we'll never say die
Hurrah we're outward bound
Hurrah we're outward bound

Oh, when we arrive in New Bedford
From any distant port you've heard
Some large sperm whales we've taken you know
And home to the Vineyard boys, we'll go
Hurrah we're homeward bound
Hurrah we're homeward bound

When we arrive in New Bedford docks
The bloomers they come down in flocks
The pretty girls you'll hear them say
Here comes my sweetheart with twelve months pay
Hurrah we're homeward bound
Hurrah we're homeward bound

THE GAM

Next we go to the dog and bell
Where there's good poison for to sell
When in comes Archie with a smile
Oh drink it, boys, it's worth your while
For I know you're homeward bound
For I know you're homeward bound

Next to the boarding house we go
Where the pretty dame cuts a pretty fine show
She sits at the table and serves out the tea
Drink it Jack ain't you game to treat me?
For I know you're homeward bound
For I know you're homeward bound

When poor Jack's money is gone and spent
There's no more to be had no more to be spent
Then in comes Archie with a frown
Say, Rise up Jack let Bill sit down
For I know you're outward bound
For I know you're outward bound

So there sits Jack with his empty pot
Not a poor fellow to pity his lot
When in comes Poll with a jig and a skip
Why the devil, Jack don't you look for a ship
For I know you're outward bound
For I know you're outward bound

Ship Minerva Smythe 1852

This song was called "Homeward Bound" just about as often as "Outward Bound." Indeed, Whall in his *Sea Songs and Shanties* calls it "Homeward Bound." It is from Whall's song that the melody used here is adapted. Whall says that it was a prime favorite and was "sung all the world over." And Hugill in *Shanties from the Seven Seas* says that occasionally it was used as a pumping or capstan chantey.

It is from Ephraim Flanders' journal that this song is taken, however he did not finish the voyage but left the ship in the Azores and came home on another vessel. Perhaps he was sick or perhaps he jumped ship. The master of

SONGS OF WHALES AND WHALING

the *Minerva Smythe* voyage was Austin Smith, of Chilmark, a fine whaleman but a notoriously hard master.

Doerflinger, *Shantymen and Shantyboys*, p. 87; Harlow *Chanteying Aboard American Ships*, p. 136; Hugill, *Shanties From the Seven Seas*, p. 541; Kidson, *Traditional Tunes*, p. 107; Shay, *Iron Men and Wooden Ships*, p. 135; Whall, *Sea Songs and Shanties*, p. 6.

THE OLD OAKEN BUCKET

How dear to my heart are the scenes of the whaleship
When fond recollections bring them all back to me
The windlass the tryworks the boats at the davits
The men at the masthead looking far out to sea

Chorus
The old oaken bucket the tar covered bucket
The ironbound bucket we all knew so well

The wide spreading top's'l the stays'l that's nigh it
The crossjack the spanker the courses the bell
The fo'c'sle hatch and the roundbuse near by it
And there the old bucket we all knew so well

Reynolds Leaflet

The melody is "The Old Oaken Bucket" of course, but it was necessary to doctor it slightly to make it fit the words. The particular old oaken bucket in the song was the whaleship's sanitary facility. And "tar covered" could be changed to a much less polite phrase. The roundhouse was the seagoing version of backhouse.

THE GAM

THE WONDERFUL WHALERS

Fathers of the oratory
List to my surprising tale
Hearken to a wondrous story
More than very like a whale
Each mesmeric marvel monger
Lend to me your ears likewise
If for miracles you hunger
You shall ope both mouth and eyes

In the ship Ann Alexander
Cruising in pursuit of whales
Bold John S. Deblois commander
With a crew so gallant sails
In the South Pacific Ocean
Reaching to the Off-Shore Ground
'Mong the waves in wild commotion
Several monstrous whales they found

These two boats did follow after
Larboard boat and starboard too
And with shouts of glee and laughter
The Leviathans pursue
When the larboard boat commanded
By the stout first mate did soon
In the whale with force strong handed
Deeply plunge a sharp harpoon

Off the mighty monster started
Pain and anguish gave him cause
Suddenly he backwards darted
Seized the boat between his jaws

SONGS OF WHALES AND WHALING

Into smithereens he cracked it
Or as witnesses declare
Who beheld the thing transacted
Bits no bigger than a chair

In the starboard boat the captain
Quickly to the rescue struck
And although the boat was snapt in
Pieces saved the crew by luck
Now the good Ann Alexander
To their aid the waist boat sent
Half the band then having manned her
At the whale again they went

Soon the ocean giant nearing
They prepared to give him fight
Little thinking never fearing
That the beast again would bite
But without their host they reckoned
At their boat he also flew
Like the first he served the second
Snapped it into pieces too

Sure his jaws together clapping
Had the gallant seamen crushed
But when they perceived him snapping
Straight into the sea they rushed
To afford the help they needed
Bold Deblois repaired again
Once more also he succeeded
In the aim to save his men

Tired perhaps of sport renewing
To their ship this time they hied
When behold the whale pursuing
With his jaws extended wide
Gloating with revenge he sought 'em
But with blubber pierced and gored
He was crippled or had caught 'em
But they all got safe on board

THE GAM

Risk the heroes little cared for
Speedily they set their sail
In the ship herself prepared for
One more tussle with the whale
Now they reached him plunged a lance in
The infuriate monsters head
Then of course they had no chance in
Close encounter onward sped

For the ship they saw him making
But the chase he soon gave o'er
Which the animal forsaking
Down on him again they bore
Fifty rods below the water
There they saw the monster lie
So despairing him to slaughter
Thay resolved no more to try

At this time Deblois was standing
Sternly on the larboard bow
Ready with harpoon his hand in
To inflict a deadly blow
Up he saw the monster rising
With velocity and power
At the rate of speed surprising
Of full fifteen knots an hour

In an instant Heaven defend us
Lo the whale had near the keel
Struck with such a force tremendous
That it made the vessel reel
And her bottom knocked a hole in
Into which the water poured
And the sea so fierce did roll in
That the billows rushed and roared

Yet the ship was saved from sinking
Though so riddled by the whale
And Deblois and his unshrinking

Crew survived to tell the tale
Strong are those daring fellows
Doubtless the harpoon to throw
And to judge from what they tell us
Stronger still to draw the bow

       Ricketson, *History of New Bedford* 1858

Ricketson says that this song was published in the *New Bedford Mercury* which copied it from the *London Punch* of December 6, 1851.

Because it was printed in the New Bedford paper it may have had some currency. However, it does not tell the true story of the *Ann Alexander*, for she was indeed sunk by that fighting whale. She sank slowly enough so that all the crew had time to get into the whaleboats which were picked up by the whaler *Nantucket* of Nantucket and carried into the port of Paita.

Sometimes ships were attacked by fighting sperm whales, although it was usually just the whaleboats that were attacked and often smashed. The ships *Union* of Nantucket and *Essex* of New Bedford, like the *Ann Alexander* were both sunk by whales.

The melody used here is supplied.

THE SEA GIRT ISLE

Oh I have roamed in many lands
And many friends I've met
Not one fair scene or friendly smile
Can this fond heart forget
But I'll confess that I'm content
No more I wish to roam
I'll steer my bark for the sea girt Isle
The sea girt Isle's my home

THE GAM

If England was my place of birth
I'd love her tranquil shore
But as Columbia is my home
Her freedom I adore
Tho pleasant days in both I've passed
I dream of days to come
I'll steer my bark to the sea girt Isle
The Sea Girt Isle's my home

Ship Clarkson 1842

Was the sea girt isle Nantucket or Martha's Vineyard? Because Nantucket vessels fitted out for the voyage in Edgartown there were almost always some Vineyard men in the crews.

The *Clarkson* was condemned at Talcahauno when the voyage was nearly complete, and the oil was transshipped home. When a vessel was condemned as no longer seaworthy, the United States consul in the port where she was condemned would try to find berths for her men in another whaler. If he was unable to do so he must somehow provide for their passage home.

The source of the melody is not known, perhaps it was supplied.

A VOYAGE ON NEW HOLLAND

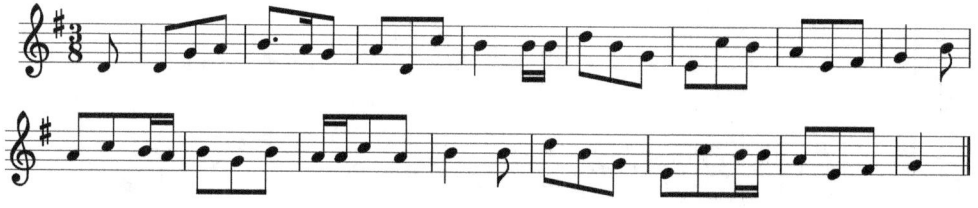

Come all you bold whalemen that plow the rough main
Off the coast of New Holland or off that of Spain
Give ear to my ditty I'll tell you what I've seen
While cruising the ocean in the bold Kathleen

Dear friends you've all heard of that city no doubt
Where sharks in men's clothing go prowling about
Where they fit out bold seamen and send them away
With a box of sea clothing and the 200th lay.

SONGS OF WHALES AND WHALING

If you cruise down South Water street there you may see
JBW Wing's shop as snug as can be
There we all signed our names a fine crew to be seen
For a thirty month voyage in the Bark Kathleen

Near the last part of August on the 25th day
With colors all flying we got under way
Bid adieu to New Bedfords sweet maidens so fair
With their low necked pink dresses and black curly hair

Now were on the Atlantic and the voyage is begun
If you don't like the business there's no chance to run
You can mourn for your sweethearts and they may for you
But the day you left New Bedford is the day you will rue

Our course is not eastward and our mast heads all manned
Our harpoons are ready and lances at hand
Our small boats in order each man knows his place
And all hands seem eager the prize for to chase

We touched at the Azores and then bore away
To the Cape De Verde Islands and there stopped a day
We next saw the Trusteens and then took a slope
And with a fair breeze passed the Cape of Good Hope

While on the Trusteen ground we had lowered for right whales
And trying to work careful took paddles and sails
But the whales smelled a rat and they gave us the slip
So the whales went to windward and us back to the ship

Now whaling in Wing's shop is all very fine
Or up to Spink Greens Hall when sipping your wine
With a girl on your knee you can cut in with ease
But it's different business when on the sale seas

The first whales we saw we down boats and got three
And got two alongside as snug as could be
But night coming on and one boat out of sight
And the weather looked stormy that very same night

THE GAM

The Capt in order to save the boats crue
We cut from the whales what more could he do
The crew in the boat they got tired of the chase
So they came alongside and we spliced the main brace

We arrived off Cape Leuwin in season to see
The Pamela cutting right under our lee
The Lapwing a boiling off our weather beam
A fine place for sperm off Cape Lewin it would seem

After cruising a few days and seeing no spout
For Geograph Bay then we tacked ship about
We passed by Cape Natches oh there is the rub
And in two hours time anchored off the tub

We'll gam with old Forest of course as we pass
And he'll sell us poor liquor for sixpence a glass
From Forest's to Carnshaws oh yes its all right
And by that time of course you'll be pretty tight

Now adieu to Australia's fair maids for a while
We're going off the west coast to cruise for sperm oil
From there to the Rosemary Isles in July
We to make out six hundred this season must try

Now we're off the west coast of New Holland all right
A cruising for sperm what a beautiful sight
We see old square head alongside of the ship
And the Capt singing out there boys heave and slip

For the owners at home a few words I will say
We'll do all the work and they'll get all the pay
You will say to yourself tis a curious note
But don't growl for some day you may chance steer a boat

When you're fast to the whale running risk of your life
He's shingling his houses and dressing his wife
He's sending his daughter off to high school
When you're up to your middle in grease you great fool

SONGS OF WHALES AND WHALING

We took a few good cuts between March and June
Of regular old sperm oil oh that is the tune
We then went to Bally which lies down in nine
We got some good water but not so good wine

To the Rosemary Islands our ship she went
To capture the humpbacks it was our intent
We thought that for two months four hundred would pay
So in July we anchored in deep water bay

We lay there at anchor quite nice for a while
Then dropped our ship down towards spectacle Isle
The Capt. Aloft with a glass in his hand
Sings out for a cow and a calf close to hand

A word about humpbacks now my dear friends
So you that to try this fine business intend
So see what fine sport it is cutting them in
And we skin the gut fat off as clean as a pin

We got the poor humpback and eat up her calf
And to see how the deck looks I bet you would laugh
All covered in gurry guts, flukes and big fins
And to get around deck you may break your poor shins

We took most seven hundred then got under way
And being short of water we went to Meiu Bay
On the island of Java got water and wood
Then put her for Anger as fast as we could

Of the maidens of Anger I'll tell you some day
Why don't he tell now I suppose you will say
But twoud injure the feelings of shipmates I fear
So you'll get all the news from old Mrs. Burtonear

Now we'll boldly up anchor from Anger my men
And try our luck off Cape Leuwin again
Old Leuwin received us as it done before
The seas mountains high and the tempest did roar

THE GAM

When Leuwin bore NE a big whale hove in sight
But our boats were turned up for it blowed so that night
And the gale still continues so we lay there hove to
And looked at old square head what more could we do

Next morning we manned our mast heads at daylight
For the gale it abated in the course of the night
We soon saw a big whale bound into the land
And the Cpt sings out lower the boats bear a hand

The mate lowered and struck one and turned him fin out
We took him alongside with many a shout
He made 70 barrels we then bore away
For that place famed for beuty called Geograph Bay

We attended the races this time in the bay
Saw fighting and fooling saw dancing and play
Saw old mother Forest selling poor gin
And Mary her daughter dressed neat as a pin

The race being over Ben Bolt won the prize
But to see all the fair sure it dazzled my eyes
But it dazzles them more to see Duff day come round
And its so with the most of the crew I'll be bound

Now we've started again on a cruise Jolly tars
And got a few miles out and in comes the Mars
We shipped some oil by her for home or elsewhere
Which made Katy's crew for to grumble and swear

Now adieu for the last time to this city of sand
Adieu to the maids of this far distant land
Good by uncle Herring look out for the mail
Our anchor is catted and we're under sail

To the port of Freemantle our course is now laid
We're going to touch there to seek medical aid
We stopped there one week then we made sail again
To cruise for sperm whales and to plow the rough main

SONGS OF WHALES AND WHALING

Now sad is the story I'm going to relate
The loss of our shipmate oh sad was his fate
He was called from our number he the summons obeyed
And his body down deep in the ocean is laid

No pale slab points out where he sunk in the deep
No loved ones ere stands o'er his grave for to weep
But the stormy winds whistle their dirge o'er his head
As he lies far from home in his deep ocean bed

But the Lord he knows best when to call us away
May each one be prepared for that much dreaded day
Farewell to our shipmate we'll neer see him more
Till the dead shall arise from the sea and the shore

Now the wheel of dame fortune is rooled around anew
But did not forget Kathleen and her crew
She showered down her blessings and our ship fills up fast
We've taken 400 since we sailed from port last

Of the ships on New Holland I'd have you to know
Some sails very fast and some sail very slow
There's the Oriole, Swallow and Eagle likewise
To beat little Katy the whole of them tries

There's the Mars and the Martha are cruising about
There's the Draco and Dunbar they lately come out
And last but not least in the list to put down
Is the clipper bark Sunbeam of fame and renown

She's commanded by Cromwell not Cromwell of old
But of a more recent date I am told
With his cutlass in hand he will chop off your head
So you wake up next morning to find yourself dead

He half starves his crew and he locks up the bread
And goes growling around like a dog with aore head
But he missed just one figure devilish old bihp
When he trod on the toes of his mate Mr. Tripp

THE GAM

We cruised until August and the season being o'er
The Capt says boys we will cruise here no more
So we then spoke the Eagle and the Capts agreed
They'd go to Mauritius with all haste and speed

We arrived at Mauritius all safe and all sound
Cruised over the city all through and all round
We recruited our ship and we then put to sea
And we'll be home in April the Capt tells me

We stood to the windward and at night shortened sail
In hopes to fall in with a good large sperm whale
With the island of Bourbon close under our lee
And our foretopsail in we're as snug as can be

One day we raised whales with the Sunbeam in sight
Her 3rd mate he struck one, of course he done right
But he being a kind hearted and jenerous man
Says, stern, Out of the way boys as fast as we can

Our boats being close, we will mate was the cry
And they soon made the blood from his spouthole to fly
So Katy being close and to in search of her prey
She backed her foretopsail and quietly lay

So we've got him alongside the Kathleen now
He's fast by a fluke chain to our starboard bow
Where many just like him have been fast before
And in hopes before long we'll see one or two more

Next morning at daylight we overboard hook
And off of this whale his jacket we took
We hove in his head, his case and his junk
While the only dry place in the ship was your bunk

We worked here in water chock up to our knees
Our bark she lay rooling and shipping in seas
Our chain straps they parted and our hooks they tore out
While Katy lies rooling and tumbling about

SONGS OF WHALES AND WHALING

Now our try works is going and the fires blazing bright
And the oil slewing out what a beautiful sight
Blind Jack's at the wheel and the watch gone below
You landsmen would enjoy our <u>comfort</u> I know

So we'll cruise the wide ocean where stormy winds blow
It's hard to leave home such a long time we know
But if duty commands it we'll never say die
And our motto while cruising is always <u>we'll try</u>

Next with the ship Martha we mated one day
She got a big whale while to windward we lay
She saw Katy coming at a double quick rate
So they run up their ensign at the mizzen to mate

Our Capt says boys now come set ours with speed
And twas lucky we did so quite lucky indeed
Our Capt he smiled for he very well knew
That ½ of the whale was for Katy and her crew

Now we'll ship by the Martha our share of this whale
And for Madagascar we'll quickly make sail
We arrived off Fort Dauphin and took a look around
We saw plenty of ships but no whales on the ground

Now boys says the Capt with his good natured smile
We'll go around the Cape and there cruise for a while
So we made sail next day for the Capt thought best
To set the sea watches and steer off South west

We took one more whale then went into Cape Town
The day before Christmas our anchor went down
Oh the Cape is a fine place and girls likes a beer
I won't say much more for friend Borden is near

Our stay at the Cape was quite brief it is true
So our course to the westward again we'll persue
In long de three east we wore ship around
And cruise and look over the Waldwich Bay ground

THE GAM

We arrived on the ground and we cruised east and west
And to raise a sperm whale why each man tried his best
But our search it was fruitless and never would pay
So for St. Helena we then bore away

Now about St. Helena a few words I will say
My friend lost his boots while ashore there one day
And instead of his boots he found gaiters I vow
A very good swap I suppose I suppose you'll say now

Next morning quite early the boots hove in sight
But he hang to the gaiters and I think he done right
For they was a nice pair and they fit to a T
But you won't hear no more about gaiters from me

Now all brother seamen whose boots needs repair
Of whose fancy gaiters I'd have you beware
For you know they cost money as well as I do
When the money's all gone then the gaiters gorn to

*Stanza 66 is missing the manuscript

Now the voyage is most over and our ships Homeward Bound
We'll all jump for joy at that thrice welcome sound
For we're thirty months absent from our dear native shore
And to get to New Bedford will take us two more

Oh the 18th of February was a fine pleasant day
When the Mars and the Kathleen they got under way
With a fair wind a blowing and studding sail set
We'll beat the old Mars to New Bedford I'll bet

Now we're rooling along with the wind at South East
Our good ship is plowing four knots at least
We're bound for New Bedford for our cruising is o'er
And we're steering the good course of NW once more

Now the hardships and the dangers of the Voyage are all past
Our ship lies snug in New Bedford at last

SONGS OF WHALES AND WHALING

Her sails are all furled and her anchor is down
And she rides at anchor off New Bedford Town

Hurrah for our good Bark ahe's carried us safe o'er
The dark stormy waters where tempests do roar
Through cold and through tempest and rain
And landed us safe in New Bedford again

So good by to old Ocean I'm done with you now
No more o'er your dark stormy billows I'll plow
Our friends here at home they all greet us with joy
Welcome home welcome home to the Bold Sailor Boy

A voyage on New Holland is from the Marble family papers 1837–1851 in the Kendall Whaling Museum archives. The Bark *Kathleen* sailed from New Bedford for the Indian Ocean, May 4, 1852 and returned February 17, 1855 with a good voyage.

Albumen print; starboard view of whaling vessel *Charles W. Morgan*

Songs of the Sea and Ships

While not all sailors were whalers, all whalers were sailors. As such they shared with merchant seamen the beauty and mystery of the sea, its lore, its dangers and the songs that dealt with the sea. Whether the songs were songs made by sailors themselves, such as "Shipwreck Near Gay Head" and "The Loss of the Albion," or art songs composed by landsmen, like "Pirate of the Isles," sailors embraced them, as long as the spirit and terminology rang true. As did whalemen.

SHIPWRECK NEAR GAY HEAD, JANUARY 14, 1782

On the fourteenth day of January last
Be sure it was a dismal night
The famous ship away was cast
It was sometime before twas light

THE GAM

The captain being something ill
Down in his cabin he did lay
The wind sprung up and blew so hard
The mate unto him did say

We must either go to sea
Or surely run the ship ashore
The captain says do as you please
For I am sick I can do not more

The men was all for going to sea
And all agreed with one consent
The pilot chose to run her ashore
Which proved to all their discontent

Whilst they all stood consulting there
What was best for them to do
The ship was fast upon the rocks
Which quickly stove her bottom through

There were five boats all on the deck
Then suddenly she gave a screen
A terrible wave made them a wreck
And quickly swept her decks clean

The mainmast and the yards came down
Which put the men into a fright
Knowing not which course to take
It being a dark and stormy night

The ship was split from stem to stern
Which filled their hearts with surprise
When these poor mortals came to see
Surprising death before their eyes

Don't you think this must be shocking
If you could hear their dismal cries
Whilst on the bar the ship was rocking
The seas they ran full mountains high

SONGS OF THE SEA AND SHIPS

On broken pieces of the ship
These poor distressed men were tossed
All striving for to get on shore
Till in the ocean they were lost

Twelve men hung to the quarter deck
If I do rightly understand
And nine of them was drownded
The other three got to land

There were fifteen poor souls in all
The raging ocean proved their grave
I hope for mercy they did call
Though but little warning seemed to have

No man could grant to them relief
Poor souls they were in great distress
But when the news got to their friends
Be sure it filled their hearts with grief

There were a few poor souls preserved
Beyond what they could think or see
Whilst others perished in their sight
Their time was come so it must be

All those that were preserved and kept
The fatal news to tell
They all hung fast upon the rock
'twas where the foaming billows swell

It was sometime the following day
The people did the wreck espy
They brought twelve living souls ashore
And two of them did quickly die

A shocking sight for to behold
To see them out into a cart
And carried to Chilmark meeting house
The sight would pierce you to the heart

THE GAM

Six men belonged to Edgartown
They left four widows in distress
And parents did for their sons mourn
And twenty six little children fatherless

The other six that strangers was
Next day the people did provide
To lay their bodies in the dust
There were six graves side by side

Not far from Gay Head was the place
Where these poor creatures lost their lives
The young men left friends to mourn
The others left both children and wives

I hope all of them that was preserved
Will bear in mind their great distress
And will not forget to prepare
For their eternal happiness

DCHS archives

"Shipwreck near Gay Head" is from a typed copy in the archives of the Dukes County Historical Society. Perhaps whoever typed the original, corrected some of the spelling. Also, in 1782 Gay Head was usually spelled as just one word — Gayhead. The rock to which the survivors clung is probably the "Great Rock" which is on the north side of the Gay Head peninsula.

The fact that there were six boats on deck, which were swept away, also the large size of the crew, would seem to indicate that the vessel was a whaler bound out on a voyage. A whaler always carried spare boats, and the pilot always stayed with the vessel until she was well past Gay Head.

Perhaps the pilot thought that he was more to the eastward than he actually was. If that had been the case when they put her ashore, the vessel would have gone onto sandy bottom with no loss of life. Perhaps the pilot made a mistake, but on the other hand if he had put her to sea as most of the men wanted she would perhaps have gone onto the Devil's Bridge in which case there might well have been no survivors.

SONGS OF THE SEA AND SHIPS

Parson Joseph Thaxter, the Edgartown minister for so many years, notes the wreck in his death records but he does not give us the name of the vessel. He does, however, give us the names of those lost, who were from Edgartown and says that they were buried in the New Burying Place.

This, of course, is a local ballad and perhaps had little currency but all local ballads were sung to one tune or another. The melody used here is "The Good Ship Mary Cochrane," No. 745 of Sam Henry's "Songs of the People," adapted to fit the words of the first stanza.

THE LOSS OF THE ALBION

Come all you jovial sailors
Come listen unto me
It is a story I will tell
That happened on the sea
The loss of the Albion ship, my boys
Upon the Irish coast
Where most of her crew and passengers
They were completely lost

It was on the first of April
From New York we set sail
Kind Neptune did protect us
With a sweet and pleasant gale
Until about the twentieth
A storm it did arise

THE GAM

The raging billows aloud did roar
And dismal was the skies

It was on one Sunday afternoon
The land we did espy
And at nine o'clock we made Cape Clear
The seas ran mountains high
The southerly wind began to blow
And bitter squalls came on
Which caused our passengers to weep
Our sailors for to mourn

All prudent sail we carried
To keep her clear from land
Expecting every moment
Our vessel she would strand
Our foretopsail was split my boys
Our foreyard took away
The mainmast by the deck was gone
The mizzen swept away

We had a lady fair aboard
Miss Powell was her name
Whose name deserves to be engraved
Upon the list of fame
She asked to take her turn at pump
Her precious life to save
No sooner was her wish denied
She met a watery grave

All night in this condition
We were tossing to and fro
At nine o'clock next morning
We were in the midst of woe
With twenty-five souls on deck
And each a broken heart
The Albion struck against a rock
And amidships she did part

SONGS OF THE SEA AND SHIPS

O now that noble ship
The Albion she is lost
And many is the times
The Atlantic she has crossed
Our noble captain he is lost
A man, a sailor bold
Many a gallant soul is lost
Many a heart made cold

We had twenty-five passengers
When from New York we came
And twenty-five bold seamen
As every crossed the main
Full fifty-four we had on board
When first we did set sail
And only nine escaped the wreck
To tell this woeful tale

DCHS archives
Ship *Sharon*, 1845

"The Loss of the Albion" is one of the better known of the songs of shipwreck. The melody to which the song was usually sung seems to have been "Caroline of Edinburgh Town." The version of that melody used here is No. 148 of Sam Henry's "Songs of the People."

There is a version of "The Loss of the Albion" in the DCHS archives with a four-measure refrain.

For references see Laws, *Native American Balladry*, p. 162.

THE GAM

A NEW SONG MAIDE

The 30th August twas on that Verry day
Our Captain come along side our orders was away
With our ankers waid all on our Bows and our topsails spread a clew
God prosper the Ship Olive Branch and all her jovel Crew

The wind Being aft SW my boys we quickly left the Land
Till 7 a Clock in the after noon as you shall understand
All in a squall the wind did hall which proved a Dismal Strook
We lost our fore and main mast and our mizzen top mast Break

Then we went to work our Riggen for to save
Thinking for to git Back again twas all that we did Crave
Att 9 a clock our fore sail we did set as you shall understand
And headed for the westward all for to make the land

Airly next morning our decks Not yet being clear
All hands was called to get to work and come up with good cheer
At 8 a clock our main Sail (set) as you shall understand
We maid Cape Cod (?) bairing west souwest all under the high land

All hands was to work a Clearing of decks the Biggest Part of that day
And cep her by the wind my Boys as near as she would lay
And the wind Being to the laward as it was the day Before
At Eight a clock we ankard all under the Cape Shore

SONGS OF THE SEA AND SHIPS

Early next morning the wind Being but small
We let her lay till 6 a clock Before we have a call
Then the wind Breased at souwest my boys and Blew a Pleasant Gail
We got our ankers on our bows and hoisted up our sails

We got up a fore top mast and top gallant mast Like wise
Set a Single reeft top Sail unto all our great joys
With our jury (?) sails and jig (?) sails yet she was a dismal Sight
We ankerd in Cape Ann harbour by 8 a clock that night

It was thirsday morning the day we left Cape ann
On Saturday we ankered all under the high Land
On Saturday Night we got back again unto our hearts Content
On Sunday hould along side of the wharf
      and on Monday our Sails we unbent

Then we went to work again all with a good chear
To fit for sea a gain Nothing did we fear
But the time it being delaid for 5 weeks or more
Twas the 6th of October we left our Native Shore

Twas at 12 a clock that Verry Day the Pilot Come on Board
Then we went our good Ship to unmoore
With the wind breased at southeast my Boys
      Come whistling threw the treas
We hoisted up our Top Sails and trimd them to the Breas

Ship Polly 1794

A good subtitle for this song would surely be "Jury-rig." The melody is adapted from "The Jolly Roving Tar" No. 670 in Sam Henry's "Songs of the People." The second melody is supplied.

THE GAM

THE WRECK OF THE CITY OF COLUMBUS I

'Twas the wreck of the fatal Columbus
On the Devil's Bridge rocks of Gay Head
Where the lives of one hundred poor people
Were lost in the wild waves 'tis said

Chorus
Nearly all were asleep as the ship plowed the deep
And the wind blew the waves very high
With a terrible shock she struck on a rock
And many were doomed there to die

The people were wild with excitement
Their cries were so sad for to hear
Loudly calling for someone to save them
But alas none to save them were near

Captain Wright tried his best to console them
But to calm them in vain he did strive
Yet he bravely remained on his vessel
Till the last man had left her alive

All the blame has been placed on young Harden
Who steered from his course toward the shore
It was little those poor souls were dreaming
Such a sad fate for them was in store

SONGS OF THE SEA AND SHIPS

But I can't help condemning the captain
Of the Glaucis that swiftly sailed by
Leaving forty poor souls in the rigging
From exposure to suffer and die

Harris the cook

THE WRECK OF THE CITY OF COLUMBUS II
(THE ILL-FATED STEAMER)

As the City of Columbus
On that lovely winter's day
Bade her last farewell to Boston
And sailed proudly down the Bay

When the last good-bye was said,
The last kisses thrown to shore
Little were those friends a-thinking
They would never see them more

And the passengers were happy
Thinking soon that they would be
In the bonny land of flowers
Far across the deep blue sea

Soon the darkness overtook them,
Still they were a happy band
They supposed their lives were trusted
Safely in the captain's hands

Later mothers kissed their children
Layed them in their berths to sleep
Soon they also shared their slumbers
Tossed upon the hungry deep

THE GAM

Hours had passed in peaceful dreaming
And the moon was shining bright
But how little they were dreaming
That it was a fateful night

Soon the pilot had deserted
And the captain was asleep
They were at the point of danger
Out upon that fateful deep

Then the cry of danger roused them
And the steamer struck a rock
And they staved the stateroom doors in
Where they all were locked

Ah, distracted were those dreamers,
And they screamed and wrung their hands
Earnest prayers went up to heaven
All were begging for the land

Wind and waves were dashing o'er them
Mother clinging to her child
All so frozen, so exhausted
On the ocean, oh so wide

THE WRECK OF THE CITY OF COLUMBUS III
(THE CITY OF COLUMBUS)

Some were clinging to the rigging
Many perished there and died
Some were saved to tell the story
Not a woman or a child

SONGS OF THE SEA AND SHIPS

Where were friends upon the shore then,
Dreaming sweetly then of those
Who had left them for a visit
To the lovely orange groves?

Ah! That steamer in the morning
Lay heeled over on her side
When the sun arose in splendor
All were buried in the tide

What a picture can we realize,
Crazed with sorrow and with pain
When the news came to the mainland
That the waves our dear ones claimed

Friends on shore were half distracted
Knowing of their heavy loss
Lives of dear ones from us taken
And into the billows tossed

We, alas, ourselves must comfort,
Thinking they have gone before
They have crossed life's sea of trouble
Landed on the other shore

Some their bodies have recovered,
Others at a loss to know
Must they drift to foreign countries?
Are they in the deep below?

They are in the land of flowers,
Sweeter than the orange groves,
Where our message cannot reach them
There soon or later we must go

Can we lay it to the captain,
And was carelessness the cause?
Can we say they were not thoughtful
Of the lives that were on board?

THE GAM

>Must he never be forgiven,
>Must his license be deprived?
>Shall he ne'er command a steamer
>With a load of human lives?
>
>Dreadful sounds the name "Columbus,"
>Dreadful sounds the name of waves
>Sweetly sounds the name of heaven
>Lonely is the sound of graves
>
> RAG DCHS Archives

The *City of Columbus* was a Savannah Line steamer bound for the South. She struck on the Devil's Bridge off Gay Head early in the morning of January 18th 1885. It was a clear night, very cold and with a strong northwesterly wind blowing. Why she was off course is not clear even to this day. Young Harden, on whom "all the blame has been placed," was the man at the wheel; he was steering the course that had been given him by the captain or first mate. He probably had his eye on the compass card and so did not notice the Gay Head light shining so brightly, and much too close over his left shoulder. But much worse, after she struck the captain gave the order for full speed astern so that she hauled off the rocks and sank in deep water.

The reason why this song is included in a book of songs that whalemen sang is because those who went in the boats to rescue those from the *City of Columbus* who were rescued from the rigging were almost all Gay Head Indian whalemen.

Strangely, this version of a Vineyard song didn't come from the Island but from Long Beach, California, where in 1929 I was working in a hole-in-the-wall restaurant, washing dishes and typing menus for my meals. I learned this from Harris the cook who was a mountain man from Tennessee, hence the credit to him.

George A. Hough Jr. who was long the Editor of the *Falmouth Enterprise* wrote the whole story of the tragedy in a fine little book called *Disaster on Devil's Bridge*.

The *Glaucis* in the last stanza was a coasting schooner, and "as she swiftly sailed by." The helmsman was perhaps the only man on deck and with his eyes on the compass card it is entirely possible that he did not see the *City of Columbus* on the rocks.

No references were found for this song.

The other two *City of Columbus* ballads are from the archives of the Dukes County Historical Society, the gift of Dorothy Scoville of Gay Head, a former curator of the Society.

SHIPWRECK ON LONG ISLAND SHORE

Ho Mr. editor stay your pen
I've sorry news to tell
All in the blinding storm and dark
The good ship Ocean Belle
With half a hundred souls and more
Went down last night on Long Island shore

Westward bound three weeks ago
Three weeks ago today
The sun shone bright and the wind blew fair
As she stood out of Dublin Bay
With a captain aboard of as right a sort
As ever voyaged from port to port

What kind of weather if fair or foul
That goodly ship befell
Till she felt the storm on our coast last night

THE GAM

No human tongue can tell
For all who sailed out of Dublin Bay
On the Ocean Belle they are dead today

A wilder storm has been seldom known
Than that of yester night
And the barren coast for many a mile
With the breakers foam was white
And not a boat be it ever so staunch
In that boiling sea could we wreckers launch

Even less than this might I have to tell
Of the storm of yester night
But for bits of wreckage that came ashore
At early morning light
And the corpse of a sailor lad that lay
On the cold wet sands at the break of day

Some mother's darling the poor boy was
Perhaps her only one
From a letter hidden on his chest
From a mother to her son
And the name of the lad as I wrote it down
In my rough handwriting was Walter Brown

So Mr. editor pause a while
And listen I pray to me
And print the story I tell you here
Print it for all to see
So the mother that's waiting for Walter Brown
Will know the corpse of her boy was found

Bark *Andrew Hicks* 1879

I have never seen this sad song of shipwreck anywhere else but in Sam Mingo's *Andrew Hicks* journal. The last two lines of the last stanza had to be supplied because part of a page was torn from the journal. And they may or may not be close to the original. And of course the melody had to be supplied, too. If it is sung as given here the last two lines of every stanza must be repeated.

The wreckers in the fourth stanza were salvagers who saved whatever they could from wrecked vessels for their own profit. But in the days before the establishment of the United States Life Saving Service — later to become a part of the United States Coast Guard — they saved plenty of lives, too. Everywhere, that is, except on Block Island, where, at least according to Vineyard tradition, the rule was, "A dead man tells no tale."

There is a story of a Block Island woman who was beachcombing after a storm, who came on a victim of the storm who had been washed up on the sand. He was still alive and he recognized his mother. "Mother," he said, "Mother don't you know me?"

"Son," she said, "remember the law of Block Island," and she conked him with her wrecking bar.

Captain Donald LaMar Poole of Manemsha is responsible for that Block Island tradition.

THE OCEAN KING

Ho ye ho messmates we'll sing
The glories of Neptune the ocean king
He reigns o'er the waters the wide seas his home
Ho ye ho in his kingdom we roam

He spreads a blue carpet all over the sea
O'er which our ship walks daintily
Though down at the bottom the old monarch hails
He blows the fresh wind right into our sails

THE GAM

Landsmen who live on the dull tame shore
Love their homes but ours we love more
Oh a ship and salt water messmates for me
There's nothing on earth like the open sea

Landsmen are green boys I have a notion
They don't know the fun that's had on the ocean
But contented they live in one spot all their lives
Like honey bees messmates they stick to their hives

What though we have storms they have earthquakes on shore
And though we have trouble they surely have more
We gather rare foods mong the isles of the sea
Where the tropical fruits grown there boys are we

Oh give me the ocean naught but the salt sea
Is a fit home messmates for hearts that are free
Ho boys ho then let us all sing
To the glory of Neptune the ocean's king

Ship *Nauticon* 1848

It seems as though I should have found a reference for this song, but I did not. The melody is supplied, and the meter is so irregular that if the song is sung the value of the notes will have to be changed for every stanza.

This was the *Nauticon*'s maiden voyage. She was built in Mattapoisett, and launched in that same year of 1848.

Not located.

SONGS OF THE SEA AND SHIPS

NAUTICLE FILOSOPHY
(BARNEY BUNTLINE)

One night came on a hurricane
The sea ran mountains high and rolling
Barney Buntline turned his quid
And says to Billy Bowline
Oh a strong sou'wester's blowing Bill
Oh can't you hear it roaring now
God help 'em how I pities them,
All them unhappy folks ashore now

Refrain
Bow wow wow rum ti iddy rum ti iddy bow wow wow

Foolhardy chaps as lives in towns
What dangers they are always in
And now are quaking in their beds
For fear the roof it should fall in
Poor creatures how they envies us
And wishes now I have a notion
For our good luck in such a storm
To be way out upon the ocean

THE GAM

And often as we seamen know
How men are killed and all undone
By overturns in carriages
And Thieves and Fires in London
And we've heard what risks all landsmen run
From noblemen to tailors
So Bill let us thank Providence
That you and I are sailors

Them as has been kept out all day
On business from their houses
Now late at night are walking home
To cheer their babes and spouses
While you and I upon the deck
Are comfortably lying
My eye see what tiles and chimney pots
About their heads are flying

Ship Frances Henrietta 1835

NAUTICAL PHILOSOPHY
(SECOND VERSION)

One night 'twas in a hurricane
The sea was mountains rollin
When Barney Bunkline turned his quid
Says he to Billy Bowline
Thars a sou wester comin Billy
Don't you hear it roar now
Lord help 'em — how I pitties 'em
Unhappy folks on shore now

Fool hardy chaps as lives in towns
What danger they are all in
At night lie quaking in their beds
For fear the roof will fall in
Poor critters how they envies us
And wishes I've a notion
For our good luck in such a storm
To be out on the ocean

SONGS OF THE SEA AND SHIPS

And as to them that's out all day
On business from their houses
And late at night are going home
To cheer their babes and spouses
While you and I upon the deck
Are comfortably lying
My eye what tiles and chimney pots
Around their heads are flying

Bill you and I have seen
How folks are bruised and (?)
By overturns in carriages
By thieves and fires in London
We've heard what risks all (?)
From noblemen to tailors
Then Bill lets thank Providence
That you and I are sailors

Ship Hillman 1854

The proper title of this song is "Barney Buntline"; "Nauticle Filosophy," however you spell it, will do. The two versions here are quite similar except that the second does not have the refrain. The melody used here was traditional on Martha's Vineyard. However, Chappell in *Popular Music of the Olden Time*, has a song called "The Barking Barber," and the melody for that is probably the parent melody of "Barney Buntline." In *The Book of Navy Songs*, the title is "A Sailor's Consolation." For some background on the song, see Johnson, *Our Familiar Songs and Those Who Wrote Them*.

The Book of Navy Songs, p. 68; Chappell, *Popular Music of the Olden Time*, p. 717; Hugill, *Songs of the Sea*, p. 139; Johnson, *Our Familiar Songs...*, p. 114; Wier, *The Book of a Thousand Songs*, p. 43.

THE GAM

THE BOATSWAIN'S CALL
(Unmooring....)

All hands on deck the boatswain cried
His voice like thunder roaring
All hands on deck the boatswain cried
The signal for our leaving
Your messenger bring
To heave your anchor to the bow

Chorus
And we'll think of the girls when we're far away
And we'll think of the girls when we're far away

Our anchor in sight the boatswain cried
Vast heaving boys vast heaving
Next over your fish and cat
Your handspikes nimble leaving
Then obey the boatswain's call
And walk away with your cat fall

It's loose your topsails next he cries
Topgallant sails and courses
Your jibs and staysails see (?) all clear
Haul home your sheets my hearties
Then with a sweet and pleasant gale
We will crowd aloft all sail

SONGS OF THE SEA AND SHIPS

Adieu to friends adieu to foes (?)
Adieu to all kind relations (?)
I'm going across the briny sea
Bound for the West India station
As we cross the raging main
The stars and stripes we shall proclaim

It was on the twenty first of June
From Mobile Bay we were leaving
There Kate and Sue two charming maids
Tears down their cheeks were coursing
As they watch our noble bark
As she ploughs the waters dark

Bark *Pacific* 1870

"The Boatswain's Call" is a capstan chantey, one of the very few chanties ever found in any of the whalemen's logbooks or journals, the reason being that seamen did not consider chanties songs at all but only a part of the work. Nor were there ever any boatswains on American whalers. One of the mates would give the orders that were given by the boatswain on merchant vessels. But chanties were used, the seaman with the best voice, or perhaps the loudest, singing the lead.

Bringing up the anchor was the heaviest work performed on board ship, and then securing the anchor to the cathead had to be done with extreme care. An anchor on a large whaleship or merchant vessel weighed several tons and it had to be secured so that it could not break loose in the heaviest sea. The messenger in the first stanza was the chain by which the anchor was secured to the capstan.

In the bark *Pacific* version of the vast heaving is written "fast heaving," probably in the same sense that a line or rope was made fast. The usual order, of course would be "vast heaving." The melody used here is adapted from Whall.

Whall, *Sea Songs and Shanties*, p. 26.

THE GAM

THE SAILOR

The sailor on the ocean wide
Thinks little of his life
He laughs to see the wind and tide
Engaged in endless strife

He laughs to scorn to hear the roar
Of breakers all around
And steers his ship from off the shore
Whence comes the dismal sound

Away he flies before the gale
And singing as he goes
His men he tells to trim the sails
And snug the hatches close

A brave man he who thus can dare
The wrath of nature grim
But naught thinks he of fright or care
If his stout ship is trim

Tis calm at last the sky serene
Looks down upon the ship
It seems as though no storm had been
Disturbing its fair trip

All things are close the ropes are taut
And jolly sings the crew
Their songs of war as if they sought
To bring the storm anew.

Ship *Lydia* 1855

SONGS OF THE SEA AND SHIPS

Sailors loved to glorify themselves, and the dangers of their calling in song. And surely in the days of sail that calling was as dangerous as any could be.

The melody is as Willard Marden used to play it. And it more or less fits the words. Willard Marden was a Nantucket man who married a Gay Head Indian girl.

BEN BACKSTAY'S WARNING

Ben Backstay was our boatswain
A very jolly boy
No lad than he more merrily
Could pipe all hands ahoy
And when it chanced his summons
We did not well attend
No lad than he more merrily
Could handle his ropes end

One day our jovial skipper
Who was a jolly dog
Served out to every mess sir
A double share of grog
Ben Backstay he got tipsy
Quite to his hearts content
And being half seas over
Why overboard he went

A shark was on our lee sir
And sharks don't never understand
But grapple all they see sir
Just like the sharks on land

THE GAM

We threw poor Ben a bit sir
To save him we had hope
But the shark had bit his head off
So Ben couldn't see the rope

One night our first dog watch was set
Ben came out on the wave
His head was gone and to us all
A warning thus he gave
By drinking grog I lost my life
So when with friends you meet
Never mix your grog boys
But always take it neat

Ship *Hillman*, 1854

In the references below, the song is called just "Ben Backstay." In *The Scottish Students' Song Book* there is a version consisting of eight four-line stanzas and a long nonsense chorus that begins "With a chip chop cherry chop folderol riddlerop" that certainly does not sound as though it had ever gone to sea.

Grog was a mixture of rum and water. The water was there, of course, to save rum. Ben Backstay's warning was that such parsimony was dangerous.

The first line of the melody is from *The Scottish Students' Song Book*. The second line is supplied to take care of the last four lines of each stanza in the Ship *Hillman* version.

Dibdin, *Songs of Charles Dibdin* (credited to D. Dibdin Jr.), p. 265; *The Scottish Students' Song Book*, p. 128; Hugill, *Songs of the Sea*, p. 52; Shay, *Iron Men and Wooden Ships*, p. 123; Stone, *Sea Songs and Ballads*, p. 46.

SONGS OF THE SEA AND SHIPS

BERING SEA

Full many a sailor points with pride
To cruises o'er the ocean wide
But he is naught compared to me
For I have cruised the Bering Sea

Chorus
Oh, Bering Sea, bleak Bering Sea,
So long we've hoped to sail on thee
For ne'er can sailor salty be
Until he's cruised the Bering Sea
And viewed Alaska's dreary shore
To fill himself with Arctic lore

Columbus and Balboa too
With nelson form a salty crew
But they are fresh compared with me
They never sailed the Bering Sea

Old Noah has our great respect
And yet he was not quite correct
Instead of Ararat, you know
He should have touched at Bogoslow

THE GAM

We breakfast, dine, and sup on fat
Eat walrus blubber and all that
Bull seals and whales are our delight
And polar bears we love to fight

The years you've spent on fishing bank
Or slaver's deck or pirate plank
On Spanish main or Crusoe's isle
Just make us Arctic heroes smile

Just think of all our dreary tracks
To yield the jaunty sealskin sacks
To have old England laugh in glee
While Yankees guard the Bering Sea

And when they sound our funeral knell
They'll say we've had our share of hell
Our welcome sure in bliss will be
Because we've braved the Bering Sea

                                    DCHS Archives

This song is in the Emma Mayhew Whiting papers of the Dukes County Historical Society in a letter written home in 1906 saying that it is to be sung to the tune of "Beulah Land." Then no one would have had to ask "What tune is that?" For "Beulah Land" was one of the best known and best loved of the old gospel songs.

The chorus gets a little tiresome if it is sung after every stanza. If sung after every second stanza it is a little better.

In the *Book of Navy Songs* collected and edited by the Trident Society of the United States Naval Academy and published by Doubleday Doran & Company in 1930 there is an almost identical version of the song called "Behring Sea" and also sung to the tune of "Beulah Land." It has one more stanza than our version which goes,

> So when you boast of fiercest gale
> That every ocean you did sail
> You cannot salty sailor be
> Until you cruise the Behring Sea.

The Book of Navy Songs, 84.

SONGS OF THE SEA AND SHIPS

SHIPS IN THE OCEAN

I wonder who first invented
The ships in the sea for to swim
For to cross the ocean to and fro
How happy was him

He might have been called some goddest
Or one that came from Spain
To whom she had found it out
A-sailing over the main

To the island of Dumbago
For any sparkling wine
Had it not been for shipping
We would have no seamen so brisk and fine

All points for the compass
We had for to steer
Some up the straights some down the straights
And some to the Baltic seas

Some to the distant islands
Where monstrous fishes be
The blessings of the Lord be theirs
As well as on the sea

Sometimes we met with hurricanes
And sometimes with dismal storms
When death a fury in all his shapes
And all his graceful forms

THE GAM

Still all hands being and doing
As fast as ever we can
To save our founding vessel
That she may carry us safe to land

When all the storms are over
All things are past and gone
The pretty girls will come on board ship
As we come over the main

Pretty little lasses
That use to prove so kind
And fickle of their fancy
And pleasure of their mind

There's none on board our vessels
Hain't half so blest as we
For we spend all our money
In mirth and jollity

You see we have no riches
We value not our store
We spend our money on the pretty girls
And go to sea for more

Sloop *Nellie* 1769

This song was difficult to set up because in the Journal it has no stanza pattern whatsoever. And also some of the lines are jumbled.

As Roy Palmer pointed out to me, the opening stanzas are reminiscent of "The Leather Botel," so that is the melody that is used here. Also the ideas found in the last stanzas are also found in "America, Commerce and Freedom." Perhaps Alexander Reinagle who wrote that may have known "Ships in the Ocean."

SONGS OF THE SEA AND SHIPS

UP ANCHOR FOR HOME BOYS

Up anchor for home boys, our cruise is complete
The billows are dancing our good ship to greet
Far away, far away o'er the ocean's blue breast
Smiles a home of bliss in the land of the West

There are pleasures abroad boys, but none to compare
With the glad shout of welcome awaiting us there
There are beauties abroad, boys for ages confest
But more beautiful far is the land of the West

Then up anchor for home boys we must not delay
For the breeze freshens fast that will bear us away
Spread our sails to the wind, let our flag be unfurled
It's the banner of freedom the hope of the world

Adieu to Italia her mountains and plains
To her kings and her scepters her captains and chains
Her children lies prostrate by tyrants opprest
But Liberty dwells in the land of the West

In the land of our fathers our own happy home
Where our hearts cling the closer the farther we roam
In the depth of whose shadows the Sun sinks to rest
As he lingering smiles on the land of the West

Bark *Vernon* 1854

This homeward bound song is from a paper in the archives of the Dukes County Historical Society. On the reverse side of the paper there is some information regarding the song that is not entirely clear. It may have been written by an officer on the USS *Independence* and "Heartily sung by

THE GAM

the crew when she left for home." The officer may have been Richard T. Parton. Also the song was printed in *The Friend*, the whalemen's newspaper published in Honolulu.

There is also this notation: "On board Barque Vernon at sea. July 3rd, 1854, Luther Little, Master."

The melody is adapted from "The Land of the West," No. 677 in Sam Henry's "Songs of the People." This was probably a merchant voyage for the *Vernon* listed in Starbuck.

BURY THE DEAD

List shipmates list that solemn call
Falls heavy on the ear
Tread lightly ye that bear the pall
A noble heart rests here

How short the time since him we bear
Ne'er thought of danger o'er his head
Whose hope of long life seemed so fair
Yet now alas he's dead

Aye place him on his lowly bier
Around him shipmates crowd
A sailor's burial he has here
His hammock is his shrowd

No proud display of hired mutes
With wailing mockery pains the ear
But o'er his corps with saddened hearts
You've dropped the bitter tear

The last sad rites are paid to him
The sea receives the dead
The ocean bird with heavy wing
Still flutters o'er his head

SONGS OF THE SEA AND SHIPS

'Tis past 'tis gone with the waters close
Around his senseless form
And onward still our good ship goes
All heedless of the storm

On coral bed serene he lays
Beneath the blue sea's angry wave
It's been his home since boyhood days
'Tis fit that it should be his grave

Ship Lexington 1853

Captain Hilliard Mayhew, of Quitsa on Martha's Vineyard, was the master of the *Lexington* on that 1853 voyage. A cove on Squibnocket Pond on which he had his small subsistence farm has been named after Captain Hilliard. After he retired from the sea Captain Hilliard and his two sons William and Hilliard Jr. went dory fishing from Squibnocket Landing. At one time codfishing brought almost as much money to New England as did whaling.

According to Starbuck that 1853 voyage of the *Lexington* was not a successful one. In the 1850s so many vessels were whaling that whales were ever becoming harder to find. But nineteenth century whaling could hardly have brought whales to the edge of extinction as have the modern factory ships of the Russians and Japanese.

The melody is supplied.

THE GAM

THE WHITE SQUALL

The sea was bright and the bark rode well
And the breeze bore the tone of the vesper bell
'Twas a gallant bark with a crew as brave
As ever was launched on the heaving wave
She shone in the light of declining day
Each sail was set and each heart was gay

They neared the land wherein beauty smiles
The sunny shore of the Grecean Isles
All thought of home and the welcome there
That soon shall greet each wandering ear
In fancy fain the social throng
In the festive dance and the joyous song

But a white cloud glides o'er the azure sky
What means that wild despairing cry
Fare ye well scenes (?) of home
The cry is help where no help can come
The white squall rides on the singing wave
And the bark is gulfed in an ocean grave

Bark *Pacific* 1870

SONGS OF THE SEA AND SHIPS

White squalls certainly did occur but usually the worst that happened was that the vessel might be dismasted.

This is a literary song; for the background see Johnson, *Our Familiar Songs*.

The Book of Popular Songs, p. 212; Johnson, *Our Familiar Songs...*, p. 115.

THE SAILOR'S GRAVE

Our bark was far far from the land
When the fairest of our gallant band
Grew deathly pale and pined away
Like the twilight of an autumn day
We watched his through long hours of pain
Our care was great but our hopes in vain
At death's stroke he gave no coward's alarms
But smiled as he died in his comrade's arms

We had no costly winding sheets
So we placed two round shot at his feet
And he lay in his hammock as snug and sound
As a king in his long shroud armour bound
We gaily decked his funeral best
With the stars and stripes upon his chest
We gave him this as the badge of the brave
And then he was fit for a sailor's grave

Bark *Stella* 1860; Ship *Abraham Barker* 1871; Bark *Andrew Hicks* 1879

THE GAM

THE SAILOR'S GRAVE (Second Version)

A bark was far far from the land
When the fairest of our gallant band
Through death and pain had passed away
Like a twilight hour on an autumn day

We watched with him through hours of pain
We wept but all our tears in vain
Death came but him did not alarm
As he smiled and died in his comrade's arms

We had no costly winding sheets
We placed a round shot at his feet
He lay in his hammock as snug and sound
As a king in his shroud all marble bound

We decked him in his funeral best
With the stars and stripes all on his chest
We gave them as a badge of the brave
That he was fit for a sailors grave

Ship Lydia 1855

Death at sea was a sad and lonely business and burial over the side of the vessel made a lasting impression on all who witnessed it. Countless songs about death at sea have been written. One, "Burial at Sea" has the recurring line "Oh, bury me not in the deep deep sea," from which came the cowboy song, "Oh Bury Me Not on the Lone Prairie." But "The Sailor's Grave" seems to have been the best known of all such songs.

SONGS OF THE SEA AND SHIPS

The first version is very similar in all three of the journals in which it was found. But the second version is different enough to show that the song was traditional.

The melody for the first version is pretty close to what may have been the original melody. The melody for the second version is as Willard Marden of Gay Head used to play it.

Beck, *The Folklore of Maine*, p. 176; Colcord, *Songs of American Sailormen*, p. 162; Doerflinger, *Shantymen and Shantyboys*, p. 161; Hugill, *Songs of the Sea*, p. 55.

THE BOLD PRIVATEER

Our anchor is stopped and we are under way
Farewell my dear Ellen I can no longer stay
Our ship she is a waiting so fare you well my dear
And I must go to sea aboard the bold Privateer

Oh Johnny dearest Johnny what makes you go to sea
How many have been slain since the war first began
You'd better stay at home with the girl that loves you dear
Than venture your sweet life on the bold Privateer

Oh Ellen dear Ellen your parents me dislike
And you have got two brothers and they threaten me my life
You hear from your angels for we'll steer clear (?)
And I must go to sea aboard the bold Privateer

THE GAM

Oh Ellen dearest Ellen what makes you grieve so soon
There are prizes to be taken in May and in June
There are prizes to be taken on the coast of France and Spain
So you my dearest Ellen shall be taken care of the same

And when we are on the oction so gallant we will fight
We'll haul down our colors by day and by night
We'll haul down our colors and on them we'll steer
And we'll let them know we're the bold Privateer

And when the war is over soon to you my dear
We'll fill our sails till (?) we come near the pier
We'll furl all our sails as we come near the pier
And we'll bid adieu to the bold Privateer.

Bark Pacific 1870

"The Bold Privateer" is a quite rare folksong and quite old too. It goes back at least to the time of the Napoleonic Wars.

During our second war with England, the War of 1812, many American privateersmen did indeed become wealthy: Quite wealthy enough to satisfy Ellen's two brothers. Other privateersmen died a miserable death in the British prison hulks, for England did not recognize privateers — vessels with letters of marque from the President of the United States — as lawful war vessels, and the men in the hulks died of starvation, disease and brutal treatment.

The first melody used here is from Sam Henry's version of the song; the second melody is supplied.

The Book of Popular Songs, p. 147; Eddy, *Ballads and Songs From Ohio*, p. 196; Henry, "Songs of the People," No. 514; Huntington, "Folksongs From Martha's Vineyard," *Northeast Folklore*, VIII: p. 34; Kidson, *Traditional Tunes*, p. 101; Laws, *American Balladry From British Broadsides*, p. 241; Sharp, *English Folk-Songs From the Southern Appalachians*, Vol. II: p. 175; Stubbs, *The Life of Man*, p. 16.

SONGS OF THE SEA AND SHIPS

THE SAILOR'S FAREWELL

Fare thee well my dearest friend
Thy husband now must go
To greet his native element
Where winds and tempests blow

And blessings rest with my dear
My prayers thus overflow
While crossing o'er the pathless deep
Where winds and tempests blow

And you my little girls for you
A father's feelings glow
With nameless wishes for your good
Where storms and tempests blow

His greatest wish and strong desire
Is that your joys may flow
From sins forgiven through Jesus name
Where winds and tempests blow

And now through life we'll sweetly steer
Together onward go
Till we arrive at that blest port
Where storms will cease to blow

Ship *Lotos* 1833

THE GAM

I do not find the Ship Lotos in Starbuck, so evidently this "Sailor's Farewell" must be from a merchant voyage. Nor am I sure of the source of the melody but I think it is one of Bill Tilton's. The second melody is supplied.

THE DEEP DEEP SEA

A noble ship lay motionless
Far on the deep blue sea
The winds were hushed
The waves were still in quiet harmony

No sound of mirth was heard on board
For one we loved had gone
Had left us for a better land
In life's full early morn

Ah sadning thoughts for one so brave
For one so loved as he
Should lay beneath the cold dark wave
Far on the deep blue sea

Chorus
The deep the deep the deep
The deep blue sea
He lays beneath the cold dark wave
Far on the deep deep sea

Bark *Edward* 1849

This very sad song is quite likely an original. It is included here for just one reason, it is one of the very few songs found in the logbooks and journals that includes the musical notation to go with the words. The notation changes slightly for each stanza. But as there is no improvement, only the music for the first stanza has been used.

THE MARINER'S GRAVE

    I remember the night was stormy and wet
    And dismally dashed the dark wave
    While the rain and the sleet
    Cold and heavily beat
    On the mariner's new dug grave

    I remember 'twas down in the darksome dale
    And near to a dreary cave
    Where the wild winds wail
    Round yonder pale
    That I saw the mariner's grave

    I remember how slow the bearers trod
    And how sad was the look they gave
    As they rested their load
    Near its last abode
    And gazed on the mariner's grave

    I remember no sound the silence did break
    As his corps to the earth they gave
    Save the night bird's shriek
    And the coffin's creak
    As it sunk in the mariner's grave

THE GAM

I remember a tear that slowly slid
Down the cheek of a messmate brave
It fell on the lid
And soon was hid
For closed was the mariner's grave

Now o'er his lone bed the brier creeps
And windflowers mournfully wave
And the willow weeps
And the moonbeam sleeps
On the mariner's silent grave

Ship Cortes 1847

This rather dismal song must have had some currency, for there are broadsides of it in Harvard's Houghton Library. The melody is supplied.

THE DROWNDED MINER

Come gentle muse assist my song
My feeble mind inspire
In morning cordance gain along
To charm selestial choir

'Tis a dismal news we have of late
That ecoes through the town
Of this young man's unhappy fate
It soared all around

This miner in his blooming years
Was drownded in the deep
With sorrow now in briny tears
Has left his friends to weep

SONGS OF THE SEA AND SHIPS

He was at sea and homeward bound
When stormy winds did rise
The heaving waves did them surround
Black clouds did fill the skies

The foaming billows loud did roar
The waves run mountain high
Then distant far from any shore
This miner's doomed to die

And on the ocean he must die
And bid his friends a Due
His sole at once do mount on high
As if on wings it flew

And on the ocean he did die
Nor a funeral there made
His body now beneath doth lie
And lacks a sartain grave

But a lase now he is gone
Where we all shall go too
Where all the rest shall follow on
And not of us a few

A las he's gone in instant flight
And will be seen no more
To regions of eternal light
Unto some radient shore

He's gone I hope to rest on high
With the angelick train
He is called from earthly unity
To join the heavenly plain

And there to live amongst the blest
Where joys shall never cease
Where no one shall disturb his rest
Nor none anoy his peace

THE GAM

While the pale carcase thoughtless lies
In the raging sea
His sole I hope doth rest on high
And ransomed will be

For ever more to live in peace
And there in safty dwell
In oceans of eternal bliss
To triumph over hell

He beats the air with eagle's wings
And chiding passes on
Glory to the emortal king
While serphims join the song

His aged parents left behind
Now swallowed up with grief
A las no comfort can they find
Nor can they gain relief

Their son is gone in prime of life
Into eternity
I hope to sing his maker's praise
With Serphims on hy

Sloop Dolphin 1790

This and a few other songs like it have been included because death was the constant companion of the men who went to sea one and two centuries ago, and they sang these songs. It seems doubtful if anyone will want to sing this today, but if there are any, the melody has been supplied. The first line of music for the first stanza, the second line for the second stanza, and so on.

SONGS OF THE SEA AND SHIPS

PITY THE POOR SEAMAN

O think on the mariner tossed on the billow
Far from the home of his childhood and youth
No mother to watch o'er his sleep broken pillow
No father to counsel no sister to soothe

Alone mid the wastes of the desolate ocean
His prison floats at the sport of the wind
Leaving all that his bosom regards with devotion
Society kindred and country behind

Ah little know ye that are peacefully sleeping
On home's downy pillow unwakened and warm
The woes of the seaman his dreary watch keeping
Mid all of the horrors of midnight and storm

O say shall the wretch thus to banishment driven
From all that entwines round the bosom below
Be sternly shut out from communion with heaven
And end his sad life in a mansion of woe

Pour pour on his pathway of tempest and gloom
The radiant light of the gospel of peace
And Bethlemen's star shall his passage illumine
To the heaven where darkness and tempest shall cease

Ship Lotos 1833

The melody is "The Bright Rosy Morning" from DeVille's *The Violin Player's Pastime*, 9.

THE GAM

SERENADE SONG OR HURRAH FOR THE ROVER AND HIS BEAUTIFUL LASS

My boat is by the tower my barque is in yon bay
And both must be gone at the dawn of the day
The moon is in her shroud to guide thee afar
On the deck of the Daring that love lighted star

Then forgive my rude mood unaccustomed to sue
I would not perhaps as your landlubbers do
My voice has been tuned to the note of the gun
That startles the deep when the combat's begun

How heavy and hard was the grasp of that hand
Whose love has been ever the guards or the band
There is an isle on the face of the deep
Where the leaves never wither and the skies never weep

And there if thou wilt thy bower shall be
When we leave the green woods for our home on the sea
And there thou shalt sing of the deeds that were done
When we loose the last blast and the last battle won

Then huzzah the black banner we nail to the mast
Hurrah for the rover and his beautiful lass

Bark Roscius 1858

There is a quite different version of this song in Burl Ives, *Sea Songs*, where it is called "The Pirate Song." The melody here is adapted from Ives but put in 4/4 time as Willard Marden of Gay Head used to play it.

Ives' version has a chorus, and perhaps the last two lines here are a chorus, or they can be repeated for a fifth stanza.

Ives, *Sea Songs*, 40

SONGS OF THE SEA AND SHIPS

THE BUCCANEER'S BRIDE

Away away o'er the boundless deep
On merrily on they roam
Wake lady disturb the mermaid's sleep
With the songs of thy Highland home

On the deck they stand that gallant band
To bear my love o'er the sea
To the spicy isles where the bright sun shines
And a home in the woods for me

Look up look up my bonny bride
Say where does thy fond heart roam
Does it sigh for Glenlock with its silvery sky (?)
Or the halls of thy Highland home

Sleep on sleep on that virgin sleep
That dreams of thy Highland halls
Thy brothers shall watch for the buccaneer
Till no dew by the twilight falls

Ship *Hillman* 1854

THE GAM

SECOND VERSION

Away away o'er the boundless deep
We merrily merrily roam
Come ....
While the mermaid sleeps
With the song of your island home

With my gallant band
To guide my love o'er the sea
To the spicy isles
Where the bright sun smiles
With its golden fruit for you

Sleep on sleep on my virgin bride
And dream of your island home
We brothers will watch
By the buccaneers bride
Till the dew of (?) the twilight falls

Bark *Pacific* 1870

These two versions of "The Buccaneer's Bride" were recorded in the respective journals sixteen years apart and so the song must have had some currency among whalemen. Still it seems to be quite rare.

ROLLING HOME

SONGS OF THE SEA AND SHIPS

Call all hands to man the capstan
See the cable running clear
Heave away and with a will boys
For New England we will steer

Chorus

Rolling home, rolling home
Rolling home across the sea
Rolling home to old New England
Rolling home dear land to thee

Round Cape Horn one frosty morning
And the sails were full of snow
Wear your sheets and sway your halliards
Swing her off and let her go

Many thousand miles behind us
Many thousand miles before
Oeac lifts her winds to bring us
To that well remembered home

Welcome Tilton

SAILING HOME FROM ENGLAND (Second Version)

Sailing home sailing home
Sailing home across the sea
Sailing home from dear old England
Fare thee well farewell to thee

Fare thee well ye Spanish maidens
It is time to say adieu
Happy times we've had together
Happy times we've had with you

Round Cape Horn one frosty morning
And the sails were full of snow
Wear your sheets and sway your halliards
Swing her off and let her go

Alton Tilton

THE GAM

Rolling Home was one of the most popular of seagoing songs. It was sung on both British and American ships and also in foreign vessels in various languages — see references and notes in Stan Hugill's *Shanties from the Seven Seas*. It was so popular because going home was always a happy time.

My daughter had difficulty in getting Alton Tilton's version. She finally went around to his place with a bottle of rum and that got the song.

Doerflinger, *Shantymen and Shantyboys*, p. 155; Harlow, *Chanteying Aboard American Ships*, p. 133; Hugill, *Songs of the Sea*, p. 39; Hugill, *Shanties from the Seven Seas*, p. 187; Hugill, *Shanties and Sailor's Songs*, p. 119, 148; Huntington, *Folksongs from Martha's Vineyard*, p. 75; Ives, *Sea Songs*, p. 90; Whall, *Sea Songs and Shanties*, p. 9.

THE PIRATE LOVER

Thou art gone from thy lover thou lord of the sea
The illusion is over that bound me to thee
I cannot regret thee though dearest thou wert
Nor can I forget thee thou lord of my heart

SONGS OF THE SEA AND SHIPS

I loved thee too dearly to hate thee and live
I am blind to the brightest my country can give
But I can not behold thee in plunder and gore
And thy Minna can fold thee in fondness no more

Far over the billow thy black vessel rides
The wave is thy pillow thy pathway the tides
Thy cannons are pointed thy red flag is on high
Thy crew are undaunted but yet thou must die

I thought thou wert brave as the sea kings of old
But thy heart is a slave and a victim to gold
My faith can be plighted to none but the free
Thy low heart has blighted my fond hopes in thee

I will not upbraid thee I have thee to bear
The shame thou hast made thee its danger and care
As thy banner is streaming far over the sea
Oh my fond heart is dreaming and breaking for thee

My heart thou hast broken thou lord of the wave
Thou hast left me a token to rest in my grave
Though false mean and cruel thou still must be dear
And thy name like a jewel be treasured up here

Ship Cortes 1847

This is a parlor song and how much currency it had on the sea is a question that will never be answered. The first melody is from sheet music published by G. Willig, Philadelphia with no date and credited to J. Aykroid and J.G. Perceval. The second melody is supplied.

Griggs' Southern and Western Songster, p. 238

THE GAM

THE PIRATE OF THE ISLE

Now I command a lusty band
Of pirates bold and free
No laws I own my ship's my throne
My kingdom is the sea

Chorus

I'm a pirate I'm a pirate
I'm a pirate of the isle

Tall ships of Spain across the main
And men whose hearts have burned
Came o'er the sea to conquer me
But never back returned

But a ship that night hove into sight
An American seventy-four
Who when she saw the pirate dark
A broadside in did pour

The pirate soon returned the boon
And on his foe did smile
But a fatal ball proved the downfall
Of the pirate of the isle

In the briny deep he lies asleep
…

SONGS OF THE SEA AND SHIPS

...
...

> *Final Chorus*
> He was the pirate he was the pirate
> He was the pirate of the isle
>
> Joseph Chase Allen

Both the words and music of this song are from Joe Allen, but unfortunately he could not remember the last three lines of the final stanza. The second melody is supplied.

Harlow, *Chanteying Aboard American Ships*, p. 172; Huntington, *Songs the Whalemen Sang*, p. 74.

NED BOLTON

A jolly comrade in the port
A fearless mate at sea
When I forget thee, to my hand
False may my cutlass be
And may my gallant battle flag
Be stricken down in shame
If when the social can goes round
I fail to pledge thy name
Up up my boys his memory
We'll give it with a cheer
Ben Bolton the commander
Of the Blacksnake Privateer

THE GAM

Poor Ned he had a heart of steel
With neither flaw nor speck
Firm as a rock in strife or storm
He trod the quarter deck
He was a welcome man I trow
To many an Indian dame
And Spanish planters crossed themselves
At mention of his name
But now Jamaica girls may weep
Rich Danes securely smile
His bark will take no prize again
Nor e'er touch Indian Isle

S'blood twas a sorry fate he met
While on his mother wave
The foe far off the storm asleep
And yet to find a grave
With store of the Peruvian gold
And spirit of the cane
No need would he have had to cruise
In tropic climes again
But some are born to sink at sea
And some to hang on shore
And fortune cried God-speed at last
And welcomed him no more

While off the coast of Mexico
The tale is bitter brief
The Black Snake under press of sail
Struck fast upon a reef
Scarce one good league from land
But hundreds both of horse and foot
Were ranged along the strand
His boats were lost while off Cape Horn
And with an old canoe
E'en had he numbered ten to one
What could Ned Bolton do

SONGS OF THE SEA AND SHIPS

Six days and nights the vessel lay
Upon the coral reef
Nor friendly sail nor favring gale
Brought prospect of relief
For a land breeze the wild one prayed
Who had never prayed before
And when it came not all his call
He bit his lip and swore
The Spaniards shouted from the beach
But dared not venture near
Too well they knew the mettle
Of the daring Privateer

Up sprung the gale the seventh day
Away away to sea
Off went the bark with riven planks
Over the waters free
Their battle flag these rovers had
Then hoisted Topmast high
And to their swarthy foe sent they
A fierce defying cry
One last broadside Ned Bolton cried
Deep boomed the cannons roar
And echoes hollow growl returned
The answer from the shore

The thundering gun the broken song
The mad tumultuous cheer
Ceased not so long as ocean spared
The shattered Privateer
I saw her as like lightning we
Swept by her in the gale
We strove to save and tacked
And fast we rattled in our sail
I knew the wave of Ned's right hand
Fare well you strive in vain
Nor he nor one of that brave crew
E'er entered port again

                                                Ship *Hillman* 1854

THE GAM

Here is another song glorifying the pirate. For pirate is what Ned Bolton sounds like in spite of the fact that his vessel was called the *Blacksnake Privateer*. Buccaneers and pirates liked to call themselves privateers which they were not. A true privateer was a letter of marque vessel commissioned by the government to prey on the enemy, but that cargo of Peruvian gold and rum sounds much more like piracy than privateering.

UNDER WAY

Hurrah my lads get underweigh
Right welcome comes the warning
Up up on deck all hands obey
We're homeward bound this morning

Chorus
You Tom and Dick and Joe and Jack
Stand by to get your anchor
Here Boy lay aft to the Mizzen Gaff
And loose away the spanker

Heave, heave my souls and forge ahead
The Breeze is gently Blowing
And while the morn is tinged with red
We're off with sheets aflowing

Then walk him round we're homeward bound
Each moment brings us nearer
So heave and haul my hearties all
For friends and home thats dearer

SONGS OF THE SEA AND SHIPS

Ho — short speak loud loud comes the hail
Avast boys vast your heaving
Jump up aloft loose every sail
Your handspikes nimbly leaving

Let fall let fall loud comes the call
Haul home your sheets like horses
Now halyards sway and sheets belay
Avast — hold on your courses

Once more your windlass man my boys
And walk her up so cheerily
Heave round and break her there she starts
Your anchors up or nearly

Now overhaul cat tackle fall
And with your fish be handy
Up with your jibb and staysail glib
So well there that's the dandy

Let fall your courses next the cry
Round in your weather braces
Board tacks and sheets my lads be spry
See all things in their places

And along we swim in gallant trim
And glad hearts warmly burning
With thoughts that roam towards far off home
To which we're fast returning

Homeward bound ah magic word
How sweet the hearts emotion
So memory strikes the magic chord
Afar upon the ocean

Then Ho for home we come we come
All dangers nobly braving
Look out Look out for our welcome shout
And Banners Proudly waving

Ship *Java* 1854

THE GAM

The orders for getting ship under way would, of course be the same for a merchantman or a whaler. For pure landlubbers perhaps some little explanation of the orders given may be in order. "Heave, heave my souls and forge ahead," means heave at the windlass or capstan — some vessels used one and some the other — to take in the scope of the anchor chain that was lying on the bottom. Then the order, "Avast boys, vast your heaving," means that the anchor chain was up and down and would hold the ship while the sails were being set.

The order, "Heave round and break her," means break the anchor out of the mud and start it up to be catted — secured on the bow. The other orders of course are for setting sails.

As always, being homeward bound was a happy time. This song may have been written by George E. Mills who was the second mate on the *Java* on that voyage. The melody used is an adaptation of "The Kilkenny Girl," No. 752 in O'Neill's *Music of Ireland*. However it sings just as well or better if put in 2/4 time.

SPANISH LADIES

Adieu to you you ladies of Lisbon
Adieu to you you ladies of Spain
For we have received orders to sail to old England
We hope on a short time to be with you again

Chorus
We'll rant and we'll roar boys like brave English heroes
We'll rant and we'll roar upon the salt seas
Until we strike soundings in the channel of old England
From Nohant to Scully is thirty-five leagues

SONGS OF THE SEA AND SHIPS

The first land we made it was called the deadman
The ramhead of Plymouth doth start London white
Sailed east beachy ship past folly and Underneys
Until we roused the Forlan light

The signal being made our grand fleet to anchor
All in the down that night for to sleep
It was stand by your stoppers let go your shank painters
Haul up your clew garnets stick out your fore sheets

Let every man loft of his full bumper
Let every man taste of his full bowl
It will furnish the blood it will drive away all sorrow
So here is a health to all seamen so bold

It will drive away all of your sorrows
It will drive away all melancholy
So here's a good health to all brave hearted and bold
Here's a health to each jovial and true hearted soul

Sloop Nellie 1769

This version from the sloop *Nellie* journal is both jumbled in spots and also hard to decipher, but what we have here is surely essentially what was intended.

Peter Pease, master mariner, who kept the journal was not only a whaleman, but a merchant seaman, too, and during the Revolution for a short time he was also a privateer. This 1769 passage was a merchant voyage from Dartmouth to London and very likely the cargo was whale oil. Joseph Rotch Jr. was the owner of the *Nellie* and even if it takes up a little space we must include some of his instructions to Captain Peter Pease as found in a letter in Dukes County Historical Society for a passage of the sloop *Union* to London in 1771.

> Captain Peter Pease
> Inclosed you have several letters which on your arrival in London I desire you will immediately deliver with your own hand.
> I have put on board the Union four birds in a cage. See that they are carefully taken care of and if they live over the passage present them with my best respects to Mr. Samuel Enderly.

THE GAM

I have also put on board five boxes of Spermaceti candles which you are to deliver to Mr. Bassall Latham march't in Bassinghall Street.
You may bring me the following Articles:
> Three suits of clothes from William Sutin at 14 Princes Street Lothbury I have wrote to him to have them ready and you are to pay for them.
> 2 Flying squirrel cages
> 2 Gray squirrel dto From some shop in Crooked Lane
> 2 good double Glouster Cheeses
> 4 hampers Porter which I desire your people not to broach on the passage as they did the last Voige
> 2 Neck clothes of Mr. Benj. Glover in Threadneedle Street such as he used to make me
> Inclosed you have a Bill on Buxton & Enderby for thirty pounds Sterling which will more than amount to the above.

Recollecting nothing more at present I remain with wishing you a good Voige & safe Return

Your assured Friend
Jos. Rotch Jun.

This very old and very good song seems always to have been sung to the same melody. This particular setting, however, is traditional on Martha's Vineyard.

Anderson, *Colonial Ballads*, p. 153; Creighton and Senior, *Traditional Songs From Nova Scotia*, p. 233; Dixon, *Ancient Poems, Ballads and Songs of England*, p. 235; Hugill, Stan, *Songs of the Sea*, p. 27; Karpeles, *Folk Songs From Newfoundland*, p. 155; Ranson, *Songs of the Wexford Coast*, p. 25; Sharp, *One Hundred English Folk Songs*, p. 183; Shay, *Iron Men and Wooden Ships*, p. 10; Stone, *Sea Songs and Ballads*, p. 183; Whall, *Sea Songs and Shanties*, p. 18; Woodgate, *The Penguin Song Book*, p. 9.

A FLOATING HOME

SONGS OF THE SEA AND SHIPS

Huzza huzza for a floating home
A good ship tight and free
There is naught like being water borne
On this the home for me

There's music in the freshening gale
While o'er the combing sea
Our gallant bark with press of sail
Bounds right gallantly

And now boys now we're homeward bound
What joy what rhapsody
Will fill our hearts if home is found
As we would have it be

Our early homes our friends and fair
Shall we meet them again
Grant do grant the sailor's prayer
Nor shall we ask in vain

With praises to that glorious king
Who has safely brought us on
Let sailors make the welkin ring
And bow before his thrown

Land land in sight my native land
Its rocks and trees I see
Oh may it for the ages stand
Home of the brave and free

Ship Uncus 1843

There is some very good original verse in the *Uncas* journal of which this homeward bound song is a part and which may have had no or very little currency. The melody used is "O for the Wings of a Dove," from DeVille's *The Violin Player's Pastime*, p. 9.

THE GAM

TARPAULIN JACKET

I am a young jolly brash sailor
Delights in all manner of sport
When I'm in liquor I'm mellow
The girls I then merrily court
But love is surrounded with trouble
And put such strange thoughts in my head
Is it not a terrible story
That love it should strike me stone dead

Have I not been in stormy weather
Have I not been in heat and cold
Have I not been with many a brave fellow
That has ventured his honor for gold
But now the wars are all over
And I am safe landed on shore
And the devil shall have me for ever
If ever I enter any more

SONGS OF THE SEA AND SHIPS

Come where is the girl that will love me
And lay with me this very night
Come jig it away with the fiddle
A country dance or a hornpipe
Let the weakest not go with the strongest
But let them be equally yoked
For the strongest will last out the longest
The jacket n'er values the stroke

Here's a health to my friends and acquaintance
When death it for me doth come
And let them behave in their station
And send me a cach of good rum
Let it be good loyal stingo
With three barrels of beer
To make my friends the more welcome
When they meet me at derry down fair

Let there be six sailors to carry me
Let them be damnable drunk
And as they are going to bury me
Let them fall down with my trunk
Let there be no sighing or sobbing
But one single favor I crave
Take me up in a tarpaulin jacket
And fiddle and dance to my grave

Broadside

"The Tarpaulin Jacket," or at least some stanzas of it, was known to all seamen. The melody seems always to have been the same, and this simple melody was used with many other songs. For one, see "The Noble Ship Catalpa" in this book. The second melody is supplied. The tarpaulin jacket weighted with a shot or some other heavy object was what all who died on board ship were buried in.

Anderson, *Colonial Ballads*, p. 158; *The Book of Navy Songs*, p. 122; Huntington, *Songs the Whalemen Sang*, p. 57.

THE GAM

THE MARINER'S LIFE

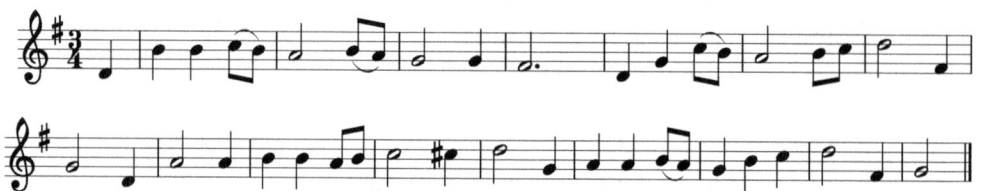

The mariner's life is the life for me
Floating along on the changeful sea
When storms are raging and winds are high
From billow to billow we quickly fly

And when all is still on the ocean's breast
We lay to sleep while the billows rest
And dream not of perils or dangers past
In the raging sea mid the stormy blast

And though far away we are doomed to roam
From all that we love in our distant home
Yet we whisper to every passing wind
A prayer for those we have left behind

And when our perils and dangers are o'er
At last we tread on our native shore
Our grateful thanks shall ascend on high
Till life's voyage is over and then happy die

Ship *Courier* 1842

The melody for this song is adapted from "What Fairy-Like Music," in DeVille, *The Violin Player's Pastime*.

SONGS OF THE SEA AND SHIPS

MARM HAUCKET'S GARDEN
(THE NANTUCKET SKIPPER)

Many a long long year ago
Nantucket skippers had a plan
Of finding out, though laying low
How near New York their schooners ran
There custom was to grease the lead
And then by sounding through the night
Knowing the soil that stuck so well
They always guessed their reckoning right

A skipper gray whose eyes were dim
Could tell by tasting just the spot
And so below he'd dowse the glim
After of course his something hot
Snug in his berth at eight o'clock
This ancient skipper would be found
No matter how his craft would rock
He slept and skippers sleep profound

The watch on deck would now and then
Run down and wake him with the lead
He'd wake and taste and tell the men
How many miles they went ahead
One night 'twas Jotham Marden's watch
A wag was Joe the peddlar's son

THE GAM

And so he mused the wanton wretch
Tonight I'll have a grain of fun

We're all a set of stupid fools
To think the skipper knows by tasting
What ground he's on. Nantucket Schools
Don't teach such stuff with all their boasting
And so he took the well greased lead
And rubbed it o'er a box of earth
That stood on deck a parsnip bed
And then he sought the skippers berth

Where are we now sir please to taste
The skipper yawned put out his tongue
Then opened his eyes in wondrous haste
And then upon the floor he sprung
The skipper stormed and tore his hair
Thrust on his boots and roared to Marden
Nantucket's sunk and here we are
Right over marm Haucket's garden

Ship *Citizen* 1844

When I was growing up it seemed as though every fisherman, ex-whaleman and 'most everybody else knew this story in one form or another. There is a version of it in Harlow's *Chanteying Aboard American Ships*, which he calls "The Nantucket Skipper," and which he credits to J.T. Fields. If it were not for that I would say that it must be the work of Charles Murphy, a famous Nantucket singer, fiddle player and song maker, because it sounds so much like him. The ship *Citizen* was a Nantucket vessel. Nantucket did indeed always boast about its schools and perhaps with good reason.

Margaret McArthur, the noted folksinger, tells me that she has been looking for a good melody for this song for years. I wish I could have found one for her. The melody used here is "Here we go round the mulberry bush." The second melody is supplied.

Harlow, *Chanteying Aboard American Ships*, p. 192.

SONGS OF THE SEA AND SHIPS

WILLIAM TAYLOR

William was a jovial lover
Alert with beauty and sweet air
Until at length he was discovered
By a charming lady fair

One day as they were a-going to be married
Dressed they were in rich array
But instead of being married
Pressed he was and sent to sea

This fair lady followed after
Dressed herself in men's disguise
With a musket all on her shoulder
Sword and pistol by her side

Then she on board of the ship did enter
By the name of Richard Carr
'twas once her hands was as white as lilys
They are now besmeared with pitch and tar

One day on board there rose a skirmish
This fair lady amongst the rest
Her under jacket being unbuttoned
The crew espied her snow white breast

The captain called for this fair lady
Saying what misfortune is brought you here
It is all for the sake of my own true lover
He was pressed the other year

THE GAM

If it's all for the sake of your own true lover
Pray come tell to me his name
William Taylor was his name sir
He lives upon the island green

If that be your William Taylor
That lives upon the island green
Tomorrow morning you shall see him
As he walks along the strand

Then she arose early next morning
Dressed herself in her own array
It was there she saw young William Taylor
Walking with a lady gay

Then she called for her sword and pistol
Sword and pistol at her command
It was there she shot young William Taylor
As he walked all on the strand

Then she wrung her hands in pity
Crying out in bitter woe
But instead of being married
This is proved my overthrow

DCHS archives

SONGS OF THE SEA AND SHIPS

WILLIAM TAYLOR (SECOND VERSION)

William was a bashful lover
William loved a lady fair
Bells a-ringing birds a-singing
To the church they did repair

Four and twenty brisk young sailors
Dressed themselves in rich array
Instead of William being married
Pressed they were and sent to sea

She followed after her true lover
Went by the name of William Carr
Her soft hands and milk-white fingers
All besmeared with pitch and tar

She dressed herself in man's array
And boldly fought among the rest
At last the wind blew open her waistcoat
And exposed her milk-white breast

Then the news went to the captain
He says Pray what wind has blown you here
Kind sir says she I'm in search of my lover
Whom you have pressed I love so dear

THE GAM

If you are in search of your true lover
Tell to me his name I pray
Kind sir says she, 'twas William Taylor
Whom you pressed the other day

If William Taylor is your true lover
He has proved cruel and severe
If you rise early in the morning
You will see him walking with his lady fair

Then she rose early in the morning
Early by the break of day
And she saw her William Taylor
Walking with a lady gay

Then she called for her sword and pistol
Sword and pistol at her command
And she shot sweet William Taylor
With his bride at his right hand

Then the news went to the captain
He heartily laughed at all the fun
Then he called her his best lieutenant
Over a ship of five hundred ton

Sloop *Nellie* 1769

BOLD WILLIAM TAYLOR (THIRD VERSION)

I'll sing you a song about two lovers
Who from Lichfield town did come
The young man's name was William Taylor
The maiden's name was Sarah Dunn

Now for a sailor William enlisted
Now for a sailor William's gone
He's gone and left his charming Sally
All alone to make me mourn

SONGS OF THE SEA AND SHIPS

She dressed herself in man's apparel
Man's apparel she put on
And for to seek her own true lover
For to find him she is gone

One day as she was exercising
Exercising among the rest
A silver locket flew from her jacket
And exposed her milk white breast

Then the captain stepped up to her
And asked her what brought her there
All for to seek my own true lover
For he has proved to me severe

If you are come to find your lover
You must tell to me his name
His name it is bold William Taylor
And from Lichfield town he came

If your lover's name is William Taylor
He has proved to you severe
He is married to a rich lady
He was married the other year

If you will rise early in the morning
In the morning by the break of day
Then you will see bold William Taylor
Walking with his lady gay

Then she called for a brace of pistols
A brace of pistols I command
Then she shot bold William Taylor
With his bride at his right hand

O then the captain was well pleased
Well pleased with what she'd done
And soon she became a bold commander
On board the ship with all the men

THE GAM

> Then the captain loved her dearly
> Loved her dearly as his life
> Then it was three days after
> Sarah became the captain's wife
>
> Broadside

How old "William Taylor" is is not surely known, but it is certainly well over two hundred years old and it has been tremendously popular with seamen and folksingers for most of that time. It tells the familiar story of the girl who dresses as a man and follows her lover to sea. According to folklore that actually happened many times, and the girl got away with it. How her sex was not discovered in the crowded quarters of a sailing vessel God only knows. Perhaps it usually was discovered as was Richard Carr's, when her waistcoat popped open.

On Martha's Vineyard there is a story of a girl who shipped on a whaler under the name of George Welden. That story is told in the *Dukes County Intelligencer*, Vol. 14, No. 4. The whaler was the *America*. Her master was Captain John A. Luce of the North Shore. She sailed from Holmes Hole on September 10th, 1862. George Welden pulled tub oar in the second mate's boat, who was Robert G. Smith of New Bedford. The entry in the ship's log for January 9th, 1863 reads "Comes with light breezes from the W the boats in chase of whales at 3 P.M. the boats came on board this day found out George Welden to be a woman first time I suspected such a thing at sunset took in sail latter part fine breezes from the S by W steering E.S.E. three sails in sight." And that is all.

Tradition says that Welden had gone for Mr. Smith in a fit of rage and tried to kill him because he had said that she was not pulling her weight. Back on board she was going to be given a taste of the rope's end and when told to strip to the waist she refused to do so and said, "I won't. I'm a woman." And so much for Richard Carr and George Weldon.

The melodies of the first two versions are from Sam Henry, the third melody is adapted from Creighton, *Songs and Ballads from Nova Scotia*. The broadside from which the third version was copied is in the Providence Public Library.

SONGS OF THE SEA AND SHIPS

There are innumerable versions of "William Taylor," and the theme is the same in all of them but in the details of the story there is tremendous variation which is one sure indication of very long oral transmission.

Clancy Brothers, p. 26; Cox, *Folk-Songs of the South*, p. 382; Creighton, *Songs and Ballads from Nova Scotia*, p. 64; Fowke, *Traditional Singers and Songs from Ontario*, p. 151; Firth, *Naval Songs and Ballads*, p. 326; Flanders and Brown, *Vermont Folksongs and Ballads*, p. 152; Greenleaf and Mansfield, *Ballads and Sea Songs of Newfoundland*, p. 49; Henry, Sam, "Songs of the People," Nos. 213 and 757; Huntington, *Songs the Whalemen Sang*, p. 94; Hubbard, *Ballads and Songs From Utah*, p. 58; Joyce, *Old Irish Folk Music and Songs*, p. 235; Karpeles, *Folk Songs from Newfoundland*, p. 171; Kidson, Ethel, *English Peasant Songs*, p. 100; Laws, *American Balladry from British Broadsides*, p. 208; Leach, *Folk Ballads and Songs of the Lower Labrador Coast*, p. 314; Mackenzie, *Ballads and Sea Songs from Nova Scotia*, p. 132; Moore, *Ballads and Folk Songs of the Southwest*, p. 171; Reeves, *The Everlasting Circle*, p. 227; Sharp, *English Folk Songs*, Vol. I: 11; Sharp, *English Folk Songs from the Southern Appalachians*, Vol. I: p. 373.

CAROLINE AND YOUNG SAILOR BOLD

Twas said of a nobleman's daughter
So comely and handsome we hear
Her father possessed a great fortune
Full thirty-five thousand a year
He had but one only daughter
Caroline was her name we are told
One day from her drawing room window
She spied a young sailor bold
His cheeks were as red as roses

THE GAM

His eyes were as the jet
Caroline then watched his departure
Went around and young William she met
Saying I am a nobleman's daughter
Possessed of five hundred in gold
Said she I'll forsake father and fortune
To wed with my sailor bold

Says William dear lady 'tis your duty
For your parents to mind
For in sailors there is no dependence
When they are on the main
Be advised and turn to your parents
And obey them in all you are told
And never let anyone tempt you
For to wed with a sailor bold

Says Caroline I am determined
And no one shall alter my mind
I'll ship and I'll cruise with my true love
And no one shall alter my mind
So she dressed herself up like a sailor
Forsook both her parents and gold
Three years and a half on the ocean
She cruised with her young sailor bold

Three times they were shipwrecked together
But always proved constant and true
Her duty she done like a sailor
Went aloft in her jacket blue
Her father long wept and lamented
His tears down in torrents did roll
At length they arrived in old England
Caroline and her young sailor bold

Strait way to her parents they did go
In her trousers and jacket so blue
The minute he received her and fainted
When first she appeared to his view
Forgive me dear father forgive me
Deny my portion of gold
But grant my request
To wed with my young sailor bold

Her father admired young William
And vowed that in sweet unity
If their lives were spared till next morning
Together they married would be
They were married and Caroline's portion
Was thirty five thousand in gold
And they live happy and cheerful
Caroline and her young sailor bold

Ship *Hillman* 1854

This typical broadside ballad in the ship *Hillman* journal is somewhat jumbled. But this must be pretty much what Martin V.B. Millard, who kept the journal intended. The melody used is suggested by the melody for the song in Creighton, *Songs and Ballads from Nova Scotia*.

Bulletin FSNE, No. 2, p. 9; Creighton, *Songs and Ballads from Nova Scotia*, p. 66; Huntington, *Songs the Whalemen Sang*, p. 103; Laws, *American Balladry from British Broadsides*, p. 211; Leach, *Folk Ballads and Songs of the Low Labrador Coast*, p. 94; O Lochlainn, *More Irish Street Ballads*, p. 78; Stubbs, *The Life of Man*, p. 22.

THE GAM

A SONG CONCERNING LOVE
(THE CAPTAIN CALLS ALL HANDS)

Fair you well my dearest Dear since I must leave you
I can no longer Stay I must go from you
I shall Pine and Dye if you go from me
So stay at home my Dear and do not leave me

Why should you go to Sea to Fight for Strangers
When you at home can stay free from all dangers
I will fold you in my arms my one Dearest juel
And I will keep you from all harms Love dont be Cruel

Down by one river as I was walking
A man and maid I Espied as they were talking
Their hands were joinded together as they were a going
Twas a Black and a Roling Eye that Proved my Ruin

Our Captain calls us now with haist and hurry
I Can no Longer Stop I must go from you
So dry up your watry tears and leave off weeping
For how happy we shall be at our next meating

Then on her neas she fell Like one a dying
And spreading her arms a broad and this Replying
Awake ye Rocks and Stones that is now relenting
All for the Sake of one I dye Lementing

Fair well you Parents Dear father and mother
You have left your daughter dear I have no other
It is vain to weep for me for I am a going
Where joys forever Be and fountains a flowing

Ship *Polly* 1794

SONGS OF THE SEA AND SHIPS

This song, its proper title is "The Captain Calls All Hands," or "Our Captain Calls All Hands" which seems to be quite rare, at least on this side of the ocean. What makes identification a little difficult is that elements of the song and even whole stanzas are found in other ballads. The melody is adapted from Purslow.

Huntington, *Songs The Whalemen Sang*, p. 99; Purslow, *The Constant Lovers*, p. 63; Reeves, *The Idiom of the People*, p. 165.

THE CHILE GIRLS

'Tis of a gallant bark I sing
That lays in Boston Bay
A-waiting there for orders
For to take us far away
A-waiting there for orders
For to take us far from home
Oh it's first we're bound for Rio boys
And it's then around Cape Horn

When we sailed out of Rio boys
It blew a pleasant gale
From ship to ship the cheers rang out
As we set every sail
As we set every sail, brave boys
For the race around the Horn
Oh, they wished us pleasant weather
While a-rounding of Cape Horn

Now rounding of Cape Horn, brave boys
We had fine nights and days
We dropped our anchor first of all
In Valparaiso Bay

THE GAM

And there them Chile girls come down
And I vow and do declare
They are far beyond our Yankee girls
With their black and shiny hair

They are waiting for a sailor man
To go upon a spree
To laugh and merry, merry
Spend his money free
And when his money is all gone
Now what do you suppose
They are far beyond our Yankee girls
For they'll rob him of his clothes

So farewell Valparaiso Bay
It's farewell for a while
And farewell all ye Chile girls
Who did them times beguile
And if ever I live to get paid off
I will sit and sing a song
All about them little Chile girls
That I met while round Cape Horn

Bark Andrew Hicks 1879

This song is usually called "Round Cape Horn," or "The Girls around Cape Horn," and sometimes "The Girls of Valparaiso." It seems to have been fairly well known and was sung by both whalemen and merchant seamen.

The "Rio" in this song is not Rio de Janeiro, but Rio Grande Do Sul in southernmost Brazil. There ships bound west around Cape Horn in the last century would often put in to refit before attempting the passage. That explains the lines "From ship to ship the cheers rant out. As we set every sail." For rounding the Horn from east to west was something to look forward to with dread because of the prevailing westerlies that often, perhaps usually, blew at gale force. Only very occasionally was the passage an easy one as in this song.

My father made the passage in a full rigged ship in 1892, and two men were lost, one was washed overboard and the other fell from aloft.

SONGS OF THE SEA AND SHIPS

The melody used here is adapted from Sam Henry's melody for the song, No. 539 of "Songs of the People."

Colcord, *Songs of American Sailormen*, p. 177; Henry, "Songs of the People," No. 539; Hugill, *Shanties from the Seven Seas*, p. 53; Purslow, *The Foggy Dew*, p. 80; Vaughan Williams and Lloyd, *The Penguin Book of English Folk Songs*, p. 90.

BLACK-EYED SUSAN

Well in the Downs the fleet was moored
The streamers waving in the wind
When Black Eyed Susan came on board
Oh where shall I my true love find
Tell me jovial sailors tell me true
Does my sweet William sail 'mongst you

William was high upon the yard
Rocked by the billows to and fro
Soon as her well known voice he heard
He signed and cast his eyes below
The cord glides swift through his glowing hands
And quick as light on the deck he stands

So does the lark high poised in air
Shut close his pinions to his breast
If chance his mate's shrill call he hear
And drops at once into her nest
The noblest captain in the whole British fleet
Might envy William those kisses sweet

THE GAM

Oh Susan Susan lovely dear
My vows shall ever true remain
Let me kiss off that falling tear
We only part to meet again
Blow as ye list ye winds my heart shall be
The faithful compass that still points to thee

Believe not what the landsmen say
Who tempt with doubts thy constant mind
They'll tell that sailors when away
In every port a mistress find
Yes do believe them when they tell thee so
For thou art present where ever I go

If to fair India's coast we sail
Thine eyes are seen in diamonds bright
Thy breath in Africa's spicy gales
Thy skin in ivory so white
Thus every beauteous object that I view
Wakes in my soul some charm of Sue

Though battle calls me from thy arms
Let not my pretty Susan mourn
Though cannons roar yet safe from harm
William shall to his dear return
Love turns aside the balls that around me fly
Lest precious tears should dim Sue's eye

The boatswain gave the fatal word
The sails their swelling bosoms spread
No longer must she stay aboard
They kissed she sighed he hung his head
Now her lessening boat rows to the land
Adieu she cried and waved her hand

Bark *Catalpa* 1856

SONGS OF THE SEA AND SHIPS

SECOND VERSION

All in the downs the fleet lay moored
The streamers waving in the wind
When black eyed Susan comes on board
Oh where shall I my true love find
Tell me you jovial sailors tell me true
If my sweet William sails among your crew

O William high upon the yard
Rocked by the billows two and fro
Soon as her well known voice he heard
He heaved a sigh and cast his eyes below
The cord glides swiftly through his glowing hand
And quick as lightning on the deck he stands

Oh Susan lovely Susan lovely dear
Let me kiss of that falling tear
We only part to meet again
If to fair India's coast I sail
Come let prepare the ………

DCHS archives

"Black-Eyed Susan" was very popular among nineteenth century seamen and that in spite of the fact that it started life as a purely literary song. It does not sound traditional but it is. The melody is adapted from the one for the song in John, *Our Familiar Songs*.... The second melody is supplied.

The Antihipnotic Songster, p. 16; Chappell, *Popular Music of the Olden Time*, Vol. II, p. 640; Creighton, *Maritime Folk Songs*, p. 90; Creighton and Senior, *Traditional Songs from Nova Scotia*, p. 131; Griggs, *Southern and Western Songster*, p. 107; Johnson, *Our Familiar Songs...*, p. 125; Laws, *American Balladry From British Broadsides*, p. 239; Ramsey, *The Tea-Table Miscellany*, p. 207; Stone, *Sea*

THE GAM

Songs and Ballads, p. 159; Reddall, *Songs that Never Die*, p. 42; Wier, *The Book of a Thousand Songs*, p. 45.

PRETTY POLLY
(THE TARRY TROUSERS)

As I walked out one fine may morning
To view the fields and take the air
I overheard a tender mother
A talking to her daughter dear

O daughter O daughter I rather you'd marry
No longer lead a single life
Oh no said she I'd much rather marry
For I choose to be a bold seamans wife

O sailors you know they are apt to ramble
And to some foreign parts will go
First they will court you and then they will leave you
And that will prove your overthrow

Mother you would have me marry a farmer
And I never would enjoy my hearts delight
But I'd have the man with the tarry trousers
They shine to me like diamonds bright

SONGS OF THE SEA AND SHIPS

The wind is a blowing and the anchor is a weighing
And he has come to take relief
And as it is so that I can no longer tarry
My charming girl you must not weep

Hark do you hear the loud guns roaring
Likewise the small arms making a noise
Polly has a true love a true love in the battle
Crying out fight on my brave yankee boys

Now the war is over and Polly is married
Married to her hearts delight
And see how neatly in trim he keeps her
She shines in silks like diamonds bright

Bark John Dawson 1863

This is an unusual version of "The Tarry Trousers," though actually versions of "The Tarry Trousers" do vary a great deal one from another. In some versions the girl follows her man to sea and in others she does not. Of course all sailors liked the idea that a girl would prefer a sailor to the security of a man on shore who had money. The melody here is from Sam Henry's "Songs of the People," changed a little to fit this version. The second melody is supplied.

Creighton and Senior, *Traditional Songs From Nova Scotia*, p. 212; Greenleaf and Mansfield, *Ballads and Sea Songs of Newfoundland*, p. 69; Henry, "Songs of the People," No. 532; Huntington, *Songs the Whalemen Sang*, p. 96; Karpeles, *Folk Songs From Newfoundland*, p. 201; O Lochlainn, *Irish Street Ballads*, p. 243; Palmer, *The Valiant Sailor*, p. 9; Sharp, *English County Folk Songs*, p. 48; Sharp, *English Folk Songs From the Southern Appalachians*, Vol. II, p. 168.

THE GAM

THE SAILOR'S RETURN
(GREEN BEDS)

A story, a story, I will tell you of one
It's of a gallant sailor and his name it is John
He has been on a gallant voyage and has lately come on shore
In his rags he appears like one that is poor

He went to an ale house he used to lodge in
But he seemed so poor they would scarce let him in
Welcome home they grumbled welcome home from sea
For last night my daughter was dreaming of thee

Call down your daughter Molly and set her on my knee
Call down your daughter and set her down by me
My daughter Molly's busy Jack and can not come down to thee
Nor neither will I trust thee for one pot or two or three

Johnny being drowsy he hung down his head
And asked for a candle to light him to bed
My beds are all engaged Jack and have been for this week
So that poor Johnny has his lodging for to seek

Come tell me proud landlady come tell me what I owe
Come tell me what I owe and the debt it shall be paid
It is nine and forty shillings that thou woes me of old
With that he pulled out two hands full of gold

SONGS OF THE SEA AND SHIPS

> The sight of the gold made this old whore to rue
> Saying Johnny you're in earnest and I was but in jest
> Upon my reputation young Johnny I love best
> I'll call my daughter Molly and set her on thy knee
> I'll call my daughter Molly and let her set by thee
>
> She kissed him she hugged him she called him her dear
> Saying the green bed is empty and Johnny shall lie there
> Before I lie in the green bed I will lie on the floor
> Before I lie in a poor man's bed I will lie out the door
>
> For when a man's got money he can boldly rant and roar
> But when he has got nothing they will kick him out the door
>
> Come all you brother sailors that plough the raging main
> Come all you brother seamen that stands both cold and rain
> When you have got money pray lay it up in store
> For when you have got nothing they will kick you out the door
>
> DCHS archives

The theme of this ballad — that the sailor is only welcome for his money — is quite common in sailors' songs. The lines "He has been a gallant voyage and has lately come on shore/in his rags he appears like one that is poor," sound as though Johnny may have been a whaleman, for just as the whaler — the vessel — was recognized by her begrimed and smoke-stained sails, the whaleman was notorious for his patched and repatched clothing, for no cloth, however stout would last out a three or four-year voyage.

The extra line in the sixth stanza can be omitted or sung to the last four measures of the tune. And the two-line stanza can be repeated to make four lines.

The melody is adapted from the melody for the song in Sam Henry's "Songs of the People." The second melody is supplied.

Belden, *Ballads and Songs*, p. 160; Eddy, *Ballads and Songs from Ohio*, p. 95; Fowke, *Traditional Singers and Songs...*, p. 29; Gardner, *Ballads and Songs of Southern Michigan*, p. 91; Greig, *Folk-Song of the North-East*, CVX; Henry, "Songs of the People," No. 779; Laws, *American Balladry from British Broadsides*, p. 159; Leach, *Folk Ballads and Songs...*, p. 166; Mackenzie, *Ballads and Sea Songs...*, p.

245; Palmer, *Songs of the Midlands*, p. 97; Purslow, *The Wanton Seed*, p. 48; Sharp, *Southern Appalachians*, Vol. 1, p. 365; Thompson, *Body, Boots and Britches*, p. 211; Vaughan Williams and Lloyd, *English Folk Songs*, p. 48.

OH CAPTAIN, CAPTAIN TELL ME TRUE (THE SAILOR BOY)

Oh captain captain tell me true
Does my sweet William sail with you
He sails across the deep blue sea
And never never thinks of me

Oh father father build me a boat
So o'er the ocean I may float
And any ship that I pass by
I'll think I hear my Willie cry

Oh gypsy, gypsy tell me true
Please tell me something I can do
I'd give this whole big wide world
To keep him from another girl

Mildred Huntington

This little three-stanza fragment is all that Mildred Huntington can remember of what was a long and very popular broadside ballad. It has many titles, but "The Sailor Boy" is the one by which it is best known.

Mil learned this either from her grandfather Welcome Tilton or from one of her whaleman great uncles. The melody she uses with this fragment is almost exactly the same as the melody to which she sings "The Butcher Boy."

SONGS OF THE SEA AND SHIPS

Baring-Gould, *A Garland of Country Song*, p. 20; Baring-Gould and Cecil Sharp, *English Folk-Songs for Schools*, p. 80; Barry, *The Main Woods Songster*, p. 58; Belden, *Ballads and Songs...*, p. 186; Creighton, *Songs and Ballads from Nova Scotia*, p. 89; Eddy, *Ballads and Songs from Ohio*, p. 77; Gardner, *Ballads and Songs of Southern Michigan*, p. 94; Greig, *Folk-Song of the North-East*, LXIV; Henry, *Folk Songs from the Southern Highlands*, p. 189; Hubbard, *Ballads and Songs from Utah*, p. 90; Karpeles, *Folk Songs from Newfoundland*, p. 159; Kenedy, *The Universal Irish Song Book*, p. 97; Laws, *American Balladry from British Broadsides*, p. 146; Moore, *Ballads and Folk Songs of the Southwest*, p. 174; Palmer, *The Valiant Sailor*, p. 48; Scarborough, *A Song Catcher in Southern Mountains*, p. 319; Vaughan Williams and Lloyd, *The Penguin Book of English Folk Songs*, p. 94.

MY WILLIE'S ON THE DARK BLUE SEA

My Willie's on the dark blue sea
He's gone far o'er the main
And many a dreary a day we'll pray
E're he come back again

Then blow gentle wind o'er the dark blue sea
Bid the storm king stay his hand
And bring my Willie back home to me
(blurred line)

I love my Willie best of all
He was ever true to me
And lonesome weary are the hours
Since first he went to sea

There is danger on the mighty deep
I hear the billows cry
And morning voices seem to speak
From out the cloudy sky

THE GAM

I see the vivid lightning flash
And hear the thunder roar
Oh father save my Willie from
The storm king's mighty power

And as she spoke the lightning flashed
Hushed was the thunder roar
And Willie clasped me in his arms
To roam the sea no more

Now blow gentle wind o'er the dark blue sea
No more will stay thy hand
Since Willie is safe at home with me
In his own dear native land

      Ship *Three Brothers*, 1851; Ship *Hillman*, 1854

This began as a very popular parlor song but it seems to have become traditional with whalemen. The melody used here is from the playing of Willard Marden. Bill Tilton sang the song to a quite similar melody, but I never learned the song from him considering it much too simple.

The Book of Popular Songs, p. 22; *The Golden Wreath*, p. 52; Grover, *A Heritage of Songs*, p. 146; Huntington, *Songs the Whalemen Sang*, p. 234.

THE FEMALE CABIN BOY

It was of a pretty fair maid as you shall understand
She had a mind for roving unto some foreign land
Attired in Sailors clothing so boldly did appear
And with a captain did agree to serve him for a year

SONGS OF THE SEA AND SHIPS

She engaged with the captain as a cabin boy to be
Our ship she being ready we soon did put to sea
The captains lady being on board who was so full of joy
So glad the Captain had engaged this handsome cabin boy

So sprightly was this pretty maid and did her duty well
But what soon followed after the thing itself will tell
The Captain with this pretty maid did oftimes skip and toy
Till he soon found out the secret of the handsome cabin boy

So sprightly was this pretty maid and with her side locks curled
The sailors oftimes smiled and said she looked just like a girl
By eating of the captains biscuit her color it did destroy
The waist was swelled of lovely Ann the handsome cabin boy

As through the bay of Biscay our gallant ship she ploughed
One night among the sailors there was a bit of a row
They bundled from their hammocks their rest it did destroy
The swore about the groaning of the handsome cabin boy

Oh doctor oh doctor the cabin boy did cry
The sailors swore by all twas good the cabin boy would die
The doctor ran with all his might and laughed at the fun
To think the cabin boy should have a daughter or a son

Now when the sailors heard the news they all began to stare
The child belonged to none of them they solemnly did swear
Now says the captain's lady My dear I wish you joy
For either you or I have betrayed the handsome cabin boy

Come lets fill up our glasses and drink success to trade
Likewise to the handsome cabin boy whether a man or maid
And if the seas should rise again our sailors to destroy
We will ship a few more men like the handsome cabin boy

Bark Champion 1842

Here is a ballad in which the girl goes to sea dressed as a sailor and comes to grief as a result of it. The captain's lady seems to have been

THE GAM

exceedingly broad minded. The melody used here is the melody for "The Lily of the West," also found in the bark *Champion* journal one of the very few times when the melody is included with the words in any of the journals or logbooks.

Buchan and Hall, *The Scottish Folksinger*, p. 115; Gardner, *Ballads and Songs of Southern Michigan*, p. 399; Hugill, *Shanties and Sailors' Songs*, p. 16; Hugill, *Shanties and Sailors*; Laws, *American Balladry From British Broadsides*, p. 209; Peacock, *Songs of the Newfoundland Outports*, p. 280; Purslow, *Marrow Bones*, p. 32; Reeves, *The Idiom of the People*, p. 110.

THE FEMALE SAILOR

Come all good people far and near
Attend unto my ditty
Near Gravesend lived a comely maid
And she was both young and pretty

Her lover was pressed
And drowned in a foreign sea
Which caused this fair maid for to say
I'll be a rambling sailor

From stem to stern she boldly goes,
She braves all dangers, she fears no foes,
And you soon shall hear of the overthrow
Of the rambling female sailor

SONGS OF THE SEA AND SHIPS

In jacket blue and trousers white,
Just like a sailor so neat and tight
The sea it was the heart's delight
Of the rambling female sailor

It's in a calm this damsel young
She charmed the sailors with her tongue,
And as she walked the deck she sung
Remember the queen of beauty

It's in a storm or up aloft
She's ready at her station.
From stem to stern she boldly goes
She likes her occupation

This maiden gay did a wager lay
She'd go aloft with any
So up aloft she boldly goes
Where oft times she had been merry

This maiden gay 'tis sad to tell
She missed her hold and down she fell
And calmly bid this world farewell
Did the rambling female sailor

When her white breasts in view first came
It proved it was a female frame
Rebecca Young it was the name
Of the rambling female sailor

Her hair hung o'er her pallid cheeks
She looked like a drooping willow,
And the sailor gazed and said,
"Farewell unbounded billow."

May laurels green grow o'er her grave
And at her feet be planted
May willows sweet grow at her feet
Of her who died undaunted

THE GAM

> May a marble stone be inscribed upon
> "Here lies a maid that has lately gone"
> No fairer maid did the sun shine on
> Than the rambling female sailor
>
> Bark Roscius 1858

This is not a very good song. Indeed it is the sort of thing that has given broadside ballads a bad name in many quarters, and that in spite of the fact that many are good and some are beautiful.

The melody is adapted from a song called "The Female Smuggler," which also is not edifying published by Wm. Hall & Son, New York in 1858 as sheet music. The second melody is supplied.

LADY FRANKLIN'S LAMENT FOR HER HUSBAND

You seamen bold that have with stood
The storms that roll oer yon briny flood
Attend these lines which soon will seeme
To put you in mind of a sailors dream

It was homeward bound one night on the deep
While swimming in my hammock I fell asleep
I dreamed a dream that I thought was true
Concerning Franklin and his brave crew

SONGS OF THE SEA AND SHIPS

I dreamed as I neared the English shore
I heard a lady sadly deplore
She wept a while and then did say
Alas my Franklin is long away

It is seven long years since a ship of fame
Did bare my husband fare oer the main
With a hundred seamen bold and stout
To fin a northwestern passage out

To find a passage around the north pole
With a hundred hearts so brave and bold
Tis more than any one can do
With hearts undreaded and courage true

Tars capt brown of scafesbrough town
Brave imbil and perry of high renown
Thers capt ross and many more
That have been cruising on that shore

They sailed east and they sailed west
Around grunlands cost where they thought best
Through hardships and dangers they nightly strove
On mountains of ice their ships were drove

These sad forlornings give me pain
Oh my long lost Frankling fare oer the main
Ten thousands pounds I would freely give
To know that on earth my husband lives

But seven long years have gone and past
And many cold and winter blasts
Blow oer the graves where poor seamen fell
By induring sufferings one though cant tell

In baffings bay whare the wright whales blows
The tail of frankling no one knows
Which causes many a wife to mourn
And weep in sadness till they return

Bark *Morning Light* 1861

THE GAM

Sir John Franklin with two ships and some two hundred men was searching for a long dreamed of northwest passage. The hope of finding such a passage had been a dream since the days of Henry Hudson's expedition which cost him his life when his crew refused to continue the search and cast him adrift in Hudson's Bay in a small boat.

Sir John Franklin and his expedition were last reported by a whaler on July 26th 1845. Lady Franklin spent a fortune trying to find out what had happened to her husband and his men.

The song is sometimes called "A Sailor's Dream." The melody used here is adapted from the one that Sam Henry uses in "Songs of the People."

Creighton, *Folksongs from Southern New Brunswick*, p. 202; Creighton, *Maritime Folksongs*, p. 145; Doerflinger, *Shantymen and Shantyboys*, p. 146; Greenleaf, *Ballads and Sea Songs of Newfoundland*, p. 300; Greig, *Folk-Song of the North-East*, LXXXVI; Henry, "Songs of the People" No. 815; Laws, *American Balladry from British Broadsides*, p. 144.

THE FLYING DUTCHMAN

'Twas on a dark and stormy night
Far southward of the Cape
When from a strong norwester
We had just made our escape
Like an infant in the cradle
The sea was hushed to sleep
And peacefully we sailed along
The bosom of the deep

SONGS OF THE SEA AND SHIPS

At length the helmsman gave a cry
Of terror and of fear
Just as if he'd gazed upon
Some sudden danger near
As looking round the ocean
Just upon our lea
We espied the flying Dutchman
Flying furious o'er the sea

Take in your blowing Canvass
Our watchful master cried
For me and my ships company
Great danger doth betide
The billows crest all white with foam
All anger doth appear
The wind springs up a hurricane
For Vanderdecken's near

On the flying Dutchman comes
On o'er each lofty spray
Deceived by the tempest dire
He makes for Table Bay
Like a bird on wing he's born before
The wind and howling blast
But ere he can cast anchor there
His day alas has past

Now mourn for Vanderdecken
How miserable is his doom
And all around that stormy Cape
It is his living tomb
It's there the Dutchman beats about
Forever night and day
And tries in vain his home to gain
By entering Table Bay

Bark *Pacific* 1870

THE GAM

The "Flying Dutchman" appears to be a quite rare song, and that in spite of the fact that the story of the flying Dutchman was known to every deep water sailor of the last century.

Both Doerflinger's and Ranson's versions are quite close to the version from the Bark *Pacific* journal, and that would seem to indicate that all three derived from the same broadside.

Ranson says that the song was sung to the melody for "The Banks of Newfoundland." So it is Ranson's melody for "The Banks of Newfoundland," that we have here. Actually there are two entirely different ballads called the "Banks of Newfoundland," and a number of different melodies. So if you don't like this particular one, look for another that will fit, or use the melody in Doerflinger. The second melody is supplied.

Doerflinger, *Shantymen and Shantyboys*, p. 148; Hugill, *Songs of the Sea*, p. 183; Laws, *American Balladry from British Broadsides*, p. 152; Ranson, *Songs of the Wexford Coast*, p. 45.

SWEET WILLIAM
(WILLIAM AND NANCY)

It was on one Sunday morning all in the month of May
Our ship she weighed her anchor for we were bound to sea
The sun did shine most glorious for Lisbon we were bound
The hills and dales all furnished with pretty girls all round

SONGS OF THE SEA AND SHIPS

I spied a fair damsel all in her blooming years
Her heart was filled with sorrow her eyes were filled with tears
All for her best beloved whom you shall understand
He had a mind for roving into some foreign land

She had no thought of parting with her own hearts delight
Until he came and told her he was going abroad to fight
All for to defend his country and the land that they lived on
So kindly he saluted her and these words she sung

Come marry me sweet William Come marry me I pray
Come marry me sweet William before you sail away
Tis the cause of all my grieving to you it is well known
So come marry me sweet William and don't leave me alone

If I should meet a damsel both proper tall and gay
And if I should take a liking my love what would you say
Would you be all offended Oh no I should love her too
I would stand one side sweet William while she did talk with you

My love these words are pleasing both pleasing fair and kind
And we will have a wedding but you must stay behind
For in the din of battle what would you do then
While we are all bold sailors and valiant fighting men

Where cannons loudly roaring and bullets swiftly fly
Where drums and trumpets sounding a drown the dismal cry
Poor sailors they lie bleeding 'tis a horrid sight to see
So stay at home sweet Polly and don't you go with me

Oh! Do not talk of dangers and try to frighten me
For I am full resolved to keep you company
And if it be your hard fortune all in the sea to die
I never will forsake you but down by your side lie

Bark *John Dawson* 1863

This was a very popular ballad and, as would be expected it has many titles among them "William and Nancy," "Lisbon," and "Men's clothing I'll Put on." The melody used here is adapted from Sam Henry's version of

THE GAM

the song called "Lovely Annie," in his "Songs of the People." The second melody is supplied.

Henry, Sam, "Songs of the People," No. 561; Huntington, *Songs the Whalemen Sang*, p. 266 (a fragment); Karpeles, *Folk Songs from Newfoundland*, p. 178; Laws, *American Balladry from British Broadsides*, p. 206; O'Shoughnessy, *Twenty-One Lincolnshire Folk Songs*, p. 14; Peacock, *...Newfoundland Outports*, p. 202; Vaughan Williams and Lloyd, *The Penguin Book of English Folk Songs*, p. 58.

CONSTANT LOVERS
(THE SILK MERCHANT'S DAUGHTER)

Both young men and damsels that to love belong
Come near and listen awhile to my song
I make no grate question but that this new ditty
Unto many people well pleasing may be

This of a rich merchant in London I right
He had a fair daughter his hearts Chief delight
She loved a Porter and to prevent the day
Of marriage he forced this young man away

For to serve the Queen and when gone from the shore
This forsaken damsel was grieved full sore
Then in Mans apparal in a merchants ship
She ventured her life over the raging deep

SONGS OF THE SEA AND SHIPS

Then when come to anchor near some foreign land
Where she ventured ashore as I do understand
A sword of the Captains in her hand she took
A way she did wander her love for to look

Then going thro a forest long time before night
A couple of Indians appeared in her sight
When drawing near to them these two brethren they
Intended to take this fair maids life away

But her having a sword her life to defend
From Blood thirsty ones who did murder intend
Thro mercy she conquerd One of them she killed
And forced the other to quit the field

She ambled along till some Smoke did appear
Which made her to think that some houses were near
But as she sought truly in the Evening tide
She came to a town that stood by the sea side

In this hour there was a ship bound to see
With all expedition unto Jamaica
In which she did sail and come to Kingston
Where to her great joy unexpected she found

Her love this young Porter was walking the street
She made it her business this young man to meet
And said what ship brother pray tell unto me
He told her and said bound to England we be

She said unto Long I am willing to go
But how to git thither I do not well know
I am not a sailor but if you want a man
For my passage I will do the best I can

Not knowing who it was he took her on bord
The Captain said what do you want with a sword
Account of her travels unto him she gave
And told him how that sword once her life did save

THE GAM

They set sail for England and now pray give ear
What sudden destruction to them did appear
The ship Sprung a leak and to the bottom she went
When out at main seas to their great discontent

Thirty seven hands were confined in a boat
In which small allowance of Room they did float
Food being all gone death appeared so nigh
The Captain made them lots to see who might die

They were made of paper as the Captain thought fit
To draw for life fairly on them to be writ
A number of figures beginning one
Unto thirty seven which things were soon done

Then in a small bag together they were shook
And so at a venture each one his lot took
This poor damsels lot was to draw least
For one might die first to feed all the rest

They drawed lots again that they fairly might see
Who among them all her butcher might be
It was a hard lot you will say when you hear
She was to be slain by that young man her dear

For whose sake so far she had ventured her life
For to do his office he come with a knife
Another with a bowl the blood for to take
At which motion she sighed and these words she spake

Spare me a few minutes I have something to say
Unfortunate creature this unhappy day
I might have escaped if I had been wise
Lord have mercy upon me and hear my sad cry

Must I who have ventured so many score miles
Through forests and hedges high mountains and stiles
Shund so many dangers and last indeed
Die a sacrifice to hunger a man for to feed

SONGS OF THE SEA AND SHIPS

Round the neck she caught him and with a kiss said
You are going to kill a poor innocent maid
A rich merchants daughter of London I be
See what I am come to by loving of thee

She shewd him a ring that between them was broke
He knowing the token then and with a sigh spoke
Alas poor Lady my heart it will burst
For hopes of your Long Life I'll die first

With tears running down each other embraced
To satisfy hunger the rest were in haste
The Captain said if you loves debt you will pay
Prepare now for death I can no longer stay

Like a noble martyr this loving young man
Said to him that stood with a knife in his hand
Be quick to your office my business is done
Before the stroke was given they all heard a gun

At which this young man cryd out hold thine hand
I did hear a gun we are near some ship or Land
Within half an hour then the ship did appear
Bound for Ireland which sight them did cheer

They were taken up and to Dublin conveyd
This Captain and couple it is now said
They came to fair London Powder (?) day
And there at a tavern this couple did stay

While the Captain unto her father did go
And asked for his daughter his answer was so
This twenty five weeks my dear Child has been lost
To be sure she is dead with my life it will cost

My heart it will break for the lost of my Child
To hear these expressions he said with a smile
She has been near death But now is alive and well
Nor (?) your souls grief in Earth can her sorrows excel

THE GAM

Account of her travels unto him he gave
And told him how such a young man did her save
Well if it be so She shall be his wife
And I shall adore him all the days of my life

The Captain sent......

Ship Polly 1794

The proper title of this song is "The Silk Merchant's Daughter." Unfortunately the last stanza or stanzas of this ship *Polly* version are lost with part of a page missing from the journal. But there is enough left to see that there is a happy ending, and after all the poor girl had gone through there should be.

For references see Laws, *American Balladry from British Broadsides*, N. 10, also Purslow, *The Constant Lovers*, p. 91–92, and it is from Purslow that the melody used here has been adapted. The second melody is supplied.

Laws, *American Balladry from British Broadsides*, p. 207; Purslow, *The Constant Lovers*, p. 91.

Platinum print photograph of coopers at Merrill's Wharf, New Bedford

Traditional Songs and Ballads

Here are some songs in which whaling and the sea are absent, or only incidental. They are, for the most part, old songs which have been sung for many years in England, Ireland, Scotland and more recently in the United States. Many of these are ballads, songs which tell a story; often a tragic one. A large number of these songs have been collected in the southern Appalachians, but those tend to be fragmentary, and less complete than those collected in New England. This is not surprising, considering the close ties that many New Englanders had with the "old country" as well as the frequent encounters that sailors from Great Britain and Ireland had with their Yankee counterparts.

Whalers, like most other folks, recognized good stories and good tunes when they encountered them, and adopted many of them as their own.

THE GAM

A SONG OF LOVE (HIGH GERMANY)

Abroad as I was walking
And a-walking along
I espied two lovers talking
And a-walking along
Says The young one
To the fair one
Bonny lassie it's away
For the king he has commanded
And his orders we must obey

Oh that's not what you promised me
When me you did beguile
You promised for to marry me
If I proved with child
So it's do not me forsake
But pity on me take
For great is my woe
Through Scotland Spain and Ireland
It's along with you I'll go

Over hills and lofty mountains
It would hurt your tender feet
Over hills and weary traveling
It would cause you for to weep
Besides you would not yield to lie
In the open fields with me all night long
And your parents would be angry
If along with me you should gang

TRADITIONAL SONGS AND BALLADS

Oh my parents I value not
Nor my ties do I fear
It's along with you my jovial sailor bold
I'll travel both far and near
For gold shall never deceive me
Nor any other fee
Along with you I'll go for to fight
The French and Spaniards
Or it's any other daring foe

Oh since you have proved so venturesome
As to venture your sweet life
I will first take you and I'll marry you
And make you my lawful wife
And if anyone offend
I will attend you shall see
You shall hear the drums and trumpets sound
On the high walls of Shakespeare

Ship L.C. Richmond 1834

This version of "High Germany" seems to be pretty badly garbled in places. The meter is pretty bad in places, too, which means that the value of many of the notes will have to be changed when it is sung. Additionally, that "high walls of Shakespeare" in the last line of the last stanza must remain unexplained. The usual ending is, "In the Wars of High Germany."

There is a very nice version of this song in Baring Gould's *A Garland of Country Song*, p. 6–7 with a quite detailed discussion of the song's background. The melody used here is adapted from the version in Peacock's *Songs of the Newfoundland Outports*, 679–680.

And note, as Baring-Gould points out, that there are actually two quite different "High Germanies;" one seems to have been the more popular.

Baring-Gould, S. and H. Fleetwood Sheppard, *A Garland...*, p. 7; Baring-Gould, S. and Cecil J. Sharp, *English Folk-Songs For Schools*, p. 44; Peacock, ... *Newfoundland Outports*, p. 659; Reeves, *The Everlasting Circle*, p. 151; Reeves, *The Idiom...*, p. 125; Sharp, One Hundred..., p. 127; Sharp, *English County...*, p. 12; Sharp, *English Folk Songs*, Vol. I, p. 93.

THE GAM

TEN THOUSAND MILES AWAY

'Tis many and many a year ago
Since last I saw my Meg
She'd a pair of irons on her arm
And another on her leg
And another on her leg brave boys
And unto me did say
I'm taking a trip on a government ship
Ten thousand miles away

Then blow ye winds yo ho
A-roving we will go
We'll stay no more on England's shore
So let the music play
I'm off on the morning train
To cross the raging main
And I'll bid farewell to my own true love
Ten thousand miles away

Joseph Chase Allen

This fragment of the song, and the melody, are both from Joseph Chase Allen. This is all he can remember of the song as it was sung by Bill Tilton, the chanteyman.

Poor Meg was bound for Australia, the dumping ground for England's unwanted, unfortunate and undesirable — one of a number of songs that

TRADITIONAL SONGS AND BALLADS

deal with the transportation in one way or another. Perhaps the best known are "Botany Bay," the ancestor of the American "Boston Burglar," "Bold Jack Donahoo," "The Wild Colonial Boy," and more.

France's dumping ground for the unfortunate was Devil's Island off the north coast of South America, and Portugal's was the Cape Verde Islands.

Abrahams, *A Singer and Her Songs...*, p. 41; Colcord, *Songs of American Sailormen*, p. 159; Flanders and Brown, *Vermont Folk-Songs and Ballads*, p. 148; Harlow, *Chanteying Aboard American Ships*, p. 116; Hubbard, *Ballads and Songs from Utah*, p. 143; Hugill, *Shanties From the Seven Seas*, p. 409; Ives, Burl, *Sea Songs*, p. 46; Manifold, *The Penguin Australian Song Book*, p. 8; *The Scottish Students' Song Book*, p. 124.

THE DRUNKEN FOOL (OUR GOODMAN)

Oh the first night that I came home
As drunk as I could be
I thought I saw a horse in the stable
Where my horse ought to be

You old fool you drunken fool
As drunk as you can be
That's not a horse that's a mooly cow
That my mother gave to me

THE GAM

Now I've traveled round this wide wide world
Ten thousand miles or more
But a mooly cow with a saddle on
I never saw before

The next night that I came home
As drunk as I could be
I thought I saw a coat in the hall
Where my coat ought to be

You old fool you drunken fool
As drunk as you can be
That's not a coat that's a patchwork quilt
That my mother gave to me

Now I've traveled round this wide wide world
Ten thousand miles or more
But a patchwork quilt with pockets on
I never saw before

The next night that I came home
As drunk as I could be
I thought I saw a head on the pillow
Where my head ought to be

You old fool you drunken fool
As drunk as you can be
That's not a head that's a cabbage leaf
That my mother gave to me

Now I've traveled round this wide wide world
Ten thousand miles or more
But a cabbage leaf with a mustache on
I never saw before

The last night that I came home
As drunk as I could be
I saw a thing in my wife's thing
Where my thing ought to be

TRADITIONAL SONGS AND BALLADS

You old fool you drunken fool
As drunk as you can be
That's not a thing that's a rolling pin
That my mother game to me

Now I've traveled round this wide wide world
Ten thousand miles or more
But a rolling pin with knockers on
I never saw before

Albertus Cahoon

This is Child Ballad 274, "Our Goodman." Sam Henry in "Songs of the People," No. 21, calls the song "The Blin' Auld Man" or "The Covered Cavalier." Henry notes that the song is a Jacobite relic dating back to either the rebellion of 1715 or that of 1745 and the man in hiding was a Jacobite seeking temporary refuge in the house of a relative — the wife. The song seems to have changed a great deal over the years.

The version of the song here is from the singing of John and Beatrice Whiting of Chilmark on Martha's Vineyard who learned it from Bert Cahoon. Bert may have learned it from his father who was a captain in the United States Life Saving Service which later became part of the Coast Guard. The second melody is supplied.

Belden, *Ballads and Songs*, p. 89; Coffin, *The British Traditional Ballad in North America*, p. 143; Eddy, *Ballads and Songs from Ohio*, p. 95; Finger, *Frontier Ballads*, p. 161; Hamer, *Garners Gay*, p. 24; Henry, Sam, "Songs of the People," No. 21; Hubbard, *Ballads and Songs from Utah*, p. 34; Moore, *Ballads and Folk Songs of the Southwest*, p. 119; Peters, *Folk Songs Out of Wisconsin*, p. 168; Sharp, *English Folk Songs From the Southern Appalachians*, Vol. I, p. 267; Shay, *Barroom Ballads*, p. 178; Scarborough, *A Song Catcher in Southern Mountains*, p. 231.

THE GAM

THE SUFFOLK MIRACLE

A wonder stranger ne'er was known
Than what I now shall treat upon
In Suffolk there did lately dwell
A farmer rich and known full well

He had a daughter fair and bright
On whom he placed his full delight
Her beauty was beyond compare
She was both virtuous and fair

There was a young man living by
Who was so charmed with her eye
That he could never be at rest
He was by love so much possest

He made address to her and she
Did grant him love immediately
But when her father came to hear
He parted her and her poor dear

Forty miles distant was she sent
Unto his brother with intent
That she should there so long remain
Till she had changed her mind again

TRADITIONAL SONGS AND BALLADS

There at this young man sadly grieved
But knew not how to be relieved
He signed and sobbed continually
That his true love he could not see

She by no means could to him send
Who was her hearts spoused friend
He sighed he grieved but all in vain
For she confined must still remain

He mourned so much that doctors art
Could give no ease unto his heart
Who was so strangely terrified
That in short time for love he died

She that from him was sent away
Knew nothing of his dying day
But constant still she did remain
And loved the dead although in vain

After he had in grave be laid
A month or more unto this maid
He came in the middle of the night
Who joyed to see her hearts delight

Her father's horse which well she knew
Her mother's hood (?) and safe guard too
He brought with him to testify
Her parents order he came by

Which when her uncle understood
He hoped it would be for her good
And gave consent to her straightway
That with him she should come away

And when she got her love behind
They passed as swift as any wind
That in two hours or little more
He brought her to her father's door

THE GAM

But as they did this great haste make
He did complain his head did ache
Her handkerchief she then took out
And tied the same his head about

And unto him she then did say
Thou art as cold as any clay
When we come home a fire we'll have
But little dreamed he went to grave

Soon were they at her father's door
And after she ne'er saw him more
I'll set the horse up then he said
And then he left this harmless maid

She knocked and straight a man he cried
Who's there I she then replied
Who wondered much her voice to hear
And was possessed with dread and fear

Her father he did tell and then
He stood like an affrighted man
Downstairs he ran and when he see her
Cryed out My child and how comst thou here

Pray sir did not you send for me
By such a messenger said she,
Which made his hair stir on his head
As knowing well that he was dead

Where is he then to her he said
He's in the stable quoth the maid
Go in said he and go to bed
I'll see the horse well littered

He stared about and there could be
No shape of any mankind see
But found his horse all in a sweat
Which made him in a dearly fret

TRADITIONAL SONGS AND BALLADS

His daughter he said nothing to
Nor none else though full well they knew
That he was dead a month before
For of grieving her full sore

Her father to the father went
Of the deceased with full intent
To tell him what his daughter said
So both came back unto this maid

They asked her and she still did say
Twas he that brought me away
Which when they heard they were amazed
And on each other strangely gazed

A handkerchief she said she tied
About his head and that they tried
The sexton then they did speak unto
That he the grave would them undo

Affrighted then they did behold
His body turning into mold
And though he had a month been dead
The handkerchief was bout his head

This thing they then unto her told
And the whole truth they did unfold
She was thereat so terrify
And grieved that she did quickly die

Part not true love you rich men then
For if they be right honest men
Your daughters love give them their way
For force oft breeds their lives decay

Ship Polly 1794

"The Suffolk Miracle" is Child 272. The ship *Polly* version is very close to it with only occasional word changes, almost as though it had been copied

THE GAM

from a broadside. In the 25th stanza of the ship *Polly* version, a line is omitted in the journal. It has been supplied from Child, Vol. IV, p. 67. The addition of that line, "About his head and that they tried," makes the last four stanzas come out correctly.

For references to other American versions of the ballad see Coffin, *The British Traditional Ballad in North America*, p. 142.

The melody used here is adapted from Sam Henry's version of the song which is very different called, "The Lover's Ghost." The second melody is supplied.

Cox, *Folk-Songs of the South*, p. 152; Creighton and Senior, *Traditional Songs from Nova Scotia*, p. 88; Flanders, *et al*, *The New Green Mountain Songster*, p. 86; Flanders and Olney, *Ballads Migrant in New England*, p. 145; Henry, "Songs of the People," No. 217; Moore, *Ballads and Folk Songs of the Southwest*, p. 117; Peacock, *Songs of the Newfoundland Outports*, 407; Sharp, *English Folk Songs from the Southern Appalachians*, Vol. I, p. 261; Wells, *The Ballad Tree*, p. 21.

WILLIE BRENNAN (BRENNAN ON THE MOOR)

TRADITIONAL SONGS AND BALLADS

Tis of a bold highwayman that I'm a going to tell
Whose name was Willie Brennan in Ireland he did dwell
On the Calvin Mountains he began his bold career
And many a wealthy gentleman before him shook with fear

Chorus
Brennan on the moor Brennan on the moor
Bold gay and undaunted stood young Brennan on the moor

A brace of loaded pistols he carried night and day
But never robbed a poor man upon the King's highway
But what he took from the rich like Turpin and black bess
He willingly divided with the widow in distress

One day he robbed a packman whose name was Julius Bawn
They traveled on together until the day was dawn
The packman finding his money gone likewise he watch and chain
He soon encountered Willie and robbed them back again

When Willie found the packman as smart a man as he
He took him on the King's highway a companion for to be
The packman threw away his pack without any more delay
And proved a faithful comrade until his dying day

One day upon the Kings' highway as Willie he sat down
He met the mayor of Castleray once outside of town
The mayor knew his features young man I think says he
Your name is Willie Brennan and you must come along with me

Now Willie's wife she being in town provisions for to buy
And when she saw her Willie she began to weep and cry
Oh that I had a blunderbuss no sooner had he spoke
She handed him a blunderbuss from underneath her cloak

Now with this loaded blunderbuss the truth he did unfold
He made the mayor quake with fear and robbed him of his gold
Five hundred pounds were offered for his apprehension there
But he with horse and saddle to the mountains did repair

THE GAM

Now Brennan being an outlaw all on the mountains high
With cavalry and infantry to take him they did try
He laughed them to scorn and at length he did say
A false hearted young woman did verily me betray

In the County of Tiparery in a place called Claymore
O Brennan and his comrade were made to suffer sore
He lost his fore-finger shot off by a ball
And Brennan and his comrade were taken after all

Now Brennan being taken in irons he was bound
And taken unto Cromwell and where high walls surround
The jury found him guilty and the judge made the reply
For robbing on the King's highway you are condemned to die

Farewell unto my wife and you my children three
Farewell unto my Father who is ever dear to me
Farewell unto my Mother and to her grey locks he cried
Oh better that Willie Brennan in his cradle had died.

Bark *John Dawson* 1863

This is another one of a host of those glorifying the outlaw. Perhaps that is because the lower stratum of society — from which so many of our folksongs come — had a not so secret admiration for the outlaw. Witness the Robin Hood songs of earlier generations. Bill Tilton sang a tremendous version of "Brennan on the Moor." I wish I had learned it from him but I didn't.

The melody here is adapted from Frank Kidson's melody for the song in *Traditional Tunes*. The second melody is supplied.

Belden, *Ballads and Songs...*, p. 284; Cazden, *The Abelard Folk Song Book*, Part 1, p. 72; Creighton and Senior, *Traditional Songs From Nova Scotia*, p. 236; Glanders and Brown, *Vermont Folk Songs and Ballads*, p. 98; Ford, *Vagabond Songs and Ballads of Scotland*, Vol. II, p. 56; Grover, *A Heritage of Songs*, p. 129; Healy, *Ballads from the Pubs of Ireland*, p. 118; Hubbard, *Ballads and Songs from Utah*, p. 258; Ives, Burl, *Irish Songs*, p. 58; Jolliffe, *The Third Book of Irish Ballads*, p. 27; Joyce, *Old Irish Folk Music and Songs*, p. 186; Kennedy, *Folksong of Britain and Ireland*, p. 697; Kidson, *Traditional Tunes*, p. 123; Laws, *American Balladry*

TRADITIONAL SONGS AND BALLADS

From British Broadsides, p. 169; Lomax and Lomax, *Our Singing Country*, p. 317; Mackenzie, *Ballads and Sea Songs from Nova Scotia*, p. 309; O'Conor, *Irish Com-All Ye's*, p. 59; O Lochlainn, *Irish Street Ballads*, p. 188; Peters, *Folk Songs Out of Wisconsin*, p. 191; Sharp, *English Folk Songs From the Southern Appalachians*, Vol. II, p. 170; Shoemaker, *Mountain Minstrelsy of Pennsylvania*, p. 242; Stubbs, *The Life of Man*, p. 18; Walton's *New Treasury of Irish Songs*, Part II, p. 186; Well, *The Ballad Tree*, p. 300.

UNCLE SAM AND JOHNNY BULL

It was in merry England
The home of Johnny Bull
When Britons fill their glasses
And fill them brimming full
Here is the tost they drank
The health to Britons brave
We are the champions of the land
And (of) the wave

Up rose Uncle Sam
And he looked across the main
Saying is that English Bully
A bellowing out again
Does he not remember
The giant where upon
That used to play with lightning
When his days work was done

THE GAM

It was in merry England
All in the bloom of spring
When English Bully Champion
Was stripped off in the ring
The coppers they were tossed
And the minutes did apply
Two to one on King
But the blows come rushing by (?)

They fought like gallant heroes
Till one received the blow
And the red crimson tide
From the Yankee's nose did flow
The tiger rose within him
The lightning in his eye
Saying smile away old England
But king mind your eye

His fellows (?) they did smile
While he held King in the air
And from his grasp he flung him
How those Englishmen did stare
Come all ye English champions
Who want to have a row
Come over to America
And we'll meet you on the ground
For (?) when you fight with Yankees
You will surely have a hastle
For there stands John C. Heenan
Yankee double in his muscle

Come all ye lofty heroes
Whose fame to .... shines
Look on that lofty Eagle
And never be afraid
May our union last forever
And and her stars now be feared
May the star spangle banner proudly wave
O'er the land of the brave

Bark *Pacific* 1870

TRADITIONAL SONGS AND BALLADS

Like so many songs in the bark *Pacific's* journal, "Uncle Sam and Johnny Bull" is badly jumbled in spots with a loss of both rhythm and rhyme. There is a shorter and more coherent version of the song in Huntington, "Folksongs from Martha's Vineyard."

"Uncle Sam and Johnny Bull" is a quite rare song, however, it is closely related to "Heenan and Sayers," which is simply a story of a prize fight and much better known. The melody is adapted from the one in Huntington.

Hubbard, *Ballads and Songs from Utah*, p. 362; Huntington, "Folksongs From Martha's Vineyard," *Northeast Folklore*, VIII, p. 25.

WE MET 'TWAS IN A CROWD

We met 'twas in a crowd
And I thought she would shun me
She came I could not breathe
For her eye was upon me

I spoke her words were cold
And her smile was unaltered
I knew how much she felt
For her soft toned voice faltered

I saw my bride's robe
And I riveled its whiteness
Bright gems were in her hair
How I cherished her brightness

She called me by my name
As the bride of another
Thou hast been the cause
Of this anguish my mother

THE GAM

And once again we met
And a young man was near her
She smiled and whispered low
As I once used to hear her

She leant upon his arm
Once was mine and mine only
I wept for I deserved
To feel wretched and lonely

And she will be his bride
At the alter he will give her
The love that was too pure
For a heartless deceiver

And the world may call me gay
At the feelings I smother
O thou hast been the cause
Of this anguish my mother

And now although she has given
Those vows to another
Her heart will be mine
Still will I think of no other

And she who hung upon his arm
Once was mine and mine only
For he has no charms
He will be wretched and lonely

Fare well to thee
Whom this heart only cherished
Oh say you will forgive
Ere I lie down and perish

When you pause on my grave
Your feelings you will smother
Forgive as I do forgive
Oh forgive, my poor mother

Ship *Virginia* 1843

TRADITIONAL SONGS AND BALLADS

There is a sheet music version of this song published by E. Riley, New York, with no date given. There the song, words and music are credited to Thomas H. Bayley, Esq. That esquire after Bayley's name would seem to indicate that the song is early, and there it is entitled just "We Met."

There is a version of this song in Huntington, *Songs The Whalemen Sang*, p. 251–52, with a melody adapted from the sheet music version. As in the sheet music version, there the sexes are reversed. Spaeth, *A History of Popular Music in America*, p. 85, states that Thomas H. Bayley was born in 1797 and died in 1829. His masterpiece, "Long Long Ago" was not published until the 1840s.

See Henry, "Songs of the People" No. 638. There as in the version in *Songs the Whalemen Sang* the girl tells of her sorrow. Henry notes that he received versions of the song from more than four contributors which certainly indicates that the song had a long life. He notes that in John Masefield's "The Bird of Dawning," the men in the open boats, after they had to abandon ship, sang the old songs to keep their hearts up and pass the time. He says that "We Met 'twas in a Crowd" was the favorite. The melody used here is from "Songs of the People."

Henry, Sam, "Songs of the People," No. 638; Huntington, *Songs the Whalemen Sang*, p. 251; Johnson, Helen Kendrick, *Our Familiar Songs...*, p. 349.

THE GAM

THE WEAVER

I am a weaver by my trade
I fell in love with a servant maid
And if I could but her favor win
Then I would weave and she would spin

His father to him scornful said
How can you fancy a servant maid
When there is ladies fine and gay
Dressed like to the queen of may

As for your ladies I don't care
Could I but enjoy my only dear
I'm obliged to mourn when I thought to smile
And I will wander the woods so wild

I went unto my love's chamber door
Where often times I had been before
And I could not speak nor yet get in
To the pleasant bed my love laid in

How can you tell what a pleasant bed
Where nothing lies but a servant maid (?)
A servant maid although she be
Blest is the man that enjoys she

TRADITIONAL SONGS AND BALLADS

Pleasant thoughts come into my mind
I turned down the sheets so fine
Where I saw her two breasts hanging so low
Like two while hills covered with snow

My love she lives in the land of worth
And I myself live a great day out
And when we live in London town
We will have a veet of great renown (?)

My love she was sick and like to die
And a most unhappy poor man was I
But at last the weaver's joy was blest
He got the servant maid at last

Sloop Nellie 1769

Ethel Kidson in *English Peasant Songs* has a shorter song called "The Yorkshire Weaver," which could just possibly be a bowdlerized version of the sloop *Nellie* song. (*English Peasant Songs* contains songs from Frank Kidson's collections that had been unpublished.) It is Ethel Kidson's melody that we have used here. The second melody is supplied.

There are many songs called "The Weaver," but none of them seem to be more than distantly related to Peter Pease's song. Peter Pease was the captain of the sloop *Nellie* on that voyage in 1769. See more about Captain Pease below.

THE GAM

LITTLE BROWN JUG

My wife and I live all alone
In a snug little house we call our own
I love rum and she loves gin
And I tell you what it is we've lots of fun

Chorus
Oh ho ho, you and me little brown jug don't I love thee
Oh ho ho you and me little brown jug don't I love thee

When I go toiling to my farm
I takes little brown jug under my arm
Sets him under a shady tree
Little brown jug don't I love thee

If I had a cow that gave such milk
I'd dress her in the best of silk
Feed her on the best of hay
And milk her twenty times a day

My wife and I and a bottle of gin
Went across the crick on a hickory limb
My foot slipped and I went in
Lost my wife but I save the gin

George Fred Tilton

"Little Brown Jug" is not very old. It was first published in 1869 but in the intervening years it has become a true folksong and at least in New England it is still heard at country dances. George Fred Tilton, who sang the song, was the most famous of the Tilton brothers because of his long walk home from the Arctic to report that the whaling fleet, frozen in the ice, was running short of food. Because of that walk a revenue cutter got food to the fleet just as the ice was breaking up. For that story see George Fred's book, *Cap'n George Fred Himself*. "Little Brown Jug" was George Fred's favorite song, and he liked what was in the jug, too.

During World War I, George Fred held a commission in the United States Navy. One trip over on a transport when there were German submarines about, George Fred had an argument with his superior officer. The officer won the argument but George Fred got in the parting shot. "Young feller," he said, "I've wrung more salt water out of my mittens than you've ever sailed over."

When Mil was a small girl her uncle brought her home a pair of Eskimo boots from the Arctic. They were the pride of her life and when she outwore them they were handed down successively to her four brothers and sisters. Mil says that when they were brought in wet from playing in the snow and put by the stove to dry they gave off a most beautiful ripe Eskimo smell.

Belden, *Ballads and Songs...*, p. 261; *The Brown Collection*, Vol. V, p. 35; Ford, *Traditional Music in America*, p. 33 and 415; Hubbard, *Ballads and Songs From Utah*, p. 244; Lomax and Lomax, *American Ballads and Folk Songs*, p. 176; *The Scottish Students' Song Book*, p. 192; Shay, *Barroom Ballads*, p. 40; Spaeth, *Read 'Em and Weep*, p. 58; Wier, *The Book of A Thousand Songs*, p. 270.

THE GAM

THE RAGING CANAL

Come list to me ye heroes, ye nobles and ye braves
For I've been at the mercy of the winds and the waves
I'll tell you of the hardships to me that did befall
While going on a voyage up the Erie Can-all

From out of this famed harbour we sailed without fear
Our helm we put hard up, and for Albany did steer
We spoke full fifty craft without any accident at all
Untill we passed that-are raging Can-all

We left old Albany harbour just at the close of day
If I rightly remember 'twas the second day of May
We trusted to our driver, although he was but small
Yet he knew all the windings of that raging Can-all

It seemed as if the devil had work in hands that night
For our oil was all out and our lamps they gave no light
The clouds began to gather and the rain began to fall
And I wished myself off and safe from the raging Can-all

With hearts chock full of love we thought of our sweethearts dear
And straight for Utica our gallant bark did steer
But when in sight of that 'ere town there came on a white squall
Which carried away our mizzen mast, on the raging Can-all

TRADITIONAL SONGS AND BALLADS

The winds came roaring on just like a wild cat scream
Our little vessel pitched and tost straining every beam
The cook she dropt the bucket and let the ladle fall
And the waves ran mountains high, on the raging Can-all

Our boat did mind the helm just like a thing of life
Our mate he offered prayers for the safety of his wife
We threw our provisions overboard butter cheese and all
And was put on short allowance on the raging Can-all

Now the weather being foggy we could't see the track
We made our driver come on board and hitched a lantern on his back
We told him to be fearless and then it blew a gale
To jump up and knock down a horse, that's taking in sail

Ship Three Brothers 1851

Whalemen must have considered this an extremely humorous song. In *The Book of Popular Songs* it is stated that the song was always sung to the tune of "The Ennis Killen Dragoon(s)." So the melody here is Sam Henry's setting of that tune in "Songs of the People." No. 98. The second melody is supplied.

The Book of Popular Songs, p. 257; Cohen, *100 Plus 5 Folk Songs for Camp*, p. 20; Downs and Siegmeister, *A Treasury of American Song*, p. 239; Kindcella, *Folk Songs and Fiddle Tunes of the USA*, p. 4; Lomas and Lomas, *American Ballads and Folk Songs*, p. 455; Sandburg, *The American Songbag*, p. 171 and 178; Spaeth, *Read 'Em and Weep*, p. 115; Thompson, *Body Boots and Britches*, p. 238; Wyld, *Low Bridge*, p. 89.

THE GAM

NEW SONG

Ye Maidens Pretty in towns and Cittys
Come hear with Pity my mournful Strain
A maid Confounded in Sorrow drounded
And deeply wounded in grief and Pain

All for the Sake of a Lively Sailor
That I ly weaping in waisting tears
Whilst other maidens are fondly Playing
I am greaving for my sailor Dear

Threw hills and valleys threw Shaids of valleys
And all around each lonely grove
Rolled in Sweat Flours and rural Bouars
We spent Soft ours in mutial Love

But now my Sailor he croast the otion
And Left his juel Resting hear
Cust be the alarms that deprived my arms
Of my Sweat lovly young Salor my Dear

Although he is gone I Cannot Blaim him
For thus my Sailor he was forst away
But my hard fortune my Cruel Parents
Contrived to have him sent to Sea

My father Left Several orders
That clost confind I should Be
All in my chamber for fear of Danger
At least I should my Darlling See

TRADITIONAL SONGS AND BALLADS

Thirteen Long weaks on Bread and warter
I lived and had no other Chear
Cruel yousage to give a Daughter
For Loving off a young Sailor Dear

Five hundred Pounds Left me by my unkle
Besides five hundred Pounds in gold
It is for that Reason I do Disdain him

For he is Beneath my young Sailor Bold
Couldn I obtain the welth of Indies
And once my Sailor should appear
Then I would Resine up my golden mine
And marry a gain with my Sailor Dear

Ship Polly 1794

I am sure that I have seen this song in print, but now I am unable to find it. The melody used is "Tather Jack Walsh" in DeVille, *The Violin Player's Pastime*. The song seems to be pretty badly jumbled, and some of the spelling is indeed beautiful in its own way.

THE GAM

ELLEN THE FAIR

Fair Ellen one morn from her cottage had strayed,
To the next market town tripped the beautiful maid
She looked like a goddess so charming and fair
Come buy my sweet posies, cried Ell the fair

I've cowslips and jessamines and hair bells so blue
Wile roses and eglantines glistening with dew
And the lily the queen of the valley so rare
"Come buy my sweet posies," cried Ellen the fair

Enraptured I gazed on the beautiful maid,
For a thousand sweet smiles on her countenance played
And while I stood gazing, my heart I declare
A captive was taken by Ellen the fair

Oh, could I but gain this nymph for my wife
How gladly I'd change my condition in life
I'd forsake the gay folk of the town and repair
To swell in a cottage with Ellen the fair

But what need I care for the lordly or great
My parents are dear I've a lordly estate,
And no lady on earth nor princess shall share
My hand and my fortune but Ellen the fair

Now a little time after, this nobleman's son
Did marry the maid his affection had won
When presented at court how the monarch did stare
And the ladies all envied sweet Ellen the fair

DCHS Archives

The melody used for this song is the one that Bill Tilton sang. I liked the melody but at the time didn't think much of the song and never learned it or even took down the words, which is too bad. The second melody is supplied.

One element in many nineteenth century broadsides is the situation in which a man or girl of a lower stratum of society manages to marry above his or her station in life. One supposes that this happened much more often in broadsides than in reality.

Laws, *American Balladry from British Broadsides*, p. 228; Thompson, *A Pioneer Songster*, p. 48.

THE LILY OF THE WEST

It's when I came to Wareham some pleasure for to find
It was there I spied a pretty maid most pleasing to my mind
Her rosy cheek and rolling eyes like arrows pierced my breast
And they called her lovely Flora the lily of the west

THE GAM

Her golden hair in ringlets hung her dress was spangled o'er
With a ring on every finger brought from some foreign shore
'Twould have enticed both kings and prices so costly was she dressed
And they called her lovely Flora the lily of the west

I courted her a while in hopes her favor for to gain
But soon she turned her back on me which caused me all my pain
She has robbed me of my liberty she has robbed me of my rest
And they called her lovely Flora the lily of the west

One day as I was walking down by a shady grove
I saw a man of high degree conversing with my love
I stepped up to my rival with a dagger in my hand
And seized him from my own true love and bid him for to stand

The sight of the dagger made him tremble as he stood
I bid him defend himself or I should spill his blood
I then with desperation swore I'd pierce his breast
For I was betrayed by Flora the Lily of the west

Then I did attend my trial and boldly made my plea
A flaw was found in the indictment which soon did set me free
Now I have gained my liberty a pain is in my breast
And I'll ramble for my Flora she still disturbs my rest

Bark Champion 1842

This version of "The Lily of the West" is not very unusual. What is exceedingly unusual is that the melody is included with the words of the song in the journal. There are only two songs in the bark *Champion* journal, this and "The Female Cabin Boy," and under the latter it says, "Melody, The Lily of the West." The key of G is a little high but except for changing the value of a few notes to fit the words of the first stanza the melody is exactly as it is in the journal. The second melody is supplied.

Of course the town where Flora lived changes from version to version, but this is the first time that I have ever seen Wareham. Starbuck has the *Champion* ship rather than bark rigged, and the date of sailing from Edgartown 1841 rather than 1842.

TRADITIONAL SONGS AND BALLADS

Baring-Gould, *Folksongs of the West Country*, p. 38; Belden, *Ballads and Songs...*, p. 132; Creighton, *Songs and Ballads from Nova Scotia*, p. 84; Eddy, *Ballads and Songs from Ohio*, p. 147; Grover, *A Heritage of Songs*, p. 153; Henry, "Songs of the People," No. 578; Kincaid, *My Favorite Mountain Ballads...*(1928), p. 46; Laws, *American Balladry From British Broadsides*, p. 263; Moore, *Ballads and Folk Songs of the Southwest*, p. 191; O Lochlainn, *Irish Street Ballads*, p. 184; Peacock, *Songs of the Newfoundland Outports*, p. 473; Sharp, *English Folk Songs from the Southern Appalachians*, Vol. II, p. 199.

ON THE GREEN MOSSY BANKS OF THE LEA

When first I arrived in this country
Curiosity caused me to roam
Then I quickly sailed over to England
And left sweet Philadelphia my home
I quickly sailed over to England
Where the forms of great beauty do shine
It was there I espied a fair maiden
And I wished in my heart she was mine

It was down by a clear crystal river
Where the pure winds soft breezes do blow
It was down by a clear crystal river
Where sweet water lilies do grow
It was there I espied this fair maiden
Some goddess she appeared to me
As she stood on the bank of the river
On the green mossy banks of the Lea

THE GAM

I stepped up and asked her good morning
Her soft cheek it blushed like the rose
Says I the gay meadows are charming
Your guidance I will be if you choose
Says she I don't wish any guidance
Young man you are a stranger to me
And yonder my father is coming
On the green mossy banks of the Lea

I waited till up come her father
When I plucked up my courage once more
Saying kind sir if this is your daughter
This beautiful maid I adore
Ten thousand a year is my portion
Your daughter a lady shall be
She shall ride in a coach with six horses
On the green mossy banks of the Lea

They welcomed me home to their cottage
In wedlock so soon to be joined
It was there I erected a mansion
In grandeur and splendor to shine
And now the American stranger
All pleasure and comfort can see
With my beautiful adorable Matilda
On the green mossy banks of the Lea

Ship *Lydia*, 1855

SECOND VERSION: NO TITLE

When first to this country I came
Curiosity caused me to roam
Over Europe I resolved to be a ranger
So I left Philadelphia my home

I quickly sailed over to Ireland
Where forms of great beauty did shine
There I beheld a fair damsel
I wished in my heart she was mine

TRADITIONAL SONGS AND BALLADS

I stepped up and bid her good morning
Good morning kind sire she replied
Ten thousand is my fortune I told her
And your guardian I'll be if you desire

Kind sir I ne'er want to guardian
...look yonder my father is coming
On the green mossy banks of the Lea

I waited still and stepped up to her father
Loosening my spirits once more
I say tell me if this be your daughter
This beautiful girl I adore

Bark *Pacific* 1870

This ballad seems to have been very popular on both sides of the Atlantic. In some versions the man is from America and not specifically Philadelphia.

The melody is from the one for the song in Purslow, *The Wanton Seed*, adapted to fit.

Creighton, *Songs and Ballads from Nova Scotia*, p. 167; Gardner, *Ballads and Songs of Southern Michigan*, p. 190; Hubbard, *Ballads and Songs from Utah*, p. 86; Laws, *American Balladry from British Broadsides*, p. 233; Leach, *Folk Ballads and Songs of the Lower Labrador Coast*, p. 84; Mackenzie, *Ballads and Sea Songs from Nova Scotia*, p. 135; Peacock, *Songs of the Newfoundland Outports*, p. 523; Purslow, *The Wanton Seed*, p. 50.

THE GAM

NEVER CHANGE THE OLD LOVE FOR THE NEW

My pen is poor my ink is pale
But my love for you will never fail
And when you think on olden time
Oh, sometimes think of me

For remember well and bear in mind
That a trusty friend is hard to find
And when you find one that is true
Change not that old one for the new

Bark Andrew Hicks 1879

"Never Change the Old Love for the New" has many titles. The melody for this fragment is from Sam Henry's "Songs of the People." The second melody is supplied.

Arnold, *Folksongs, of Alabama*, p. 33; Belden, *Ballads and Songs...*, p. 487; Brewster, *Ballads and Songs of Indiana*, p. 339; Henry, "Songs of the People," No. 482; High, *Old, Old Songs*, p. 46; Randolph, *Ozark Folksongs*, Vol. IV, p. 260.

TRADITIONAL SONGS AND BALLADS

THE HIGHWAYMAN

In Dublin City I was bred and born
On Stephens Green I died forlorn
It was there I learned a sadlers trade
And I was always called a roving blade

At the age of sixteen years I took wife
I loved her dearly as I did my own life
For to maintain her both neat and gay
Lords Dukes and others I did make pay

And when my money did grow low
On the highway I was forced to go
I robbed Lords and Dukes in the dead of night
And I took their gold to my hearts delight

I robbed Lord Mansfield I do declare
On Stephen's Green I met him fair
Shut up his coach bid him good night
And took his gold to my hearts delight

Down in Strovels garden I strayed away
With my sweet girl for to see the play
Then Felins gang did me pursue
And I was taken by the cursed crew

THE GAM

When taken at last and condemned to die
For me many a pretty girl will cry
Their tears nor cries cannot pity me
Nor save me from O the fatal tree

My father cries O I am undone
My mother cries O my darling son
My darling wife tears out her hair
Where shall I flee for I am in despair

Let highway men my mourners be
Give them bright swords and liberty
That they might say and speak the truth
There goes a bold and undead youth

Let six Dublin ladies bear my pall
Give them white gowns and ribbons all
That they might say and speak the truth
There goes a bold and undead youth

DCHS Archives

This song has no title in the archives of the Dukes County Historical Society: however it is a rather unusual version of "The Highwayman."

The ballad has many other titles among them "The Rambling Boy," "The Wild and Wicked Youth," "The Robber," "Scarlet Town," and more.

The theme of the highwaymen and maidens to carry his coffin is found in the American "The Streets of Laredo," as well as in other songs as "St. James Infirmary Blues." The melody is suggested by the one in Purslow, *The Constant Lovers*. The second melody is supplied.

Baring-Gould, *Folk Songs of the West Country*, p. 56; *The Book of Popular Songs*, p. 96; Dunston, *Cornish Dialect and Folk Songs*, p. 24; Fowke, *Traditional Singers and Songs from Ontario*, p. 44; Hubbard, *Ballads and Songs from Utah*, p. 262; Huntington, "Folksons from Martha's Vineyard," *Northeast Folklore*, VIII, p. 23; Kennedy, *Folksongs of Britain and Ireland*, p. 712; Kidson, *A Garland of English Folk Songs*, p. 97; Laws, *American Balladry from British Broadsides*, p. 172; O Lochlainn, *More Irish Street Ballads*, p. 70; Purslow, *The Constant Lovers*, p. 107; Reeves, *The Everlasting Circle*, p. 152; Sharp, *English Folk Songs*, Vol. II, p. 78.

TRADITIONAL SONGS AND BALLADS

CRUISKEEN LAWN

Let the farmer praise his grounds
As the huntsman does his hounds
And the shepherd his sweet-scented lawns
While I more blessed than they
Spend each happy night and day
With my smiling little Cruiskeen lawn

In court with manly grace
Should Sir Toby plead his case
And the merits of his cause make known
Without his cheerful glass
He'd be stupid as an ass
So he takes a little Cruiskeen lawn

Then fill your glasses high
Lets not part with lips so dry
Though the lark should proclaim it is dawn
But if we can't remain
May we shortly meet again
Just to take another Cruiskeen lawn

And when grim death appears
After free and happy years
And tells me my glass it is run

THE GAM

I'll cry be gone you slave
For great Bacchus gave me leave
Just to fill another Cruiskeen lawn

DCHS Archives

The "lawns" in the third line of the first stanza corresponds to what we would call pastures. But the "Cruiskeen Lawn" at the end of each stanza is something else again. It is a play on words, a something hidden, a phrase with a secret meaning, in this case a drink of whiskey. Irish song is full of such, as "the bonny bunch of roses" for England and "the green linnet" for Napoleon.

The melody used is adapted from Chappell, *Popular Music of the Olden Time*, Vol. I, p. 120 which Chappell says is undoubtedly the parent air of Cruiskeen Lawn — see Vol. II, p. 770. The second melody is supplied.

The words of this version without the melody will be found in Vol. VIII of *Northeast Folklore*.

There is a version of the song in Kenedy, *The Universal Irish Song Book* with a chorus in Gaelic.

The Book of Popular Songs, p. 169; Fowke, *Traditional Singers and Songs from Ontario*, p. 16; *Gems of Irish Songs*, p. 12; Griggs, *Southern and Western Songster*; Ives, *Irish Songs*, p. 49; Kenedy, *The Universal Irish Song Book*; O'Conor, *Irish Com-All-Ye's*, p. 54; Sparling, *Irish Minstrelsy*, p. 485; *Walton's New Treasury of Irish Songs and Ballads*, Part I, p. 25; Welsh, *The Golden Treasury of Irish Songs...*, Vol. II, p. 374.

ACROSS THE FIELDS OF BARLEY
BILL GRIMES

TRADITIONAL SONGS AND BALLADS

Tomorrow morn I'm sweet sixteen
And Billy Grimes the drover
Has popped the question to me ma
He wants to be my lover
And so he said to me mama
To be up bright and early
And take a pleasant walk with him
Across the fields of barley

You shall not go my daughter dear
And there's no use in talking
You shall not go my daughter
With Billy Grimes a-walking
To think of him my daughter dear
That ugly dirty drover
Some other man of high estate
Will have to be your lover

Old Grimes is dead you know mama
And Billy is so lonely
Old Grimes is dead and you must know
That Billy is the only
Surviving heir to all that's left
Not land and housen merely
But income from the old estate
A half a thousand yearly

My daughter dear, I did not hear
Your last remark quite clearly
But Billy is a clever lad
And no doubt he loves you dearly
So then be sure my daughter dear
To rise up bright and early
And take a pleasant walk with him
Across the fields of barley

Joseph Chase Allen

THE GAM

There is a sheet music version of this song in the British Museum by Arthur Henry Brown, with no date, called "Across the Field of Barley" subtitled "A very Old Song," but with a quite different melody. Is it possible that this is the parent version of the song? Or is it only Arthur Henry Brown's setting of a very old song? At any rate, the version here, words and music are from Joseph Chase Allen who may have learned it from Bill Tilton. Joe Allen says that "housen" in the third stanza was how the plural of house was spelled on Martha's Vineyard when he was a boy, and how it was pronounced.

Belden, *Ballads and Songs...*, p. 251; Hubbard, *Ballads and Songs from Utah*, p. 104; Manny, *Songs of Miramichi*, p. 218; Sharp, *English Folk Songs from the Southern Appalachians*, Vol. II, p. 248; Vincent, *Lumberjack Songs*, p. 38.

THE BUTCHER BOY

In Boston town where I did dwell
A butcher boy I love too well
He courted me my heart away
And then with me he would not stay

There is a tavern in the town
And there my true love sets him down
He takes a strange girl on his knee
And tells her things he won't tell me

Oh yes, I know the reason why
'Tis that she has more gold than I
But gold will melt and silver will fly
Some day she'll be as poor as I

TRADITIONAL SONGS AND BALLADS

I went upstairs and I made my bed
And not a word to my mother I said
My mother she came up to me
And says Dear daughter what ails thee

Oh mother, oh mother you do not know
My pain and sorrow grief and woe
I'll get a chair and set me down
With pen and ink I'll write it down

On every line she dropped a tear
While thinking of her Willie dear
Her father he came home at night
And says where is my daughter bright

He went upstairs and the door he broke
He found her hanging by a rope
He took his knife and cut her down
And on her breast these lines be found

Oh dig my grave both wide and deep
Place tombstones at my head and feet
And on my breast please place a dove
To show the world I died for love

Mildred Huntington

Mildred cannot remember whether she got this song from her grandfather, Welcome Tilton, or from one of her great uncles. It is a traditional ballad. The name of the town changed according pretty much to the singer's origin. Sometimes it is London town, sometimes Dublin town and sometimes even Jersey City.

A few of the references are related or ancestral versions of "The Butcher Boy."

Arnold, *Folksongs of Alabama*, p. 66; Belden, *Ballads and Songs...*, p. 206; Broadwood, *English Traditional Songs and Carols*, p. 95; Cox, *Folk-Songs of the South*, p. 430; Creighton, *Songs and Ballads from Nova Scotia*, p. 33; Dunston, *Cornish Dialect and Folk Songs*, p. 42; Eddy, *Ballads and Songs from Ohio*, p. 129; Flanders and Brown, *Vermont Folksongs and Ballads*, p. 115; Gardner, *Ballads and*

THE GAM

Songs of Southern Michigan, p. 117; Grover, *A Heritage of Songs*, p. 18; Hamer, *Garners Gay*, p. 61; Henry, "Songs of the People," No. 683; Hubbard, *Ballads and Songs from Utah*, p. 63; Hudson, *Folksongs of Mississippi*, p. 160; Joyce, *Old Irish Folk Music and Songs*, p. 134; Karpeles, *Folksongs from Newfoundland*, p. 243; Kincaid, *My Favorite Mountain Ballads and Old Time Songs*, p. 43; Laws, *American Balladry from British Broadsides*, p. 261; Mackenzie, *Ballads and Sea Songs from Nova Scotia*, p. 157; Owens, *Texas Folk Songs*, p. 89; Peacock, *Songs of the Newfoundland Outports*, p. 707; Peters, *Folk Songs Out of Wisconsin*, p. 204; Reeves, *The Idiom of the People*, p. 90; Reeves, *The Everlasting Circle*, p. 96; Robinson, *Country Songs and Ballads*, p. 15; Scarborough, *A Song Catcher in Southern Mountains*, p. 283; Shay, *Barroom Ballads*, p. 12; *Songs Lincoln Loved*, p. 179; Spaeth, *Weep Some More My Lady*, p. 128.

TRADITIONAL SONGS AND BALLADS
THE NIGHTINGALE

As I walked out one May morning
My fortune for to seek
It's who should I find but a fair pretty maid
And her hands were soft as silk

Her cheeks were a rosey rosey red
And her eyes were as black as the sloes
And she is the beauty of this whole world
For she is blessed where ever she goes

I says my pretty fair maid where are you going
What makes you ramble so soon
I'm going to yonder green grove
To hear the sweet nightingale tune

Then I says my pretty maid may I walk along with you
And I hope there will be no harm done
Oh yes kind sir you may walk along with me
Although you are nothing but a poor mans son

Oh we walked till we came to the side of the grove
Where I played her a virginy tune
Oh when shall we be married oh kind sir she said
And I hope it will be very soon

THE GAM

Oh little did I think on that very morn
As I came out of my door
That ever I should wed with a gay lady
That would roll me any riches in store

For the drum shall beat and the fife shall play
And we will bid old England defy did I call for more
And we'll rant and we'll roar all boldly
What a rakish young fellow am I

Ship *Lydia* 1855

This seems to be a strange and very different version of "The Nightingale." It is told in the first person by the man who does play the girl a "virginy tune" but there is no mention of the fiddle. Nor when the girl asks him to marry her does he tell her that he already has a wife and children. Indeed, the song is so very different that it may be only related to the more familiar "The Nightingale."

The melody is adapted from the one in Belden, *Ballads and Songs*.... The second melody is supplied.

Abrahams, *A Singer and Her Songs...*, p. 24; Baring-Gould, *Folk Songs of the West Country*, p. 98; Baring-Gould, *Folksongs for Schools*, p. 63; Belden, *Ballads and Songs*, p. 239; Cox, *Traditional Ballads and Folk-Songs Mainly from West Virginia*, p. 94; Flanders and Olney, *Ballads Migrant in New England*, p. 164; Karpeles, *Folk Songs from Newfoundland*, p. 232; Kinscella, *Folk Songs and Fiddle Tunes...*, p. 4; Laws, *American Balladry from British Broadsides*, p. 255; Moore, *Ballads and Folk Songs of the Southwest*, p. 211; Purslow, *Marrow Bones*, p. 60; Sharp, *English Folk Songs from the Southern Appalachians*, Vol. II, p. 192; Wells, *The Ballad Tree*, p. 222; Wyman, *Lonesome Tunes*, p. 68.

TRADITIONAL SONGS AND BALLADS

AN OLD SONG

One morning being fair I rode to take the air
Down by one river clear alone she did go
So advancing by the side whair the streams did gently glide
Twas there I first espeyed my Sweet Collen reu

As I stood gaising in transported a musing
With intamfis (?) my Bosom did glow
There a lone She was Lean She was the fairest on the green
That Sweet Butiful Queen and my Sweet Combeana

She was soft in her fetures and Sweet in her Stature
And I find by all Nature she was comly not low
She was pleasing and sweet sincere modest and desent
And all Pleasures doth agree with my Sweet Combeana

Now threw the groves in search of my Love
Each day I will Rove the grove threw and threw
I will search out every shade until I find out that maid
That hath my heart betraed my Sweet Combeana

One night all alone by the light all alone
By the light of the moon over hills and over Dails
And over valleys that's low
Thrir no comfort could I bear but search out my dear
But in sorrow I will spend the year for my Sweet Combeana

Ship Polly 1794

It certainly seems as though this song, called only "An Old Song" in the ship Polly journal, should have been located, but it was not. Nor is it a strange version of "The Colleen Rue." The melody is not supplied. But where was it found or what is lost? So the whole song is a mystery. In addition, it seems badly garbled in spots.

THE GAM

LORD LOVEL

Lord Lovel he sat in St. Charles's Hotel
In St. Charles's Hotel sat he
As fine a cuss of a southern swell
As ever you'd wish to see see see
As ever you'd wish to see

Lord Lovel the town had sworn to defend
A-waving his sword on high
He swore his last ounce of powder he'd spend
Or in the last ditch he'd die die die
Or in the last ditch he'd die

He swore by the black and he swore by the blue
And he swore by the stars and bars
That never he'd fly by a Yankee crew
While he was a son of Mars Mars Mars
While he was a son of Mars

He had fifty thousand gallant men
Fifty thousand men had he
And all had sworn with him that they'd never
Surrender to any tarnation Yankee kee kee
Surrender to any tarnation Yankee

TRADITIONAL SONGS AND BALLADS

He had forts that no Yankee alive could take
He had iron clad boats a score
And batteries all around the lake
And around the river shore shore shore
And around the river shore

Sir Farragut came with a mighty fleet
With a mighty fleet came he
Lord Lovell instanter began to retreat
Before the first boat he could see see see
Before the first boat he could see

Oh tarry Lord Lovell Sir Farragut cried
Oh tarry Lord Lovell said he
I rather think not Lord Lovell replied
For I'm in a great hurry hurry
For I'm in a great hurry

Lord Lovell kept running all day and all night
Lord Lovell kept running kept he
For he swore that he couldn't abide the sight
Of the guns of this Yankee kee kee
Of the guns of this Yankee

When Lord Lovell's life was brought to a close
By a sharp-shootin Yankee gunner
From his head there sprouted a red red rose
From his feet a scarlet runner runner
From his feet a scarlet runner

DCHS Archives

The Civil War parody on "Lord Lovell" is from the Whiting papers in the Dukes County Historical Society's archives in Edgartown on Martha's Vineyard. The song without a melody will be found in Huntington's "Folksongs from Martha's Vineyard," *Northeast Folklore* VIII.

That scarlet runner in the last stanza is a variety of pole bean that was very popular in the last century, until better varieties of beans were developed.

THE GAM

The melody is adapted from the melody for "Lord Lovel" in Sandburg's *The American Songbag*. The second melody is supplied.

Cox, Traditional Ballads and Folk Songs Mainly from West Virginia, p. 37.

THE MAID OF ERIN

My thoughts delight to wander
Upon a distant shore
Where lovely fair and tender
Is she whom I adore
May heaven its blessings sparing
On her bestow them free
The lovely maid of Erin
Who sweetly sang to me

Had fortune fixed my station
In some propitious hour
The monarch of a nation
Endowed with wealth and power
That wealth and power sharing
My peerless queen should be
The lovely maid of Erin
Who sweetly sang to me

Although the restless ocean
May long between us roar
Yet while my heart has motion
She'll lodge within its core
For artless and endearing
And mild and young is she
The lovely maid of Erin
Who sweetly sang to me

When fate gives intimation
That my last hour is nigh
With placid resignation
I'll lay me down and die
Fond hopes me cheering
That in heaven I'll see
The lovely maid of Erin
Who sweetly sang to me

            Ship *Cortes* 1847

It seems that I should have found a reference or references for this song, but I did not. The melody is from the singing of Nan Huntington.

THE WINDS THAT BLEW 'CROSS THE WILD MOOR (MARY ON THE WILD MOOR)

One night when the winds they blew cold
And bitter across the wild moor
Young Mary she came with her child
Wandering home to her own father's door

Saying, father pray let me come in
Take pity on me I implore
Or the child at my bosom will die
From the winds that blow 'cross the wild moor

THE GAM

But her father was deaf to her cry
Not a sigh, not a sound reached the door
But the watchdogs did bark at the winds
That blew bitter across the wild moor

Now how must her father have felt
When he came to the door in the morn
And saw Mary lying there dead
With her child fondly clasped in her arms

So frantic he tore his grey hair
As on Mary he gazed at the door
Saying there Mary perished and died
Of the winds that blew 'cross the wild moor

But the old man with grief pined away
And his body to the grave was soon bourn
And no one lives there to this day
For the cottage to ruin has gone

But the villagers will point to the spot
Where the willow hangs over the door
Saying, there Mary perished and died
Of the winds that blew 'cross the wild moor

Ship *Euphrasia* 1849

Perhaps the proper title for this song is "Mary on the Wild Moor." It was very popular for a long time. Johnson in *Our Familiar Songs and Those Who Made Them* says that both the words and the melody are very old but that they were not linked as one song until Joseph W. Turner did so about 1845. The second melody is supplied.

Barrett, *English Folk Songs*, p. 76; Belden, *Ballads and Songs...*, p. 207; Cox, *Folk-Songs of the South*, p. 437; Cox, *Traditional Ballads and Folk-Songs, Mainly from West Virginia*, p. 103; Henry, *Folk-Songs from the Southern Highlands*, p. 372; Hubbard, *Ballads and Songs from Utah*, p. 212; Johnson, *Our Familiar Songs...*, p. 303; Kidson, *Traditional Tunes*, p. 77; Laws, *American Balladry from British Broadsides*, p. 158; Leach, *Folk Ballads and Songs of the Lower Labrador Coast*, p. 169; Mackenzie, *Ballads and Sea Songs from Nova Scotia*, p. 164; Munch, *The Song*

TRADITIONAL SONGS AND BALLADS

Tradition of Tristan Da Cunha, p. 102; Owens, *Texas Folk Songs*, p. 76; Peters, *Folk Songs out of Wisconsin*, p. 116; Purslow, *The Constant Lovers*, p. 57; Reddall, *Songs that Never Die*, p. 393; Scarborough, *A Song Catcher in Southern Mountains*, p. 335; Shoemaker, *Mountain Minstrelsy of Pennsylvania*, p. 114; Thompson, *A Pioneer Songster*, p. 185.

A FISHERMAN'S GIRL

It was down in the country a poor girl was weeping
It was down in the country poor Mary Anne did roam
She belongs to this nation
She has lost each dear relation
Cries the poor little fisherman's girl
My friends are dead and gone

Oh who is soft-hearted to give me some shelter
For the bitter winds do blow and dreadful is the storm
I have no father or mother
But I've a tender brother
Cries the poor little fisherman's girl
My friends are dead and gone

Oh once I knew enjoyment my parents tenderly raised me
I passed with my brother each happy night and morn
But death has made a slaughter
Poor father's in the water
Cried the poor little fisherman's girl
Whose friends were dead and gone

So fast falls the snow I cannot find shelter
So fast falls the snow I must hasten to the thorn
My shelter is the bushes

241

THE GAM

My bed is the rushes
Cried the poor little fisherman's girl
Whose friends were dead and gone

It happened as she passed by a very noble cottage
A gentleman saw her for her his heart did burn
Saying come in lonely creature
He viewed each drooping feature
Of the poor little fisherman's girl
Whose friends were dead and gone

He took her to the fire where he warmed her and fed her
The tears began to fall he fell upon her breast forlorn
Saying live with me forever
We shall part again never
You are my dearest sister
Our friends are dead and gone

She now has a home she lives with her brother
She now has a home and the needy n'er does scorn
For God was the protector
Likewise the kind conductor
Of the poor little fisherman's girl
When her friends were dead and gone

Ship *Cortes* 1847

This song is a fairly rare variant of "The Fisherman's Boy." For references for that see Laws, *American Balladry from British Broadsides*, p. 287.

Unfortunately the melody to which the song was sung was not found, so what we have here is supplied.

Eddy, *Ballads and Songs from Ohio*, p. 177; Hubbard, *Ballads and Songs from Utah*, p. 189.

TRADITIONAL SONGS AND BALLADS

POOR LITTLE JOE

As I was a-walking through London's gay throng
I spied a little boy a-singing a song
You could tell by his face that he wanted bread
Though he was singing he wished he was dead

Chorus
Cold blew the blast, down came the snow
No one to shelter him, nowhere to go
No mother to guide him in her grave she laid low
Out on the cold world was poor little Joe

A carriage rolled past with a lady inside
She was fondly caressing her own darling child
Joe followed the carriage she nodded and smiled
I looked on his face and I saw how he cried

I looked on the way and I thought it was hard
For that poor little urchin forgotten by God
As he walked down the street with his dull parting tread
Praying to heaven for rest when he's dead

THE GAM

The lights had gone out and the clock had struck one
A watchman returning his duty was done
While Joe walked the street with his dull parting tread
Thinking of starving and looking for bread

Hello, what's there? the watchman he cried
For poor little Joe on the doorstep had died
With his face turned to heaven all covered with snow
He died on the cold street had poor little Joe

Bark Andrew Hicks 1879

On the basis of internal evidence "Poor Little Joe" dates from the early years of the nineteenth century, for London's night watchmen were replaced by the famous Metropolitan Police, the "Bobbies" about 1820. Also few children died of hunger on the streets after that date. There are a number of songs of this general type. Perhaps the best known of them "The Orphan Girl," in which the waif freezes to death on the marble steps of the rich man's hall. Another is "The Flower Girl."

For references see Hubbard, *Ballads and Songs from Utah*. See also Cox, *Traditional Ballads and Folk-Songs Mainly from West Virginia*, p. 209, and the melody used here was suggested by the fragment of the song found there. The second melody is supplied.

Cox, *Folk-Songs of the South*, p. 445; Cox, *Traditional Ballads and Folk-Songs Mainly from West Virginia*, p. 209; Hubbard, *Ballads and Songs from Utah*, p. 190.

THE FLOWER GIRL

TRADITIONAL SONGS AND BALLADS

Underneath the gaslight glitter
Stands a little fragile girl
Heedless of the night winds bitter
As they round about her whirl
While the hundreds pass unheeding
In the evening's waning hours
Still she cried with cheerful pleading
Won't you buy my pretty flowers

Chorus

There are many said and weary
In this pleasant land of ours
Crying every night so dreary
Won't you buy my pretty flowers

Ever coming ever going
Men and women hurry by
Heedless of the teardrop's glitter
In her sad and wistful eye
How her little heart is sighing
In the cold and dreary hours
Only listen to her crying
Won't you buy my pretty flowers

Not a loving word to cheer me
From the passersby is heard
Not a friend to linger near me
With a heart by pity stirred
Homeward goes the tide of fashion
Seeking pleasures pleasant hours
None to hear with sad compassion
Won't you buy my pretty flowers

Ship *Eliza Adams* 1879

This is another tear-jerker from the era of tear-jerkers. The melody is from *The Mohawk Minstrel's Magazine of Favorite Songs and Ballads*.

The Mohawk Minstrel's Magazine of Favorite Songs and Ballads, Vol. I:1.

THE GAM

THE STEPMOTHER

The wedding rites are over
I turn my head aside
To keep the guests from seeing
The tears I can not hide
I could not greet the fair one
So I took my little brother
To greet my father's chosen one
But I could not call her mother

She is a fair young creature
With a mild and gentle air
Blue eyes soft and sparkling
Sunny silken hair
I know my father gives her
The love he gave another
But if she were an angel
I would not call her mother

They took my mother's picture
From the accustomed place
And placed beside my father
A younger fairer face
They made that dear old chamber
Bordeaux of another
But if she were an angel
I would not call her mother

TRADITIONAL SONGS AND BALLADS

Last night I heard her singing
A song I used to love
When those sweet words were uttered
By one who sings above
And every note was hallowed (?)
By the sweet voice of another
And if she were an angel
I would not call her mother

Bark *Pacific* 1870

There are two songs with the theme of "The Stepmother," one in which the child is blind and the other in which she is not. The songs are so close with so many interchangeable stanzas that references here are for both songs. Both songs were very popular seventy-five and more years ago, particularly so with the blind street and carnival singers, who with the coming of Social Security have almost entirely vanished.

The melody used here is adapted from Arnold's *Folksongs of Alabama*. Repeat it for the second half of each stanza. The second melody is supplied.

Arnold, *Folksongs of Alabama*, p. 79; Abrahams, *A Singer and Her songs…*, p. 53; Belden, *Ballads and Songs…*, p. 275; Fuson, *Ballads of the Kentucky Highlands*, p. 146; Henry, *Folk-Songs from the Southern Highlands*, p. 371; Huntington, *Songs the Whalemen Sang*, p. 298.

THE GAM

NORAH O'NEAL

Oh I'm lonely tonight love without you
And sigh for one glance of your eye
For there's a charm love about you
Whenever I know you are nigh
Like the beam of the star when it's smiling
Is the glance which your eye can't conceal
And your voice is so sweet and beguiling
That I love you sweet Norah O'Neal

Chorus
Oh don't think that I ever doubt you
My love I can never conceal
For I'm lonely tonight love without you
My darling sweet Norah O'Neal

Oh the nightingale sings in the wildwood
As if every note that she knew
Was learned from your sweet voice in childhood
Which reminds me sweet Norah of you
I think love so often about you
You don't know how unhappy I feel
For 'tis lonely tonight love without you
My darling sweet Norah O'Neal

Ship *Charles and Edward*, 1858

TRADITIONAL SONGS AND BALLADS

The melody is adapted from Wier, *Book of a Thousand Songs*. See also Spaeth, *A History of Popular Music in America*, p. 159 for background.

Heart Songs, p. 470; Kenedy, *The Universal Irish Song Book*, p. 161; O'Conor, *Irish Com-All-Ye's*, p. 141; Wier, *The Book of a Thousand Songs*, p. 332.

THE OLD BOG HOLE

Oh my Judy she's as fair as the flower on the lea
She is neat and complete from neck to knee
We were out the other night for to take a little stroll
And I took Judy down by the old bog hole

Chorus
Oh acushla mavoreen won't you marry me
Achusla mavoreen won't you marry me
Acushla mavoreen won't you marry me
Can't you fancy the likes of Barney Magee

Fine children we'll have and you musn't mind that
There'll be Katy and Judy and Biddy and Pat
And Mary so meek and Barney so bluff
Oh stop you sassy devil have you not got enough

I'll not got enough and I won't be content
Till ye bring me home as many as there is days in Lent
And the people will stare when we go for a stroll
And we all promenade round the old bog hole

THE GAM

....
If you should care for more delicate stuff
I'd take the little rod that my grandfather stole
And I'll go fish for eels in the old bog hold.

....
....
....................the duck loves the drake
And sweet Judy Flannigan I'd die for your sake

            Joseph Chase Allen

Joe Allen says that his grandfather used to sing this, but this is all he can remember of the much longer song. I think this much was doing pretty well, for Joe was eighty-eight years old and for many years wrote for the Oracle of *Yankee Magazine* and the editor of the Fisherman's Page of the *Vineyard Gazette*.

Ford, Vagabond *Songs and Ballads of Scotland*, Vol. II, p. 157; O'Conor, *Irish Com-All-Yes*, p. 5.

THE LAMENT OF THE IRISH EMIGRANT

I'm sitting on the stile Mary
Where we sat side by side
On a bright May morning long ago
When first you was my bride
The corn was springing fresh and green
And the lark sang loud and high
And the red was on thy lip Mary
And the love light in your eye

The place has little changed Mary
The day as bright as then
And the lark's loud song is in my ear
And the corn is green again
But I miss the soft clasp of your hand
And your warm breath on my cheek
And I still keep thinking now Mary
You never more may speak

It's but a step down yonder lane
And the little church stands near
The church where we were wed Mary
I see the spire from here
But the graveyard lies between Mary
And my step might break your rest
For they've laid my darling down to sleep
With the barley on your breast

I'm very lonely now Mary
For the poor mahee (?) has no friends (?)
But Oh I love thee better far (?)
The few our father sends (?)
And you were all I had Mary
My blessing and my pride
There's nothing left to care for now
Since my poor Mary died

I'm bidding you a long farewell
My Mary kind and true
But I'll not forget you darling
In the land I'm going to
They say there's bread and work for all
And the sun shines always there
But I'll not forget old Ireland
Were it fifty times as fair

And often in those grand old woods
I'll sit and shut my eyes
And my heart will travel back again
To the place where Mary Lies

THE GAM

And I think I'll see the little stile
Where we sat side by side
And the springing corn and the bright May morn
When first you was my bride

Ship Euphrasia 1849

The long lament is evidently slightly garbled. The melody is from Johnson, *Our Familiar Songs and Those Who Made Them*. See Johnson for the complete song with two more stanzas than the *Euphrasia* version. For more background, see Spaeth, *A History of Popular Music in America*, p. 87.

Dean, *Flying Cloud*, p. 81; *Gems of Irish Song*, p. 9; Johnson, *Our Familiar Songs...*, p. 85; Kenedy, *The Universal Irish Song Book*, p. 85; O'Conor, *Irish Com-All-Ye's*, p. 156; Peacock, *Songs of the Newfoundland Outports*, p. 462; Sparling, *Irish Minstrelsy*, p. 346; Wier, *The Book of a Thousand Songs*, p. 221.

KATHLEEN MAVOURNEEN

Kathleen Mavourneen the bright day is breaking
And the horn of the hunter is heard on the hill
The lark from his flight the bright dew is shaking
Kathleen Mavourneen what slumbering still

Oh hast thou forgotten how soon we must sever
Oh hast thou forgotten this day we must part
It may be for years and it may be for ever
Then why are thou silent thou voice of my heart

Kathleen Mavourneen awake from thy slumber
The blue mountains glow in the suns golden light
Oh where is the spell that once hung on thy waking
Arise to thy beauty thou star of my night

TRADITIONAL SONGS AND BALLADS

Mauvourneen Mauvourneen my sad tears are falling
I think that from Erin and thee I must part
Mauvourneen Mauvourneen thy lover is calling
Then why art thou silent thou voice (?) of my heart

Ship Lydia 1855

"Kathleen Mavourneen" has been a very popular song for a very long while. It was first published in 1840. Spaeth in *A History of Popular Music in America*, p. 86, calls it the Scotch "song of the year." That must be tongue in cheek, for of course it is an Irish song, and was written by "an Irish lady," Mr. Crawford.

LITTLE NELL OF NARRAGANSETT BAY

Full well do I remember my boyhoods happy hours
The cottage and the garden where bloomed the fairest flowers
The bright and sparkling waters o'er which we used to sail
With hearts so gay for miles away before the pleasant gale
I had a dear companion but she's not with me now
The lily of the valley is waving o'er her brow
And I am sad and lonely and weeping all the day
For bright eyed laughing little Nell of Narragansett Bay

THE GAM

I loved my little beauty the boat it was my first
And with her close beside me what joys the foam to ride
She laughed in tones so merrily to see the waves go by
While wildly blew the stormy winds and murky was the sky
Though lightning flashed around us and all was dark and drear
She loved to brave old ocean and never dreamed to fear
The Arrow bounded foreward and darted through the spray
With bright eyed little Nell of Narragansett Bay

One day from us she wandered and soon within the boat
The rope was quickly loosened and with the tide afloat
The treacherous bark flew lightly and swift before the tide
While home and friends and all so dear was many miles behind
Next day her form all lifeless was washed upon the beach
I stood and gazed upon it bereft of sense of speech
Tis years since she has left us and still I weep today
For bright eyed laughing little Nell of Narragansett Bay

Chorus
Then toll the bell at early break of day
For lovely Nell so quickly washed away
Toll toll the bell so sad and mournfully
For bright eyed laughing little Nell of Narragansett Bay

Bark *John Dawson* 1863

"Little Nell of Narragansett Bay" does seem to have achieved the status of a folksong although perhaps it never had very wide circulation. Even songs much more literary than this one did achieve that status, witness "The Baggage Coach Ahead," and "White Wings." Both songs undoubtedly originated as sheet music. The melody for the song here is adapted from that in Spaeth, *Weep Some More my Lady*.

Dean, *Flying Cloud*, p. 119; Hubbard, *Ballads and Songs from Utah*, p. 121; Shoemaker, *Mountain Minstrelsy of Pennsylvania*, p. 38; Spaeth, *Weep Some More My Lady*, p. 30.

TRADITIONAL SONGS AND BALLADS

GOLDEN SLIPPERS

Oh my golden slippers are laid away
'Cause I ain't going to use 'em till the wedding day
And the long tailed coat that I love so well
I'll wear it in the chariot in the morning
And the long white robe that I bought last June
I'm going get changed 'cause it fits too soon
And the old gray hoss that I used to drive
I'll hitch her to the chariot in the morning

Chorus
Oh them golden slippers, oh, them golden slippers
Golden slippers I'm going to wear because they look so neat
Oh them golden slippers, oh them golden slippers
Golden slippers I'm going to wear to walk on the golden street

My old banjo hangs on the wall
Where it ain't been tuned since 'way last fall
And the darkies all say we're going to have a good time
When we ride in the chariot in the morning
Brother Ben and sister Luce
Going to telegraph the news to uncle 'bacca juice
What a great camp meeting there will be that day
When we ride in the chariot in the morning

THE GAM

So it's good-bye children I've got to go
Where the rain don't rain where the wind don't blow
Where your Ulster coat you're never going to need
When you ride in the chariot in the morning
But your golden slippers must be nice and clean
And you age must be just sweet sixteen
And you white kid gloves you will have to wear
When you ride in the chariot in the morning

Bark *Andrew Hicks* 1879

"Golden Slippers" which began life as a black face minstrel song seems to have become truly traditional. Also, at least in the Northeast, it is widely used as a fiddle tune for square dancing.

Botkin, *The American Play-Party Song*, p. 197; Brown, *North Carolina Folklore*, Vol. 5: p. 571; Ford, *Traditional Music in America*, p. 113 and 410; Henry, *Folk-Songs from the Southern Highlands*, p. 413: Wier, *The Book of a Thousand Songs*, p. 344.

THE EASTBOUND TRAIN

The eastbound train was crowded
One cold December day
The conductor shouted tickets
In his good old-fashioned way

TRADITIONAL SONGS AND BALLADS

A little girl in sadness
Her hair was bright as gold
She said Sir I have no ticket
And then her story told

My father is in prison
He's lost his sight they say
I'm a-going for his pardon
This cold December day

My mother takes in washings
To keep us all in bread
With my poor sick blind old father
In prison almost dead

My brothers and my sisters
Would all be very glad
If I could only bring back
My poor sick blind old dad

The conductor was dumfounded
He could not make no reply
But taking his rough hand and wiping
The teardrop from his eye

He says Oh God bless you little one
Just stay right where you are
You will never need no ticket
While I am on this car

Mildred Huntington

Mildred learned this song from her grandfather Welcome Tilton. I have searched but have not found a reference for this but surely somewhere one exists. Why is it that in so many songs the train is eastbound? The second melody is supplied.

THE GAM

A LADY'S ANSWER

As I walked out one pleasant morn
I spied a lady gay and airy
I addressed her thus, made a low bow
Saying, Dear girl when will you marry
She looked about with sparkling eyes
And said Young man if you will tarry
And lend to me a listening ear
Then I'll tell you when I will marry

When misers cease to love their ore
And dead ducks fly o'er the river
When cork shall sink and millstones swim
And not till then if it is never
When Old Town streets are paved with gold
And willows bear a golden cherry
When all these things shall come to pass
Young man oh then I'll marry

When cows refuse to wear their skins
And the great sea shall cease its motion
When whales shall swim upon dry land
And crowbars float upon the ocean
When Bonaparte shall cease to fight
And England's ships on wheels be carried
When all these things shall come to pass
Then, young man, will I be married

TRADITIONAL SONGS AND BALLADS

When Aetna's flames shall cease to burn
And rocks are seen like fishes swimming
And all the rivers shall run dry
And Lucifer inhabit heaven
And every fish throws off its scales
And in their stead wears burning lava,
When all these things shall come to pass
Then young man, oh then I'll marry

When loadstones grow on pigeon's wings
And every sot refuses brandy
And grapes shall grow on cypress trees
And brimstone turn to sugar candy
When every heart shall cease to beat
And all the dead grow brisk and airy
When all these things shall come to pass
Then young man oh then I'll marry

When the hoarse raven shall sweetly sing
And Greenland's coast bears flowery meadows
And owls shall turn to kings and queens
And gravestones dread each other's shadows
And negroes turn to white men fair
And tattlers are all nicely buried
When all these things shall come to pass
Then, young man will I be married

When grapevines bear gold candlesticks
And in them candles ever burning
When lambs and lions will agree
And widowed doves shall cease their mourning
When phoenixes on earth are found
And with their mates long time have tarried
When all these things shall come to pass
Then young man shall I be married

When cranes build nests in old men's beards
And eagles dwell in haunted houses
And tortoise shell grows on cows horns
And young men wear gold dust for trousers

THE GAM

When spiders' webs make cables strong
But go, young man, you have listened long
And lent to me a listening ear
Now I've told you when I'll be married

DCHS Archives

This song is from "Hannah Smith's Book," a manuscript collection of poems in the archives of the Dukes County Historical Society in Edgartown, Massachusetts. The book was probably put together about 1830 when Hannah was forty-one years old. Hannah really was a poet and some of the shorter poems in her book show a real lyric quality, as does some of the material in her *Diurnal Records for the Year 1823*. She was entirely unknown.

Hannah certainly was no whaleman but some of her brothers and near relatives were whalemen and seamen, and Hannah may have learned the song or a fragment of it from one of them. For some of the stanzas in "A Lady's Answer" are undoubtedly Hannah's. As an example of that, in stanza two Old Town is Edgartown and in Hannah's day Edgartown's streets were notoriously sandy.

When I was a boy Chester M. Poole of Chilmark used to recite some of the song. The melody is adapted from that in Wyman's *Twenty Kentucky Mountain Songs*.

Williams, *Folk Songs of the Upper Thames*, p. 200; Wyman, *Twenty Kentucky Mountain Songs*, p. 106.

THE LETTER EDGED IN BLACK

I was standing by the window yester morning
Without a thought of worry or of care
When I saw the postman coming up the pathway
With such a happy face and jolly air

TRADITIONAL SONGS AND BALLADS

He rang the bell and whistled as he waited
And then he said Good morning to you Jack
But he little knew the sorrow that he brought me
As he handed me a letter edged in black

With a trembling hand I took the letter from him
I opened it and this is what it said
Come home my boy your dear old father wants you
Come home my boy your dear old mother's dead

The last words that your mother ever uttered
Were, tell my boy I want him to come back
My eyes are blurred my poor old heart is breaking
As I'm writing you this letter edged in black

With a trembling hand I took the letter from him
I opened it and this is what it said
Come home my boy your dear old father wants you
Come home my boy your dear old mother's dead

The last words that your mother ever uttered
Were, tell my boy I want him to come back
My eyes are blurred my poor old heart is breaking
As I'm writing you this letter edged in black

Those angry words I wish I'd never spoken
You know I did not mean them don't you Jack
May the angels up in heaven bear me witness
As I'm writing you this letter edged in black

I could hear the postman whistling yester morning
Coming up the pathway with his pack
But he little knew the sorrow that he brought me
As he handed me a letter edged in black

Mildred Huntington

Mildred thinks that she probably learned this song from Welcome Tilton her whaleman grandfather. It was a great favorite in the days of hillbilly music but Welcome Tilton must have learned it long before that. How long ago did the black-edged envelope bearing the tidings of a death in the family go out of fashion?

    Kennedy, James O'Brien, *American Ballads*, p. 131; Randolph, *Ozark Folksongs*, Vol. IV, p. 162; Richardson, *American Mountain Songs*, p. 35; Shay, *Barroom Ballads*, p. 192; Spaeth, *Weep Some More...*, p. 38; Stout, *Folklore From Iowa*, p. 74.

HIGHLAND MARY

    Ye banks and braes and streams all around
    The castle of Montgomery
    Green be your woods and fair your flowers
    Your waters never drumblie

              Chorus
    Ye golden hours on angel's wings
    Blew o'er me and my dearie
    Fair dear to me as light and life
    Was my sweet hiland Mary
    Here summer first unfolds her robes
    And there the latest tarry
    And there I took the last farewell
    Of my sweet hiland Mary

    'Twas aufful death and timely frost
    That nipped my flower so early
    Now green the sod and cold the clay
    That rapt my hiland Mary

TRADITIONAL SONGS AND BALLADS

> Pale pale now those rosy lips
> That I've kissed so fondly
> And mouldering in the silent dust
> The heart that loved me fondly
>
> Ship Euphrasia 1849

Robert Burns' love song to his Highland Mary has gone through a few changes here that perhaps do not improve its artistic quality, but do show that it had become a true folksong. Nan Huntington sang it very much as it is found in the *Euphrasia* journal.

The melody used here is from *Gems of Scottish Song*. The melody is "Katherine Ogie."

Gems of Scottish Song, p. 79; Johnson, *Our Familiar Songs…*, p. 359; Griggs, *Southern and Western Songster*, p. 192; Kidson, *Traditional Tunes*, p. 85; Reddall, *Songs That Never Die*, p. 294; *The Silver Chord*, p. 50; Wier, *The Book of a Thousand Songs*, p. 192.

BONNIE ANNIE LAURIE

Maxwell braes are bonnie where early falls the dew
It was there that Annie Laurie gave me her promise true
Gave me her promise true that ne'er forget shall be
And for bonnie Annie Laurie I would lay me down and die

Her skin was like the snowdrift and her neck was like the swan
Her face it was the fairest that ere the sun shone on
That ere the sun shone on and mild was her blue eye
And for bonnie Annie Laurie I would lay me down and die

THE GAM

Like snow on the ground lying is the fall of her silent fee
Like winds in summer sighing her voice is low and sweet
Her voice is low and sweet she is all the world to me
And for bonnie Annie Laurie I would lay me down and die

Ship Lydia 1855

Johnson in *Our Familiar Songs and Those Who Made Them*, gives us the background of the song and calls it just "Annie Laurie."

There is also some interesting background on the song in Spaeth, *A History of Popular Music in America*, p. 81.

Gems of Scottish Song, p. 44; Johnson, *Our Familiar Songs...*, p. 44; Reddall, *Songs That Never Die*, p. 121; Wier, *The Book of a Thousand Songs*, p. 22.

ROB ROY MCGREGOR-O

Pardon now the bold outlaw
Rob Roy Magriger-o
Grant him pardon gentles-a'
Rob Roy Magriger-o
Let your hands and hearts agree
Let the Highland Laddie free
Make us sing with muckle glee
Rob Roy Magriger-o

Long the state has doomed his fall
Rob Roy Magriger-o
Still he spurned the hateful law
Rob Roy Magriger-o
Scots can for their country die
N'er from Britons shall they flee
All that's past forget forgi'
Rob Roy Magriger-o

TRADITIONAL SONGS AND BALLADS

Scotland's fear and Scotland's pride
Rob Roy Magriger-o
Your reward must now abide
Rob Roy Magriger-o
Long your favor has been mine
Favor I will n'er resign
Welcome now for auld lang syne
Rob Roy Magriger-o

Ship *Galaxy* 1827

This song is quite old and should be truly traditional. Any relationship it may have to "Rob Roy," Child 225, must be exceedingly remote. The melody used here is from *Gems of Scottish Song* where it says that the melody is "Duncan Gray."

Gems of Scottish Song, p. 97.

MY HIGHLAND HOME

My Highland home where tempests blow
And cold thy wintry looks
Thy hills are crowned with driven snow
And ice bound are thy brooks
But colder far the Scotsman's heart
However far he roam
To whom these words no joy impart
My native Highland home

THE GAM

Chorus

Then come with me to Scotland dear
We n'er again will roam
And with thy smiles so bonny cheer
My native Highland home

When summer comes the heather bell
Shall tempt my feet to rove
The chashat dove within the dell
Invites to peace and love
For blythsome is the face of day
And sweet the bonny broom
And pure the dimpling rills that play
Around my Highland home

Ship *Galaxy* 1827

The melody here is adapted from that in *Gems of Scottish Song*, p. 59–60 called "My Native Highland Home." The version in the *Galaxy* journal does not include the chorus. It is added here to complete the song. It can be sung if desired to the second line of the melody.

Only *Gems of Scottish Song*, p. 59.

JESSIE THE FLOWER OF DUNBLANE

The sun had gone down on lofty Ben Lomand
And left the red clouds to preside o'er the scene
When lonely I stray in the calm summer gloaming
To muse on sweet Jessie the flower of Dunblane

TRADITIONAL SONGS AND BALLADS

How sweet is the brier with its soft folding blossom
How sweet is the birk with its mantle of green
Yet sweeter and fairer and dear to this bosom
Is lovely young Jessie the flower of Dunblane

She's modest as any and blithe as she's bonny
For guileless simplicity marks her its ain
And far be the villain divested of feeling
Who would blight in its bloom the flower of Dunblane

Sing on thou sweet mavis thy hymn to the evening
Thou so dear to the echoes of Calderwood glen
So dear to this bosom so artless and winning
Is charming young Jessie the flower of Dunblane

How lost were my days till I met with my dearie
The sports and the city seem foolish and vain
I ne'er saw a nymph I would call my deary
Till I met with sweet Jessie the flower of Dunblane

Though mine were the station of loftiest grandeur
Among its profusion I'd languish in pain
I reckon as nothing the height of its splendour
In wanting sweet Jessie the flower of Dunblane

Ship Lotos 1833

Like so many folksongs "Jessie the Flower of Dunblane" started out as a literary song. For its background see Johnson, *Our Familiar Songs*... However it does seem to have reached the status of traditional song. Sing it as though it were three eight line stanzas.

Gems of Scottish Song, p. 191; *Griggs Southern and Western Songster*, p. 31; Johnson, *Our Familiar Songs...*, p. 372; Reddall, *Songs That Never Die*, p. 382; Shoemaker, *Mountain Minstrelsy of Pennsylvania*, p. 294.

THE GAM

BRUCE'S ADDRESS TO HIS ARMY

Scots wha hae wi' Wallace bled
Scots whom Bruce has often led
Welcome to a gory bed
Or to glorious victory

Chorus
Now is the day and now is the hour
See the front of battle lower
See approaching proud Edward's power
Edward's chains and slavery

Wha can be a traitor knave
Wha can fill a coward's grave
Wha so base to be a slave
Let him turn and flee

Wha for Scotland king and law
Freedom's sword will strongly draw
Freemen stand and freemen be
Calodonia on wi' me

By oppression's woes and pains
By our son's in servile chains
We will drain our dearest veins
Then they shall be free

Lay the proud usurper low
Tyrants fall in every foe
Liberty is in every blow
Let us forward do or die

Ship *Galaxy* 1827

TRADITIONAL SONGS AND BALLADS

Robert Burns wrote this song and set it to a very old Scottish melody called "Hey Tuttie Taitie." This version from the *Galaxy* journal is interesting because it differs enough from Burns to indicate that it had become traditional. The melody used is adapted from the one in *Gems of Scottish Song*.

Book of Popular Songs, p. 429; *Gems of Scottish Song*, p. 106; *Heart Songs*, p. 429.

Captain and Mrs. James A.M. Earle and son Jamie on deck of *Charles W. Morgan*

Popular Songs of or near the Period of the Voyage

This group of songs were commercially published and intended for a general audience at a time that roughly corresponded to the great days of whaling. Whalemen generally learned them aurally, and variations and parodies crept in, but they remained essentially the same songs that were sung ashore.

THE GAM

BEN BOLT
THE ANSWER TO BEN BOLT

Oh yes I remember the name with delight
Sweet Alice so cherished and dear
I seek her grave in the hour of night
And moisten the turf with a tear
And then when the heart is overburdened with woes
I wander and muse all alone
And long for the time when my head shall repose
While Sweet Alice lies under the stone

I roam through the woods where so joyous we strayed
And recline on the green sunny hill
And things are so bright in the beautiful glade
But my heart it is lonely and chill
The hands that so fondly I pressed them in mine
And the lips that were melting with love
Are cold in the grave and I'm left to repine
Till I meet with sweet Alice above

Ah well I remember the schoolhouse and brook
And the master so kind and so true
The wild blooming flowers in the cool shady nook
So fragrant with incense of dew

POPULAR SONGS OF OR NEAR THE PERIOD OF THE VOYAGE

But I weep for these though so dear to my heart
To the friends that have left us alone
The bosom will heave and the tear drop will start
For sweet Alice lies under the stone

                                        Ship *Edward Carey* 1854

THE GRAVE OF BEN BOLT

By the side of Sweet Alice they have laid Ben Bolt
Where often he longed to repose
For there he would kneel with the early spring flowers
And plant o'er his darling a rose
His heart was as true as the star to his gaze
When tossed on the billows alone
But now it is cold and forever at rest
For he calmly lies under the stone

How often his eyes were seen brimming with tears
To mingle with others in grief
But joy would rekindle the warmth of his smile
When knowing the balm of relief
At last he has gone to the bright spirit land
And free from all sorrow and pain
He tastes the full raptures of angels above
For he meets with sweet Alice again

We'll gather the flowers from the sweet shady nook
And moss from the silent old mill
To strew o'er the grave where obscurely repose
The hearts that death only could still
And oft when the soul has grown weary and sad
Will come by the twilight alone
To muse on the bright spot where together Ben Bolt
And sweet Alice lie under the stone

                                        Ship *Edward Carey* 1854

THE GAM

PARODY ON BEN BOLT

O don't you remember the Boys Ben Bolt
The boys with noses so red
Who drank with delight whenever they met
And always went drunk to bed
In the old grave yard in the edge of the town
In corners obscure and alone
They have gone to rest and the gay young sprigs
Have dropped off one by one

O don't you remember the jug Ben Bolt
And the spring at the foot of the hill
There oft we have lain in the summer hours
And drunk to our uttermost fill
The spring is filled with mud Ben Bolt
And the wild hogs root around
And the good old jug and its whiskey sweet
Lies broken and spilt on the ground

O don't you remember the Tavern Ben Bolt
And the Bar Keeper kind and true
And the little nook at the end of the bar
Where we swallowed the rum that he drew
The tavern is burnt to the ground Ben Bolt
And the bottles are cracked and dry
And of all of the Boys that spread it there
There remains but you and I

Ship *Leonidas* 1856

Spaeth in *A History of Popular Music in America* says that Ben Bolt was one of the most popular songs of the nineteenth century. Actually it was popular well into the twentieth century. The melody here is from the singing of Nan Huntington. The parent song has not yet been found in any of the logbooks or journals studied. Perhaps it was so well known that no whaleman or sailor ever bothered to write it down.

As I remember my mother singing it the first line went "O don't you remember Sweet Alice, Ben Bolt?" As the comma was not audible I always

POPULAR SONGS OF OR NEAR THE PERIOD OF THE VOYAGE

thought the girl's name was Alice Ben Bolt. It wasn't but just "Sweet Alice." The song was written in 1848 and my mother was still singing it in 1948 at least.

"The Answer to Ben Bolt" and "The Grave of Ben Bolt" are sequels dripping with sadness. But the "Boys Ben Bolt" is something else again. In the journal of the Ship *Edward* of New Bedford there is a fragment of another parody. It would seem that Shubael Fred Chase the master of the *Edward* was no Ahab. Here is the fragment:

> Oh don't you remember old Shubael Fred Chase
> Old Shubael with his hair all so brown
> Did you weep with delight when he gave you a smile
> Or tremble with fear at his frown

In the same journal there is a crew list on verse and above it is a pen drawing of a fat sow labeled "S.C. Captain of the Edward." Here is the crew list:

> Fred Chase and Alley Simmons too
> And now you know those of our crew
> There's Wm. Clark and Johnny Band
> And R.R. Brook at your command
> There's Henry Gardner in his prime
> And Macy's not behind his time
> Frank Morris too among the rest
> And Joseph Chase too in his best
> There's David Harper up and drest
> And Johnny Links among the rest
> There's Charles Ludolph and Dennis Goff
> They're both afraid to go aloft

And then this final cut at poor Shubael:

> Oh Shubael Shubael Shubael C
> You are a cunning little duck
> Does he want some mother's T
> Or a sugar tit to suck

THE GAM

Anderson, *Colonial Ballads*, p. 34 (another parody); *The Book of Popular Songs*, p. 204; Dean, *Flying Cloud*, p. 31; *Heart Songs*, p. 96: Johnson, *Our Familiar Songs...*, p. 9; Reddall, *Songs That Never Die*, p. 224; *Songs That Lincoln Loved*, p. 54.

JINGLE BELLS

Come jump into the sleigh boys
Let's hurry up and start
There's Betty Sue and Maggie Too
To whom I gave my heart
Come jump into the sleigh boys
Let's hurry up and start
For the horse is madly prancing
And impatient to depart

Chorus
Jingle bells jingle bells jingle all the way
Oh what joy it is to ride in a one horse open sleigh
Jingle bells jingle bells jingle all the way
Oh what joy it is to ride in a one horse open sleigh

Now the town is past
As on our way we go
The horse's hoves are fast
Seen through stinging snow

POPULAR SONGS OF OR NEAR THE PERIOD OF THE VOYAGE

The snow blows thick and fast
Past Maggie Tucker's chin
And all are happy faces
As on our way we go

Six days shall't thou work
And do all thou ar't able
On the seventh holy-stone the deck
And coal-tar all the cable
We went down to the river
And came to Dinah's hut
And there we walked in hand and hand
And the rum it was so hot

Bark *Andrew Hicks* 1879

SECOND VERSION: DASHING THROUGH THE SNOW

Dashing through the snow in a one horse open sleigh
O'er the hill we go laughing all the way
Bells on bobtails ring making spirits bright
Oh what sport to ride and sing a sleighing song tonight

Chorus
Jingle bells jingle bells jingle all the way
Oh what fun it is to ride in a one horse open sleigh (repeat)

A month or two ago I thought I'd take a ride
And soon Miss Faney Bright was sitting by my side
The horse was lean and lank misfortune seemed his lot
We got into a drifted bank and we got upsot

So now the ground is white go it while you're young
Take the gals tonight and sing a sleighing song
I got a bobtail bay two forty is his speed
Hitch him to an open sleigh and crack you'll take the lead

Bark *Pacific* 1870

THE GAM

Spaeth in his *A History of Popular Music in America*, p. 132 says that the song was written in 1857 by J. S. Pierpont and that the original title was not "Jingle Bells," but "Dashing Through the Snow." Spaeth also says that there was an English version with a different chorus.

Perhaps Sam Mingo's third stanza is original with him, but because in his journal he includes it with the first two stanzas it is included here. The melody is standard and will be found in many songbooks.

Heart Songs, p. 148; *The Scottish Students Song Book*, p. 244; Wier, *The Book of a Thousand Songs*, p. 148; Woodgate, *The Penguin Song Book*, p. 12.

THE LONE STARRY FLOWER

O the lone starry flower give me love
When still is the beautiful night
Peep through the cloud's silver white
When no winds through the lone woods sweep love
And I gaze on the bright rising star
When the world is in dream and in sleep love
Then wake when I touch my guitar

When the red rosy dawn grows bright love
Far away o'er the distant sea
When the stars cease their gentle light love
I will wait for a welcome from thee

POPULAR SONGS OF OR NEAR THE PERIOD OF THE VOYAGE

> And oh if that pleasure be mine love
> We will wander together afar
> And thy heart shall be mine mine thine love
> Then wake while I touch my guitar
>
> Ship *Euphrasia* 1849

The most interesting thing about this parlor song is how greatly it changed in oral transmission. The proper title of the song is not "The Lone Starry Flower" but "The Lone Starry Hours," and there are word changes on almost every line.

The melody is adapted from the sheet music published by Oliver Ditson & Co. in 1850. That may mean that it was put in the journal after the voyage had ended. The music is by James Power and the words by Marshall S. Pike. Spaeth in *A History of Popular Music in America*, p. 594 notes that it was first published in 1849, the year the voyage began.

The Book of Popular Songs, p. 37.

THE ROSE THAT ALL ARE PRAISING

The rose that all are praising
Is not the rose for me
Too many eyes are gazing
Upon that costly tree
But there's a rose in yonder glen
That shuns the gaze of other men
For me its blossoms raising
Oh that's the rose for me
Oh that's the rose for me
Oh that's the rose for me

THE GAM

The bird that sings so sweetly
Is not the bird for me
Too many ears can hear her
Atop that lofty tree
But there's a bird that gaily sings
Though free to roam she folds her wings
To me her songs resining
Oh that's the bird for me
Oh that's the bird for me
Oh that's the bird for me

The gem a king might covet
Is not the gem for me
From darkness who would move it
Save that a world might see
But she's a gem that shuns display
And next my heart's worn every day
So dearly do I love it
Oh that's the gem for me
Oh that's the gem for me
Oh that's the gem for me

Ship *Cortes* 1847

The melody is adapted from Wier, *The Book of a Thousand Songs*

Wier, *The Book of a Thousand Songs*, p. 400

MY LOVE

My love why art thou straying
From my heart so warm and true
Why dost thou love but wander
O'er the sea so deep and blue

POPULAR SONGS OF OR NEAR THE PERIOD OF THE VOYAGE

Is there a joy in parting
With one you love when nigh
Oh tell me in a whisper
Shall I meet you bye and bye

My love the tears were falling
When I pressed your hand in mine
And quivering lips gave token
Of the love I'd give for thine
I felt that joy was passing
And life felt oh so drear
When cold farewells were spoken
And you left me lonely here

My love the years in passing
Bring you nearer to my heart
I see your fair face smiling
Though we are so far apart
I hear your loving whisper
Borne far o'er the deep blue sea
I know you soon are coming
With a heart of love for me

My love it is with pleasure
I would journey by your side
When hastening o'er the billows
You come to claim your bride
The years I've passed so lonely
Make my heart more warm and true
In depths of pure affection
And its boundless love for you

Bark *Andrew Hicks* 1879

This song is badly jumbled in the journal. It is only included here because, again, it shows that those three or four long years of waiting for the whaleman to return must have been pretty rough on the girl at home. The melody is supplied.

THE GAM

MAGGY BY MY SIDE

The land is flittering
Flittering from my view
The gale in the sail is setting
Toils a merry crew
Then let my home be on the waters wide
I'll roam with a proud heart
Maggy by my side

Chorus

Maggy dear my one love
Maggy by my side
My one loved Maggy dear
Setting by my side

Storms can apoil me never (?)
While the brow is clear
Fair weather lingers ever
When her smiles appear
When sorrow round my heart shall bide
Still may I find her
Setting by my side

Winds is howling oer the billows
From the distant glee
Storms raging round my pillow
Brings now care to me

POPULAR SONGS OF OR NEAR THE PERIOD OF THE VOYAGE

Roar on yea dark wave oer the troubled tide
I (?) heed not your anger
Maggy is by my side

Ship Hillman 1854

MAGGIE BY MY SIDE (Second Version)

The land of my home is flitting
Flitting from my view
A gale in the sails is sitting toils the merry crew
Then let my home be on the waters wide
I roam with a proud heart Maggy by my side

Chorus

My own loved Maggy dear
Sitting by my side
Maggie dear my own love
Sitting by my side

The wind howling o'er the billows from the distant sea
The storm raging round my pillow brings no care to me
Roll on ye dark waves o'er the troubled tide
I heed not your anger my Maggie by my side

Storms can appall me never while her brow is clear
Fair weather reigneth ever when her smiles appear
When sorrows breaking round my heart shall hide
Still may I find her sitting by my side

Ship Lydia 1855

This is one of Stephen Foster's much less well known songs and perhaps deservedly so. The melody is adapted from Wier, *The Book of a Thousand Songs*.

The Book of Popular Songs, p. 27; *Heart Songs*, p. 135; Wier, *The Book of A Thousand Songs*, p. 307.

THE GAM

WHY ART THOU NOT HERE

The summer stars look brightly down
Upon the tranquil sea
And evening's breath is hushed and gone
From mountain stream and tree
The promised hour hath glided by
And yet a distant sphere

Thrice have the flowers of springtide blushed
The green leaves waked in bloom
And zephyrs through the bright bowers rushed
O'er laden with perfume
And thrice the summer wreaths have worn
The brightness they now wear
Since from our shore thy bark was borne
Ah why art thou not here?

The parting words had bid me hope
At that lone eventide
Ere the best buds of spring shall open
I'll be sweet at thy side
Yet thrice the light springs' buds put on
Hath darkened o'er their bier
And thrice the stars of summer shone
Ah why art thou not here?

Ship *Three Brothers* 1851

Here are those three long years of waiting that must surely mark this as a whaleman's song. Sometimes a whaling voyage began as a one year or less plum pudding voyage, and then after refitting in Rio Grande Do Sul ended up around Cape Horn. The melody is supplied.

POPULAR SONGS OF OR NEAR THE PERIOD OF THE VOYAGE

SWEET NELLIE BROWN

Stroll through the meadows cross over the stream
You see my darling she is a poet's dream
Soft flowing tresses voice soft and sweet
None half so handsome or half so neat
I'm always lonely when she is gone
Who would not love her sweet Nellie Brown

Chorus
Yes she is my Nellie no fairer seen
Life with my darling seems like a dream
Eyes so entrancing grace like a fawn
Who would not love her sweet Nellie Brown

When we are married early in spring
There'll be rejoicing church bells will ring
And little Nellie will be my wife
Her ways so simple her thoughts so pure
She will be my darling for ever more

Bark *Benjamin Cummings* 1866

In *The American Song Folio* this song is credited to W.R. Williams and called "Sweet Nellie Bawn." And it is from that work that the melody is taken. Spaeth, in *A History of Popular Music in America* says that W.R. Williams was also known as Will Rossiter.

THE GAM

Unfortunately, I have not been able to relocate *The American Song Folio* and so cannot give publisher, place or date of publication or the page number.

WIND OF THE WINTER'S NIGHT

Wind of the winter's night whence comest thou
And whither oh whither art wandering now
Sad sad is thy voice on the desolate moor
And mournful oh mournful thy howl at my door

Say where hast thou been on thy cloud-drifted car
Say what hast thou seen on thy roaming afar
What sorrow impels thee thou boisterous blast
Thus to mourn and complain as thou journeyest past

I have been where the snow's on the chill mountain peak
Would have frozen the blood in the ruddiest cheek
And for many a dismal and desolate day
No beam of sunshine has brightened my way

I have come from the deep where the storm in its wrath
Spread havoc and death in its pitiless path
Where the billows arose and the lightning flew by
And histed their arms in the dun-colored sky

And I saw a frail vessel all torn by the wave
Drawn down with her crew to a fathomless grave
And I heard the loud crack of her keel as I passed
And the thrash of her sail and the crack of her mast

POPULAR SONGS OF OR NEAR THE PERIOD OF THE VOYAGE

> But it smote on my ear like the tocsin of death
> As I strove and struggled with the waters for breath
> 'Tis for requiem I sing as I howl through the air
> And repent of the fury that caused her to die
>
> Ship *Cortes* 1847

The song is noted in Spaeth, *A History of Popular Music In America*, p. 80. The melody used here is adapted and simplified from a long and involved sheet music version which credits it to Henry Russell and Charles Mackey. The song was written in 1836.

NELLIE

Oh Nelly dear Nelly I'm waiting for you
With the stars glimmering faintly away in the blue
And the moon's clear light is falling soft on the sea
Come Nelly sweet Nelly I'm waiting for thee

Oh Nelly dear Nelly I'm waiting for you
While quietly the flowers are supping the dew
And old ocean is murmuring sweet whispers to me
Oh Nelly sweet Nelly whilst I'm listing for thee

Oh Nelly dear Nelly I'm waiting for you
While the night world rolls on through the starlight and blue
And the horris are singing a bright future to me
Oh Nelly sweet Nelly I'm waiting for thee

Oh Nelly dear Nelly I'm waiting for you
While the light gentle breeze stirs the leaves anew
And the softest sound that's breathed over the lea
I think is Nelly sweet Nelly coming to me

THE GAM

My Nelly sweet Nelly I press thee once more
To a heart that beats now as it ne'er did before
And thou hast kept thy heart truly my angel for me
Then Nelly my own Nelly thou ever shall be

                                          Ship *Clifford Wayne* 1855

The melody is from the singing of Nan Huntington, who only remembered three of the stanzas.

ALL'S WELL

Deserted by the waning moon
When skys proclaim night's cheerless noon
On tower or fort or tented ground
The sentry walks his lonely round
And should a footstep haply stray
Where caution marks the guarded way
Who goes there stranger quickly tell
A friend the word good night all's well

Or sailing on the midnight deep
While weary messmates soundly sleep
The careful watch patrols the deck
To guard the ship from foe or wreck
And while his thoughts oft homeward veer
Some well known voice salutes his ear
What cheer oh brother quickly tell
Above below good night all's well

                                            Ship *Cortes* 1847

POPULAR SONGS OF OR NEAR THE PERIOD OF THE VOYAGE

This of course is a purely literary song and was popular for a long time. Undoubtedly it had some currency among seamen. Johnson in *Our Familiar Songs and Those Who Made Them* gives us some of the background for the song. Also the melody is adapted from Johnson.

The Book of Popular Songs, p. 205; Johnson, *Our Familiar Songs...*, p. 637.

HOME AGAIN

Home again home again
From a foreign shore
O it fills my heart with joy
To be with friends once more
Here I wept the parting tear
To cross the oceans foam
But now I'm once again with those
Who kindly greet me home

Chorus

Home again home again
From a foreign shore
And O it fills my heart with joy
To be with friends once more

Happy hearts happy hearts
With mine are lost in glee
And oh the friends I loved in youth
Seems happier seem happier than me

THE GAM

And if my guide should be the boat (?)
To bid me longer roam
I'll bid adew to all my friends
And seek my ocean home

Music sweet music sweet
Lingers round the place
And oh I feel the childhood charms
Which time can not efface
Then give me but my hometide roof
I seek no palace....
For I can live a happier life
With those I love at home

Ship Hillman 1854

"Home Again," was the work of Marshall Pike and was published in 1851. The melody is adapted from Wier, *The Book of A Thousand Songs*, p. 202. All home-going songs were popular with whalemen whose voyages were often so interminably long.

Book of Popular Songs, p. 84; *The Golden Wreath*, p. 93; *Heart Songs*, p. 327; Wier, *The Book of A Thousand Songs*, p. 202.

HER BRIGHT SMILE HAUNTS ME STILL

Tis one year since last we met
And may never meet again
I have struggled to forget
But the struggle was in vain
For her voice lives on the breeze
And her spirit comes at will
In the moonlight on the sea
Her bright smile haunts me still

POPULAR SONGS OF OR NEAR THE PERIOD OF THE VOYAGE

> I have sailed 'neath alien skys
> I have trod the desert plains
> I have seen the cloud arise
> Like a grand..........
> Many dangers I have seen
> Which and ever life can see
> In the moonlight on the sea
> Her bright smile haunts me still
>
> Bark *Pacific* 1870

Two lines of each stanza are left out in the bark *Pacific* journal, which meant that the melody had to be altered a little which does not improve it. There is a complete setting of the song in ¾ time in Wier, *Book of A Thousand Songs*.

Spaeth, *A History of Popular Music in America*, p. 170 says that this song published in 1864 is a "definite throwback to the school of self-pity with a sailor to do the complaining."

The Silver Chord, p. 56; Wier, *The Book of A Thousand Songs*, p. 192

LILY DALE

'Twas a calm still night and the moon's pale light
Shone soft o'er hill and dale
When friends mute with grief stood round the death bed
Of my poor lost Lily Dale

THE GAM

Chorus
Oh Lily sweet Lily dear Lily Dale
Now the wild rose blooms o'er the little green grave
'Neath the trees in the flowery dale

Her cheek that once glowed with the rose tint of health
By the hand of disease has turned pale
And the death damp was on the pure white brow
Of my poor lost Lily Dale

I go she said to the land of rest
But ere my strength shall fail
I must tell you where near my own loved home
You must lay poor lost Lily Dale

'Neath the chestnut tree where the wild flowers bloom
And the stream ripples forth through the vale
Where the birds shall warble their songs in the spring
There lay poor lost Lily Dale

Ship *Euphrasia* 1849

Spaeth, *A History of Popular Music in America*, p. 125, says that this song was written in 1852 by H.S. Thompson. Thus it must have been recorded in the journal near or after the end of the voyage. Spaeth also says that it was the best known of a whole series of "melancholy ditties." The melody is adapted from Wier, *The Book of a Thousand Songs*.

Belden, *Ballads and Songs...*, p. 374; *The Book of Popular Songs*, p. 96; *The Golden Wreath*, p. 98; *Heart Songs*, p. 299; Reddall, *Songs that Never Die*, p. 226; Spaeth, *Weep Some More My Lady*, p. 27; Thompson, *A Pioneer Songster*, p. 92; Wier, *The Book of A Thousand Songs*, p. 282.

POPULAR SONGS OF OR NEAR THE PERIOD OF THE VOYAGE

LONG LONG AGO

Tell me the tales that to me were so dear
Long long ago, long long ago
Sing me the songs I delighted to hear
Long long ago long ago
Now you are come all my griefs are removed
Let me forget all the times you have roved
Let me believe that you love as you loved
Long long ago long ago

Do you remember the first time we met
Long long ago long long ago
Ah yes you told me you never would forget
Long long ago, long ago
Then to all others my smiles you preferred
Love when you spoke you gave to each word
Still my heart treasures the praises I heard
Long long ago, long ago

Though by kindness my fond hopes were raised
Long long ago, long ago
You my Alan's eloquent lips have been praised
Long long ago, long ago
But by long absence your strength has been tried
Still to your accents I listen with pride
Blest as I was when I sat by your side
Long long ago, long ago

Marble family papers, 1837, 1851

THE GAM

Long Long Ago was written both words and music by Thomas Haynes Bayly about 1840 and it became very popular. Spaeth in *A History of Popular Music in America* says that this was Bayly's masterpiece and that it is still sung.

Johnson, *Our Familiar Songs...*, p. 3; *The Silver Chord*, p. 175; *The Book of A Thousand Songs*, p. 257.

DO THEY MISS ME AT HOME

Do they Miss me at home do they miss me
Twoud be an assurance most dear
To know that this moment some loved one
We're saying I wish he were here
To feel that the group at the fireside
Were thinking of me as I roam
Oh yes twoud be joy beyond measure
To know that they miss me at home
To know that they miss me at home

When twilight approaches the season
That ever is sacred to song
Does some one repeat my name over
And sigh that I tarry so long'
And is there a chord in the music
That's missed when my voice is not there
And a chord in each heart that awakens
Regret at my wearisome stay
Regret at my wearisome stay

POPULAR SONGS OF OR NEAR THE PERIOD OF THE VOYAGE

Do they set me a chair near the table
When evenings home pleasures are nigh
When the candles are lit in the parlor
And the stars in the calm asure sky
And when the good nights are repeated
And all lay them down to their sleep
Do they think of the absent and waft me
A whispering good night while they sleep
A whispering good night while they sleep

Do they miss me at home do they miss me
At morning at noon and at night
And lingers a gloomy shade round them
That only my presence can light
Are joys less invitingly welcome
Are pleasures less hale than before
Because one is missed from the circle
Because I am with them no more
Because I am with them no more

Ship *Hillman* 1854
Ship *Lydia* 1855

The *Lydia* and *Hillman* versions are quite similar with only enough word change here and there to show that at least one of them was not copied from the sheet music.

The melody is adapted from Spaeth, *Weep Some More My Lady*.

The Book of Popular Songs, p. 49; *The Golden Wreath*, p. 68; Johnson, *Our Familiar Songs...*, p. 68; *The Silver Chord*, p. 189; Spaeth, *Weep Some More My Lady*, p. 18; Wier, *The Book of A Thousand Songs*, p. 110.

THE GAM

MEET ME BY MOONLIGHT

Meet me by moonlight alone
And then I will tell you a tale
Must be told by the moonlight alone
In the grove at the end of the vale
You must promise to come for I said
I would show the night flowers their queen
Nay turn not away thy sweet head
Tis the loveliest ever was seen
Oh meet me by moonlight alone
Oh meet me by moonlight alone

Daylight may do for the gay
The thoughtless the heartless the free
But there is something the moonlight
That is sweeter to you and to me
Oh remember be sure to be there
For though dearly a moonlight I desire
I care not for all in the air
I want the sweet light of your eyes
So meet me by moonlight alone
So meet me by moonlight alone

Ship *Hillman* 1854

Johnson, *In Our Familiar Songs and Those Who Made Them* says that "Meet Me By Moonlight" was the work of J. Augustus Wade who was so poor "that in his last days he literally went begging among the music publishers."

POPULAR SONGS OF OR NEAR THE PERIOD OF THE VOYAGE

However, this song written some time before his death in 1875, became extremely popular. The opening three lines became a part of "The Jail Song," which was one of the most popular country songs of the first part of this century. The melody is adapted from Wier, *The Book of A Thousand Songs*.

Johnson, *Our Familiar Songs...*, p. 374; *The Silver Chord*, p. 124; Wier, *The Book of A Thousand Songs*, p. 302.

WHEN THE ROSES WERE IN BLOOM

When the roses were in bloom
And the leaves were green
I would join you if I could
As my queen as my queen
There was something in your glances
In the trembling of your hand
Put a summer in our fancies
And a glory in the land
When the roses were in bud
And the leaves were green
When the roses were in bud
And the leaves were green

THE GAM

When the roses were in bloom
And the leaves aflame
I whispered will you come
And you came and you came
Was there ever love like ours
As we wandered you and I
By the river and the flowers
And the crimson in the sky
When the roses were in bloom
And the leaves aflame
When the roses were in bloom
And the leaves aflame

When the roses were all blown
And the leaves were dead
And we had to own
Love had fled love had fled
With the dead leaves and the dying
Of the flowers and the trees
We had left our love a-laying there
Oh may it rest in peace
When the roses were all blown
When the roses were all blown
And the leaves were dead

Bark Andrew Hicks 1879

It seems as though I should have found a reference for this song but I did not. Sam Mingo, a Christiantown Indian kept the *Andrew Hicks* journal and there is no evidence that he was a maker of songs although he may have left a love here and there in the South Seas. I knew Addie Mingo Smalley very well. She was Sam Mingo's daughter and she said that her father was capable of anything. We do know that he was a good whaleman.

POPULAR SONGS OF OR NEAR THE PERIOD OF THE VOYAGE

THE WATCHER

The night was dark and fearful the blast came wailing by
A watcher pale and fearful looked forth with anxious eye
How wistfully she gazed no gleam of light was there
Her eye to heaven she raised in agony of prayer

Within that swelling lowly where want and darkness reigned
The precious child her only lies mouldering in his path
And death alone can fell him she feels that this must be
But oh for light to see him smile once again on me

A hundred feet are dancing within a mansion fair
A hundred lights are glancing they have not mourning there
Oh young and joyous creatures one lamp from out your store
Would give that poor boy's features to his mother's gaze once more

The sun now brightly shining she heedeth not its ray
Beside her boy reclining the pale dead mother lay
A smile her pale lips wreathing a smile of hope and love
As if her heart were beating there is light for us above

Ship Trident 1846

Here is another song of gloom and sadness to go with "Poor Little Joe," "The Flower Girl," and the like. The melody is from the singing of Nan Huntington.

Thompson, *A Pioneer Songster*, p. 183.

THE GAM

ANNIE OF THE VALE

The young stars are gleaming
Their clear light bestowing
Their radiance fills the clear summer night
Come forth like a fairy
So blithesome and airy
And ramble in their soft and gentle light

Chorus
Come come come love come
Come ere the night torchs pale
Oh come in thy beauty
The marvel of duty
Dear Annie dear Annie of the vale

The world we inherit
So charmed by thy spirit
So radient as the mild warm summer day
The watch dog is snarling
For fear Annie darling
His beautiful young friend I'd steal away

Bark *Pacific* 1870

"Annie of the Vale" was a very popular hit of its time. Belden in *Ballads and Songs* has a three stanza version that except for the chorus has been entirely changed into a Civil War song.

The melody here is adapted from sheet music published by Firth Pond & Co., New York, 1861.

Belden, *Ballads and Songs*..., p. 222–223; Tom Thumb, *A Sheaf of Songs*..., p. 32.

POPULAR SONGS OF OR NEAR THE PERIOD OF THE VOYAGE

GENTLE ANNIE

Then will come no more gentle Annie
Like a flower thy spirit did depart
Thou art gone afar like the many
That have bloomed in the summer of my heart

Chorus
Shall we never ore behold thee
Never har thy merry voice again
When the spring time comes gentle Annie
And the wild flowers are scatterd o'er the plain

We have roamed and loved mid the bowers
When thy dewy cheek was in bloom
Now I wander alone mid the flowers
Which mingle their perfume o'er thy tomb

Ah the hours grow sad while I ponder
Near the silent spot where thou art laid
And my head bows down when I wander
By the stream and meadows where we strayed

Ship *Lydia* 1855

This is one of Stephen Foster's less well known songs. The melody is from Wier, *Book of A Thousand Songs*.

The Book of Popular Songs, p. 19; *The Golden Wreath*, p. 57; *Heart Songs*, p. 354; *Songs That Lincoln Loved*, p. 12; Wier, *The Book of a Thousand Songs*, p. 172.

THE GAM

ELLA RHEE

Oh Ella Rhee so kind and true
In the little churchyard lies
Her grave is wet with drops of dew
But brighter were her eyes

Chorus
Then carry me back to Tennessee
There let me live and die
Among the fields of yeller corn
In the land where Ella lies

Her pretty eyes and gentle form
Methinks I still can see
I love the spot where she was born
Way down in Tennessee

The summer moon will rise and set
The night birds trill their lays
And the possum and coon so softly step
Round the grave of Ella Rhee

Welcome Tilton
Bark *Pacific* 1870

This is Welcome Tilton's version of "Ella Rhee." It is one of the very few songs of this type that I ever heard him sing.

Spaeth, in *A History of Popular Music in America*, p. 128, says that the song was claimed by Septimus Winner as his in 1865 but it has been traced back to C.E. Steuart and James Porter dated 1853.

Welcome Tilton seems to have combined the two songs to make one of his own that he sang with great seriousness.

POPULAR SONGS OF OR NEAR THE PERIOD OF THE VOYAGE

Dean, *Flying Cloud*, p. 96; *The Scottish Students Song Book*, p. 306; Wier, *The Book of a Thousand Songs*, p. 122.

DARLING NELLIE GRAY

There's a lone green valley on the old Kentucky shores
....
A setting and a singing by the little cottage door
Where lived My darling Nellie Gray

Chorus
Oh my poor Nellie Gray they have taken you away
And I'll never see my darling any more
I'm setting by the river and I'm weeping all the day
For you're gone from the old Kentucky shore

When the moon had climbed the mountain
And the stars were shining too
Then I'd take my darling Nellie Gray
And we'd float down the river in my little red canoe
While my banjo sweetly I would play

One night I went to see her she's gone the neighbors say
The white man bound her with his chain
They have taken her to Georgia for to wear her life away
As she toils on the cotton and the cane

THE GAM

My canoe is under water and my banjo is unstrung
I'm tired of living any more
My eyes shall look downward and my song shall be unsung
While I stay on the old Kentucky shore

My eyes are getting blinded and I cannot see my way
Hark there's somebody knocking at my door
Oh I hear the angels calling and I see my Nellie Gray
Farewell to the old Kentucky shore

Oh my darling Nellie Gray up in heaven there they say
And they'll never take her from me any more
I'm coming coming coming as the angels clear the way
Farewell to the old Kentucky shore

Bark Pacific 1870

Spaeth, in *A History of Popular Music in America*, p. 131–32 says that "Darling Nellie Gray" became a part of our folk literature. It certainly did and a part of our folk music. The melody was used as a square dance tune almost as much as the song was sung. The setting here is the melody as it was used for country dances on Martha's Vineyard.

The song was written by Benjamin Russel Hanby and published in 1856. Spaeth gives us some very interesting background for it such as that there actually was a slave named Nelly Gray who was taken away from her lover, and that Hanby's father ran a station of the underground railroad that helped escaped slaves reach freedom in the North.

The second line of the first stanza, omitted in the journal reads, "Where I've whiled many happy hours away."

Anderson, *Colonial Ballads*, p. 144; *The Book of Popular Songs*, p. 283; Downs and Siegneister, *A Treasury of American Song*, p. 274; *The Golden Wreath*, p. 152; *Heart Songs*, p. 116; Shoemaker, *Mountain Minstrelsy of Pennsylvania*, p. 139; *The Silver Chord*, p. 183; Munch, *The Song Tradition of Tristan da Cunha*, p. 114; Wier, *The Book of a Thousand Songs*, p. 112.

POPULAR SONGS OF OR NEAR THE PERIOD OF THE VOYAGE

GOOD OLD JEFF

'Tis just one year ago today
That I remember well
I sat down by poor Nellie's side
And a story she did tell
'Twas about a poor old darkey Jeff
That lived for many a year
But now he's dead and in his grave
No trouble does he fear

Chorus
For poor old Jeff has gone to rest
We know that he is free
Disturb him not but let him rest
Way down in Tennessee

She took my arm we walked along
Into an open field
And there she paused to sigh a while
Then to his grave did steal
She sat down by that little mound
And softly whispered there
'Tis me dear father 'tis thy child
And softly dropped a tear

THE GAM

But since that time how things have changed
Poor Nell that was my bride
Is laid beneath the cold grave sod
Down by her father's side
I planted there beside her grave
This weeping willow tree
And bathed its roots with many a tear
That it might shelter me

Brig Pavilion 1858
Bark Andrew Hicks 1879

Why this song was so exceedingly popular for such a long time is hard to understand. But it was. The original title was "The Poor Old Slave." It was also called "The Gold Old Slave." Spaeth in *A History of Popular Music in America* says that it was written in 1851 by G.W.H. Griffin. Many song writers of the time were trying to cash in on Stephen Foster's success.

The melody is adapted from Wier, *The Book of a Thousand Songs*.

Wier, *The Book of a Thousand Songs*, p. 388.

THE BELLE OF BALTIMORE

I've been through Carolina
I've been to Tennessee
I've traveled Mississippi
For master set me free

POPULAR SONGS OF OR NEAR THE PERIOD OF THE VOYAGE

    I've kissed the lovely creole
    By Louisiana's shore
    But I never found a gal to match
    The belle of Baltimore

    Chorus
    Oh boys belle's a beauty
    Eye so bright and cheek so sooty
    No gal I've ever seen before
    Is so sweet as the belle of Baltimore

    My belle is tall and slender
    She sings so very clear
    You'd think she was a nightingale
    If once her voice you'd hear
    I walked down to her cabin
    I rapped against the door
    I want to give my daguerreotype
    To the belle of Baltimore

    Brig *Pavilion* 1858

"The Belle of Baltimore" is a blackface minstrel song and the melody is better than many such. The mention of the "daguerreotype" in the second stanza dates it as early. Perhaps giving one's daguerreotype to a girl was the first step in getting engaged.

The brig *Pavilion* was a small vessel of only 150 tons and probably carried only three whaleboats. That voyage of 1858 was in the Atlantic.

The melody is from Wier, *Songs of the Sunny South*.

Wier, *Songs of the Sunny South*, p. 32.

THE GAM

THE VACANT CHAIR

We shall meet but we shall miss him
There will be one vacant chair
We shall linger to caress it (?)
While we breathe the evening prayer
When a year ago we gathered
Joy was in his mild blue eyes
But a golden cord is severed
And our hopes in ruins lie

Chorus
We shall meet but we shall miss him
There will be a vacant chair
We shall linger to caress him
While we breathe the evening air

At our fireside sad and lonely
Often will the bosom swell
At remembrance of the story
How our noble Willie fell
How he strove to bear our banner
Through the thickest of the fight
And upheld our country's honor
With (?) the strength of manhood's might

POPULAR SONGS OF OR NEAR THE PERIOD OF THE VOYAGE

> Time they tell us wreaths of glory
> Ever more will deck his brow
> But this soothes the anguish only
> Sweeping o'er our heartstrings now
> Sleep today O early fallen
> In thy green and narrow bed
> ....(?) from pine and cypress
> Mingle with the tears we shed

Spaeth, in *A History of Popular Music in America*, says that this song was sung by soldiers of both the North and South. The melody is adapted from Wier, *The Book of a Thousand Songs*, where the setting is in 3/4 time. We have put it in 4/4 time here, for that is how it was played traditionally on Martha's Vineyard.

Wier, *The Book of a Thousand Songs*, p. 483.

THE BELLE OF THE MOHAWK VALE

> Sweet is the vale where the Mohawk gently glides
> On its clear winding way to the sea
> And dearer than all the streams on earth besides
> Is this bright rolling river to me

> *Chorus*
> But sweeter yes dearer far than these
> Who charms where all others fail is
> Blue eyed bonny bonny Eloise
> The Belle of the Mohawk Vale

THE GAM

Oh sweet are the scenes of my boyhood's sunny hours
That bespangle the bright valley o'er
And dear are the friends seen thru memories fond tears
That have lived in the lost days of yore

Oh sweet are the moments when dreaming I roam
Through my loved haunts now mossy and grey
And dearer than all is my childhood hallowed home
That is crumbling now slowly away

Bark Pacific 1870

The proper title of this song is "Bonnie Eloise." It was written in 1858, and according to Spaeth in *A History of Popular Music in America*, p. 134, it was used as a marching tune by both North and South in the Civil War.

It was very popular in its time, and the melody, at least, has become truly traditional and is still sometimes heard at country dances in New England.

Heart Songs, p. 108; Shay, *Drawn From the Wood*, p. 115; Wier, *The Book of a Thousand Songs*, p. 51.

COLUMBIA THE GEM OF THE OCEAN

Oh Columbia's the ruler of the ocean
The home of the brave and the free
The shrine of each patriot's devotion
All nations pay homage to thee

POPULAR SONGS OF OR NEAR THE PERIOD OF THE VOYAGE

Thy banner makes heroes assemble
When liberty's form is in view
Thy mandates make tyranny tremble
When borne by the red white and blue

Chorus
When borne by the red white and blue
When borne by the red white and blue
Thy mandates make tyranny tremble
When borne by the red white and blue

When war waged its wild desolation
And threatened our country to deform
The ark then of Freedom's foundation
Columbia rode safely through the storm
With then the wreaths then of victory o'er her
So nobly she bore her brave crew
With the wreaths then of victory o'er her
So nobly she bore her brave crew

Chorus
With her flag floating proudly before her
Her boast was the red white and blue
With her flag floating proudly before her
Her boast was the red white and blue

Oh the can boys the can bring hither
And fill it high to the rim
May the memory of Washington live ever
Nor the deeds of his glory n'er grow dim
May his service never sever
From its hold on the sailors so true
The army and navy for ever
Three cheers for the red white and blue

Chorus
Three cheers for the red white and blue
Three cheers for the red white and blue
Our army and navy for ever
Three cheers for the red white and blue

Ship *Hillman* 1854

THE GAM

The title of this in the journal is just "Song." The proper title is "Columbia the Gem of the Ocean," not "the ruler." There are other changes all through the three stanzas and choruses that show that it is most certainly was not copied from sheet music or a broadside.

Spaeth in *A History of Popular Music in America*, p. 98–99 gives an interesting history of the song and notes that it was claimed by two writers, David T. Shaw and Thomas A. Becket.

The Book of Popular Songs, p. 138; Ford, *Traditional Music in America*, p. 458; Reddall, *Songs that Never Die*, p. 88; *The Scottish Students Song Book*, p. 66; *The Silver Chord*, p. 148.

LINES TO DELIA

I've wandered many a league Delia
Since last with you I met
And many more about the world
Tis will I wander yet,
Still though I'm borne from Clime to Clime
Where all seems strange and new
Remembrance brings each happier time
With absent friends and you Delia
With absent friends and you

Though brief the time which haply made
Acquainted you and I
Within my heart are gently laid
Thoughts which will never die
They mingle with the brightest dreams

POPULAR SONGS OF OR NEAR THE PERIOD OF THE VOYAGE

That ere my memory knew
And fancy brings again the scene
Of absent friends and you Delia
Of absent friends and you

Though change of scenes in foreign land
Seems pleasant for a while
The pressure of the strangers have
And welcome may beguile
Yet give me back my kindred home
With all that's prized and true
And I would wish no more to roam
From absent friends and you Delia
From absent friends and you

Three years has yet its way
Of cheerlessness to flee
Ere homeward bound my barque shall stray
In gladness ore the sea
Yet while neath stranger skies I cruise
And pays be ere so few
A solace still twill be to muse
Of absent friends and you Delia
Of absent friends and you

Ship Three Brothers *1851*

In a sheet music version of this song published by Russell and Patee, Boston, 1852 the title is not "Lines to Delia" but rather "Absent Friends and You, Mary." The song is credited to William F. Spencer, USN.

There are minor word changes throughout the song. But after the different titles and the change in the girl's name, the biggest difference is in the first line of the fourth stanza, the time of the man's absence. In the printed version it is one year, not the three years in the *Three Brothers* journal. One year of sea duty was long enough for a navy man, but for a whaleman it was almost always three years and often more.

"Abandonment of the Whalers in The Arctic Ocean September 1871" lithograph by J.H. Bufford; publisher Benjamin Russell

Miscellaneous Songs

Here is a group of 16 songs that don't fit neatly into any of the other categories. They cover a wide range, from a dissertation on chickens to two songs on women's rights, with detours along the way for commentaries on love, liquor and agnosticism.

A PSALM OF LIFE

Tell me not in mournful numbers
Life is but an empty dream
Chickens in their fitful slumbers
Are by no means what they seem

Life is real life is earnest
And the shell is not its span

THE GAM

Egg thou art and egg remainest
Was not spoken of the hen

Now enjoyment and not sorrow
Is our destined end and way
But to scratch that each tomorrow
Finds us fatter than today

Art is long and time is fleeting
Be our bill then sharpened well
Not like muffled drums be beating
On the inside of the shell

In the world's broad field of battle
In the great henyard of life
Be not like the lazy cattle
Be a rooster in the strife

Trust no hawk however pleasant
And yet never be it said
When the birds of prey were present
You were skulking in the shed

Lives of old cocks then remind us
We can make our lives sublime
And when roasted leave behind us
Hen tracks in the sand of time

Bird tracks that perhaps another
Chicken drooping in the rain
A forlorn and henpecked brother
When he sees shall crow again

Let us then be after hatching
With a heart for every fate
Ever crowing ever scratching
Learn to cackle and to prate

Brig Pavilion 1858

MISCELLANEOUS SONGS

This song is a take-off on Longfellow's poem. It dates from the time when all farm and small town families kept chickens, and the morning crowing of the roosters was a sound that was universal.

Laying hens were sometimes kept penned on the decks of whaleships and it was usually the afterguard, the captain and his officers that got the eggs.

This is from a journal kept by Elbridge Adams of Chilmark on Martha's Vineyard. The melody used is "Reuben, Reuben" as sung, hummed and whistled by my mother Nan Huntington. The second melody is supplied.

FREE THINKERS REASONS FOR REFUSING TO PREACH

I am plagued with my friends and neighbors to boot
To know what Religion my conscience would fit
If I never am saved, I'll speak as I think
I'll love mankind better and take a good drink

Some call me a Quaker, some call me a Jew
Some say I the laws of Mahomet pursue
But if I've good liquor I'll fill to the brink
I'll love mankind better and take a good drink

I've read the opinions of wise men and fools
In classical authors who taught in the schools
And Philosophy teaches me freely to think
To love mankind and to take a good drink

I hope the dissenters may all be forgiven
And Whitefield and Sandsman both go to heaven
But many poor souls to the bottom will sink
For the want of good reason as well as good drink

THE GAM

> Perhaps some may call me a bold Labertine
> But let them to reason one moment incline
> Their eyes will be opened with me they'll all think
> They'll be jovial and free and they'll all take a good drink
>
> Ship Polly 1794

This little song from the journal of the ship *Polly* and speaks for itself and a good title would be "Have a Good Drink." The original title "De Mott," which is what it is called in *The Jovial Songster II* and here is the last stanza of the song as found there. The melody is from *The Jovial Songster*.

> So here's the opinion of honest De Mott
> Who loves to enjoy both his friends and he pot
> O'er a cup of good liquor he ne'er sleeps a wink
> But is jovial and free, and will take a good drink

The Jovial Songster II, p. 22.

THE VIRGIN NINETEEN YEARS OLD

As I was a-walking one night 'neath the shade
I spied a fair damsel all nipped up so grand
She had feathers and finery and jewels and gold
She said she was a virgin, yes a virgin
Only nineteen years old

MISCELLANEOUS SONGS

Her fingers were a-tapering and her neck like a swan
Her nose it was turned up and her voice not too strong
In three weeks we married and the wedding bells told
That I'd married a virgin, yes a virgin
Only nineteen years old

The wedding party broke up a we retired to our rest
But my hair it all stood on end when my bride she undressed
For a cartload of wadding she first did unfold
Which I thought was most peculiar, yes peculiar
For one nineteen years old

She took off her right foot, she had nothing to hide
She unstuck her left ear and laid it aside
Then she pulled out her eyeball, on the carpet it rolled
Thinks I, is this a virgin, yes a virgin
Only nineteen years old

She wiped off her eyebrows and I thought I would faint
As she scraped from off her old face a whole cartload of paint
Then she took off her wig and her bald pate well told
That this was no virgin, no virgin
Only nineteen years old

She pulled out her false teeth and I jumped up in terror
For her nose and her chin they did come together
Then I out from that chamber never more to behold
A sweet young virgin, no virgin
Not nineteen years old

So young men take a warning if to church you do go
Be sure your bride is perfect from tip top to toe
Or you'll pay for your folly and like me you'll be sold
For a patched up old strumpet, no virgin
Almost ninety-nine years old

Bark Andrew Hicks 1879

THE GAM

This song seems to be better known in the British Isles than it is on this side of the Atlantic, although I do remember the trap fishermen at Menemsha singing fragments of it when I was a boy. The melody is from *The Clown's Songster*.

When Mil and I were in Belfast some years ago a singer in a pub sang a quite different and we thought not so good a version of this song. The second melody is supplied.

The Clown's Songster, p. 12

WOMAN'S RIGHTS I

The rights of woman what are they
The right to labor and to pray
The right to watch while others sleep
The right o'er others woes to weep

The right to succor in distress
The right while others curse to bless
The right to love while others scorn
The right to comfort all who mourn

The right to shed new joy on earth
The right to feel the soul's high worth
The right to lead that soul to God
Along the path the Savior trod

The path of meekness and of love
The path of faith that leads above
The path of patience under wrong
The path in which the weak grow strong

MISCELLANEOUS SONGS

Such are women's rights and God will bless
And crown their champions with success

                              Bark *Midas* 1861

This is one of several songs in this book that deals with women's rights and woman's place in society. The women's lib of today has roots that go back a long, long way.

The music is from sheet music, n.d. in the British Museum. The words are credited to Lord Houghton and the music to Marianne Mathews. The bark *Midas* version is considerably shorter than Lord Houghton's and the melody has been simplified.

The song has not been located elsewhere. The last two lines of the last stanza will sing to the last half of the music.

WOMAN'S RIGHTS II

Oh we've heard of women's rights and of woman's wrongs
In speeches in the papers and in topical songs
And there isn't any doubt in any right mind
She's a right to be loved by the whole of mankind
She's a right to be clothes as it pleases her whim
Yet not to be dowdy but natty and prim
She's a right to disport in spangles and tights
Oh there are a few of the lady's rights

THE GAM

Chorus
She's a right to a wink and a kiss in the dark
To a carriage and pair and a drive in the park
She's a right to be somebody's pretty little dear
And if she can get it a thousand a year

She's a right to be happy a right to be glad
She hasn't any right to be sulky and sad
She's a right to a dance at the fancy ball
To a seal skin jacket and an Indian shawl
She's right to a share of the cakes and ale
To a share in the palace and a share in the jail
To a share of the money and a share of the fun
And a right to be married when she's twenty-one

She's a right to be heard when she talks of her wrongs
And to fight with her tongue but not with the tongs
She's a right to a seat in a cottage or tent
But not to a seat in the parliament
She's a right to be mother a right to be wife
But no right at all to be single for life
She's a right to be missus but no right to rebel
She hasn't any right to be mister as well

She's a right to be saucy a right to be smart
But she hasn't any right to break a man's heart
To a breach of promise she has every blame
But wearing the breeches is a different game
She's a right to re-dress if she can only pay
That is to re-dress herself ten times a day
But the marriage rights are her greatest delights
Oh there are the sweetest of the ladies rights

Bark *Andrew Hicks* 1879

Here is an entirely different "Women's Rights," but note that in spite of the entirely different tone of this and "Woman's Rights I," the basic idea of the two is identical — woman's place is in the home to serve and be served but she does not intrude on man's prerogative. She is and must remain the weaker sex.

This song must have been in print but I have not been able to find it, so the melody here has been supplied.

A SONG FOR A WEDDING

When Adam was created and dwelt in Eden's shade
As Moses has related and soon a bride was made
Ten thousands time ten thousand of creatures roamed around
Before a mate was fashioned and yet no bride he found

He had no conversation but seemed as if alone
Till to his admiration he found he'd lost a bone
Great was his exultation when first he found his bride
Great was his elevation to see her by his side

He spoke as in a rapture I know from whence she came
From my left side extracted and woman is her name
So Adam he rejoiced to see his lovely bride
A part of his own body the product of his side

THE GAM

The woman was not taken from Adam's head we know
To show she must not rule him 'tis evidently so
The woman was not taken from Adam's feet we see
So he must not abuse her the meaning seems to be

The woman was extracted from under Adam's arm
So she must be protected from injury and harm
The woman was extracted from near to Adam's heart
By which we are directed that they must never part

Likewise that he should treat her and love her as his friend
Prize nothing else above her till life shall have an end
This seems to be the reason why man should love his bride
A part of his own body the product of his side

So here we see directed the duty of a bride
That she shall be subjected must never be denied
So as she was extracted from under Adam's arm
So she must be protected from injury and harm
So she must be subjected unto her husband's will
That nothing be neglected her duty to fulfill

As I have been invited to write a line or two
I hope 'twill not be slighted what I attempt to do
And now most noble bridegroom to you I turn aside
To your loyal consort and to your lovely bride

As you have been my scholars I taught you both to read
And now to what I offer I beg you will give heed
As by a sacred contract you now are man and wife
See that you both endeavor to live a Godly life

The book that's called the Bible be sure not to neglect
In every scene of action it will you both protect
There is counsel for the bridegroom and likewise for the bride
Let not this sacred volume be ever laid aside
The bridegroom is commanded in that he should live
As becomes a Christian and a house provide

MISCELLANEOUS SONGS

The bride she is commanded her husband to obey
In everything that's lawful until her dying day
Avoiding all contention nor sow the seeds of strife
These are the solemn duties of both a man and wife

           Bark *Andrew Hicks* 1879

Other titles for this song are "Wedlock" and "When Adam was Created." The woman's place is very clearly stated, but some of the duties of the man are listed too. Greig calls the song "Creation," and says that he has heard it sung to a variant of "Rosin The Beau," so that is what we have here for the melody. The last two lines of the six line stanzas can be sung by repeating the second line of the melody. The second melody is supplied.

Brown, *North Carolina Folklore*, Vol. V, p. 46; Greig, *Folk-Song of the North-East*, CXLVIII; Kidson, *Traditional Tunes*, p. 152; Sharp, *English Folk Songs From the Southern Appalachians*, Vol. II, p. 152.

WEDLOCK

Dear Lady since the single state
You've left and chose yourself a mate
Since metamorphosed to a wife
And bliss and woes insured for life

A kindly miss the way would show
To gain the bliss and miss the woe
But first of all I must suppose
You've with mature affection chose

THE GAM

And this presumed I think you may
Here find to married bliss the way
Small is the province of a wife
And narrow is her sphere in life

Within that sphere to move aright
Shall be her principal delight
To guide the hours with prudent care
And properly to spend and spare

To make her husband bless the day
He gave his liberty away
To form the tender infant mind
These are the tasks to wives assigned

Then never think domestic care
Beneath the notice of the faire
But daily those affairs inspect
That naught be wasted by neglect

Be frugal plenty round you seen
And always keep the golden mien
Be always clean and seldom fine
Let decent neatness round you shine

If once fair destiny be fled
Love soon departs the connubial bed
Not nice your house but neat and clean
In all things there's a proper mien

Some of our sense may take in this
To answer some to remiss
To early days of married life
Are oft be hurt by childish strife

Then let it be your rule and care
To keep that season bright and fare
For this is the time by gentle art
To fit your empire in his heart

MISCELLANEOUS SONGS

Kind obliging earnest strive
To keep the lamp of love alive
And should it through neglect expire
You never again would light the fire

To charm is reason dress your mind
Still love shall be with friendship joined
Right on that basis it will endure
From time and death itself secure

Be sure thou never for power contend
Nor strive by tears to gain your end
Sometimes the tears that cloud our eyes
From pride and obstenancy arise

Heaven gave to man superior sway
Then heaven and him be sure obey
Let sullen frowns your brow not cloud
Be always cheerful never loud

Let trifles never discompose
Your temper no nor your repose
Abroad for happiness ne'er roam
For happiness resides at home

Still make your partner easy there
Man finds abroad sufficient care
If every thing at home be right
He always enters with delight

Your converse he'll prefer to all
You see kind words do pleasure all
With careful cheats his cares beguile
And always meet him with a smile

Should passion ever his soul deform
Serenely meet the blustering storm
Never in wordy war engage
Nor never meet his rage with rage

THE GAM

With all sure sense and softening art
Recall lost reason to his heart
And guide his ways with prudent care
And may your wedded life be fair

Sloop Dolphin 1790

It seems natural that this song should go with the songs on women's rights, or lack of them, for "Heaven gave to man superior sway."

Benjamin Paddock, Jr. was master on that voyage "in the good sloop Dolphin of Nantucket on a whaling cruise toward the Bahamas, February 23, 1790."

Such short voyages in the Atlantic usually lasted only a few months and later came to be called "Plum pudding voyages." There is a story that on one such voyage from Edgartown, the captain didn't kiss his wife goodbye as all the visitors went ashore. And after they were underway the mate got up his courage to ask the captain why he hadn't done so. "Why should I?" the captain replied. "We'll only be gone six months or less."

A late-eighteenth or early-nineteenth century sloop was not necessarily a very small vessel. Some were larger than many of the schooners and brigs of the period and almost all of them were faster. That towering single mast with its great spread of canvas aerodynamically was the most efficient rig. But it took a good crew to handle it.

The last two lines of the last stanza have been supplied. The melody is part of the fiddle tune "Bonnie Dundee." The second melody is supplied.

THE LILY OF LAKE CHAMPLAIN

Tis of as fair a landscape as ever you did see
It lies between the Canidies and the Atlantic Sea
It's covered all over with flowers bedewed with bending grace
To me it is the fairest lands on the banks of Lake Champlain

MISCELLANEOUS SONGS

Tis on this lakes fair bosom ships may securely ride
Beneath those bright and shining waves where playful fishes glide
The birds are singing in the air of every gaitage youth
Their notes are full of melody most charming unto youth

Besides there is a maiden more fairer than the rose
Or any other flower that in this universe grows
She has caused me for to love her and for her my heart doth ache
She is my lovely Mary the lily of the lake

One day as she sat on my knees I told her my design
I pressed her to my bosom I pressed her to be my bride
She answered me with a blooming blush she said she'd be my bride
She is my lovely Mary the Lily of the lake

But now I've gone and left her the raging seas to stem
But still my memory cherishes her my lovely Elmy
And if ever I should return again unto my native state
I'm in hopes to find her unmarried the Lily of the lake

But if she has forgotten me other I never can
O be me in America or in some foreign land
O be me roving o'er the seas whatever may be my fate
With a golden chain I'm bound unto the Lily of the lake

But if she has forgotten soon her I'll bid adieu
There is a rose in New York town that is both kind and true
She claims possession of my heart sweet Catherine is her name
I'll marry the Rose and bid adieu to the Lily of Lake Champlain

Adieu you beautiful Lily adieu you beautiful beautiful rose
For I am on the ocean where stormy winds to blow
Where winds and waves they do unite to seal my dismal fate
One slender form withstood the storm 'twas the Lily of the lake

God speed our ship Elaida unto our native shore
And grant that we return again to the girls we most adore
Embrace them in arms of love and there let us remain
With the lovely rose of New York town not the lily of Lake Champlain
Bark *John Dawson* 1863

THE GAM

This song in which the man loves two girls and leaves them both to go whaling is somewhat confused. The chances are that it never had much if any currency.

The melody used here is No. 583 of Sam Henry's "Songs of the People," called "The Banks of the Dee," which is almost certainly the parent song of the American "The Banks of Lake Champlain." So it is fitting that it be used here and it seems to fit the words of "The Lily of Lake Champlain" pretty well.

SONG OF OLD

Adam the first was formed of dust
As Scripture doth record
And did receive a wife called Eve
From his Creator Lord

From Adam's side the crooked bride
The Lord was pleased to form
Ordained that they might lay
And keep each other warm

The court indeed they had no need
She was his wife at fust
And she was made to be his aid
Whose origin was dust

This new made pair full happy were
And happy might remain
If his help mate had never ate
The fruit that was ordained (?)

MISCELLANEOUS SONGS

Thus Adam's wife destroyed his life
In manner that was awful
Tis yet marriage now we all allow
To be but just and lawful

But woman must be courted fust
Because it is the fashion
And they oftimes commit great crimes
Caused by a lustful passion

And now a days there are two ways
And which of the two is right
To lie between sheets neat and clean
Or set up all the night

But some suppose bundling in clothes
Doth heaven sorely vex
Then let me know which way to go
To court the fairer sex

Whether they must be hugged and bussed
While sitting by the fire
Or whether they in bed may lay
Which doth the Lord require

Natures request is great for rest
Our bodies seek repose
Night is the time and its no crime
To bundle in our clothes

For since in bed a man and maid
May bundle and be chaste
It does no good to burn up wood
Sure tis a needless waste

Let coast and shift be thrown a drift
And breeches take their flight
An honest man and virgin can
Lay quiet all the night

THE GAM

But if there be dishonesty
Entangled in their minds
Breeches or smocks can serve for padlocks
The way lust combined

Kate and Sue both find it true
Who bundling do use
Ruth is Beguiled and got with child
Who bundling did despise

Whore will be whore and on the floor
It has been often said
To set over smoke and ashes Poke
Won't keep a girl a maid

Ship Polly 1794

One wonders if perhaps the original title of this song was "Bundling." Bundling was an amenity of the seventeenth and eighteenth centuries, and it may have lasted in a few places into the beginning of the nineteenth.

Aside from the pleasure the man and girl got from laying together its secondary purposes were to prevent the girl from "becoming with child," and to save firewood. It certainly did the latter, but whether or not it prevented many pregnancies is questionable. Vital records for those times show a great many cases where the first child came six or seven or even eight months after the marriage. Of course, we do not know in which cases the ashes were poked or in which the couple lay between the sheets.

Almost surely this song was in print, probably as a broadside but it has not been located

The melody used is "Jamie Raeburn's Farewell," No. 151 of Sam Henry's "Songs of the People."

MISCELLANEOUS SONGS

THE SPEAKING FLOWER

Our ship is ready to depart
Yet e'er I go from thee
Some proof of love to cheer my heart
I pray thee grant to me

Oh give me while the land
I leave in which we met
At least the flower that's in your hand
In token of regret

Each day in tempest and in calm
I'll wear it on my breast
And it shall be hope's soothing balm
On all my hours of rest

With pallid cheek and heaving breast
And half distracted air
The humbling maiden to heaven addressed
A faintly murmured prayer

Thou answerest not and I must go
Unloved across the main
Adieu and may thou never know
What 'tis to love in vain

The maiden gasped and could not tell
In words the love she bore
But from her hand the blossom fell
Before her on the floor

Bark *Paulina* 1849
Ship *Minerva Smythe* 1852

THE GAM

This song from Ephraim Flander's journal was recorded either on the ship *Minerva Smythe* on which he sailed from New Bedford on a whaling voyage or on the bark *Paulina* on which he returned home after he had been given his discharge in the Western Islands — the Azores.

The song surely seems to be an English version of a French song found in Laura Alexandrine Smith's *The Music of the Waters*, p. 157–58, called "Une Fleur Pour Reponse." And here is the first stanza of that song:

> *Notre vaisseau va quitter cette plage,*
> *Oh! Bien longtemps je serai sans vous voir*
> *Ne m'eloignant emporterai-je un gage*
> *Sinon d'amour au mois d'un peu d'espoir?*

We know that many folksongs, lyrics as well as ballads, have crossed over from one language to another and the "Speaking Flower" seems to be one of them.

The melody used here is an adaptation of that in *The Music of the Waters*.

MURPHY DELANY

Murphy Delany so funny and frisky
Reeled into a shebeen to get his skin full
And popped out again pretty well lined with whiskey
As fresh as a daisy and blind as a bull

MISCELLANEOUS SONGS

When a trifling accident happened to our rover,
Who took the quay side for the floor of his shed
And the heel of a coal barge he just tumbled over
And thought all the time he was going to bed

Some folks passing by hauled him out of the river
And got a horse doctor his sickness to mind
Who swore that poor Murphy no more was a liver
But dead as the devil and there was an end

They sent for the coroner's jury to try him
But Murphy not much liked this comical strife
Fell to turning and twisting the while I set by him
And came when he found it convenient to life

Says he to the jury your lordship, hard please you
I don't think I'm dead yet do what it is you do
Not dead says the foreman. Ye palp and ye beazy
Don't you think that the doctor knows better than you?

So then they went on with their business some further
And examined the doctor about his belief
Then they brought in poor Murphy as guilty of murder
And swore they would hang him in spite of his grief

Then Murphy laid hold of a clumsy shelalagh
And laid on the doctor as sly as a post
Who swore that it couldn't be Murphy Delany
But something alive Sure it must be his ghost

Then the jury began for to try him again
While he like a devil about him did lay
They sent out of hand for the clergy to shrive him
But Murphy lay the clergy and then ran away

Ship *Frances Henrietta* 1835

This song has a nice Irish melody and may have begun life in an Irish music hall. It is of the same general order as "Who Put the Overalls in Mrs. Murphy's Chowder?" and "The Wooden Wedding," songs which make fun of the Irish, some good-natured and sometimes not so good-natured. Indeed,

THE GAM

the Irish are responsible for many such songs themselves.

"Murphy Delany" is from Henry Manter's manuscript collection of songs and poems. Some of his letters are still extant and are in the archives of the Dukes County Historical Society. Particularly some of those to his wife make good reading. The melody used here is from the one in *The Songster's Museum* published by Andrew Wright in Northampton, Massachusetts in 1803. There the song is called "Murphy Delancey."

The Songster's Museum.

CHICAGO

Oh I have been east and I have been west
For in traveling a man may afar go
Before he will find anywhere in the world
A town to compare with Chicago
If you've never been a swindler in your life
And never ran away with another man's wife
And never did up to the bar go
They won't let you live in Chicago

Chorus
Oh Sodom was great and Gomorrah was some
And in Venice each man was Iago
But nothing out there can a moment compare
With the sweet state of things in Chicago

MISCELLANEOUS SONGS

Some people sends on by Adams express
Some puts their faith in Wells Fargo
But if you would go to the devil direct
Just enter yourself in Chicago
They won't let a clergyman live in the town
On such they have put an embargo
Unless he makes mutton of all his young lambs
And then he may live in Chicago

There the infants are fed on whiskey direct
For liquor they all to their ma go
And a muley cow gives as a man might expect
Rum punch in the town of Chicago
The town with fast ladies and gay gamboliers
Is as full as a ship with its cargo
And the very best men it is truthfully said
Fight cocks in the streets of Chicago

There all the boys play at poker and cram
And most of them did to the war go
They sing that wild song called I don't give a damn
All night on the streets of Chicago
But it can not be said that their morals are bad
Or that they too much below par go
For devil a moral the folks ever had
That live in the town of Chicago

Bark Abraham Barker 1871

This song which is almost not a song at all but a monologue, is from sheet music by H.M. Higgins, Chicago, 1868.

Higgins prefaces his song as follows: Some slanderous writer in a Pittsburg paper vents his spleen upon the "Queen of the Lakes" in a manner most disrespectful and cheeky. He must have fallen into very bad company when here to have formed such an unjust estimate of our city and its citizens. Chicago can "how its own row."

THE GAM

I'LL TASTE NO MORE THE POISONOUS CUP

I'll taste no more the poisonous cup
That brought on me destruction
The poisonous beverage I'll give up
And I will take instruction
Though demons rave let them beware
For with them I'll no longer tarry
But my vice sleeps one in the grave so fair
My lovely lovely Mary

For many an hour we've whiled away
To view the rose's blossom
And underneath the willow shade
I clasped her to my bosom
That happy day is past and gone
This world to me is dreary
By my cursed vice of drinking rum
I lost my lovely Mary

That happy day is spent for e'er
An outcast now I wander
There's none my drooping soul can cheer
For we are torn asunder

MISCELLANEOUS SONGS

The demon rum did me o'erpower
Broke the heart that loved me dearly
And now the green grass marks the spot
Where sleeps my lovely Mary

But lo a ray of light breaks forth
To hearts o'erfilled with horror
'Tis the temperance star shines in the north
Its light will drown all sorrow
I've signed the glorious pledge for life
Of this sad world I'm weary
Kind angels waft me to my wife
My love lovely Mary

Ship Cortes 1847

There are many temperance songs several of them called "The Drunkard's Dream," but this particular song has not been located.

In the last stanza the line that reads "I've signed the glorious pledge for life" means that the poor soul had signed a pledge saying that he would never take another drink as long as he lived. The signing of the pledge was one of the rather vicious tricks of the temperance movement. When I was eleven or twelve years old, I was subjected to a great deal of pressure to sign that pledge. Thank God I didn't sign it.

The melody used here is adapted from "St. Catherine Lane at Five" in Huntington's *William Litten's Fiddle Tunes*, p. 9. The scond melody is supplied.

THE GAM

WATER LUE

One dark and dismal morning
As I from bed did rise
I looked out from my window pane
And there to my surprise
I saw a sailor and his wife
And he kissed his little boy
And then I heard him say to her
When shall we meet again?

Chorus
With aching hearts and bitter tears
In sorrow and in pain
These parting words are oft times said
When shall we meet again?

He took the boy up in his arms
And kissed his snow white brow
He laid his wife's head on his breast
And said I leave you now
I'm going away to foreign lands
Across the raging seas
And when I'm gone love think of this
When shall we meet again?

Now very shortly after this
The boy took sick and died
She took the boy up in her arms
And in her ear he cried

MISCELLANEOUS SONGS

Oh mother mother mother
I'm full of grief and pain
Won't you please ask papa
When shall we meet again?

Now four or five months after this
A knock came to her door
A postman with a letter there
Came news to her aboard
And when she read the dreadful news
Tears to her eyes did flow
To think his ship had struck a rock
To sink and rise no more

Bark *Andrew Hicks* 1879

Sam Mingo's spelling of Waterloo in his journal is unique but it gives the idea — utter and complete defeat. One suspects that perhaps the proper title is "When Shall We Meet Again." The melody is supplied. I am sorry that I could not have made or found a better one, but at least this seems to fit the words.

THE NOBLE SHIP *CATALPA*

A noble whale ship and commander
It was called the *Catalpa* they say
Came out to Western Australia
And took six poor Fenians away

THE GAM

Chorus
So come all you screw warders and gaolers
Remember Perth Regatta Day
Take care of the rest of your Fenians
Or the Yankees will steak them away

Seven long years they had served there
And seven long more had to stay
For defending their country old Ireland
For what they were banished away

They kept them in Western Australia
Till their hair it began to turn gray
When a Yank from the States of America
Came out here and stole them away

Now all the Perth boats were a-racing
And making short tacks for the spot
But the Yankee tacked into Fremantle
And took the best prize of the lot

The corvette all armed with bold warriors
Went out the poor Yank to arrest
But she hoisted her star-spangled banner
Saying you will not board me I guess

So remember those six Fenian prisoners
And sing up this song with a will
And remember the Yankees who stole them
From that little stone house on the hill

Now they've all landed safe in America
And there they'll be able to cry
Hurrah for the green flag and shamrock
We'll fight for our land till we die

Broadside

MISCELLANEOUS SONGS

This broadside ballad sings to the tune of "Tarpaulin Jacket" which is given here in a slightly different setting. This broadside was sent to me by A.L. Lloyd who has always been as interested in whaling songs as I have been when he noticed that several songs in *Songs the Whaleman Sang* were from a journal of the ship *Catalpa*.

The *Catalpa* was a quite famous whaler entirely apart from the notoriety she gained from the voyage told about in the broadside. Indeed she actually did do some whaling on that mission to rescue the Fenians, perhaps as a cover. Zephenia W. Pease, a New Bedford newspaperman, wrote a book called *The Catalpa Expedition* which tells the whole story of the rescue voyage.

Lahey, *Australian Favorite Ballads*, p. 31; Manifold, *The Penguin Australian Song Book*, p. 20.

DRINKING GIN

A-drinking gin through all the day
And then at night attend the play
Will on a man infer a curse
And find the bottom of his purse

Our children they do cry for bread
And hungry they do go to bed
My dear my garments are so thin
Occasioned by thy drinking gin

THE GAM

If prayer or tear can ought avail
Pray husband quickly spread all sail
With Luce or Daggett sail from Linn
And bid adieu to drinking gin

Then as good Paul in ancint time
I'd recommend in any clime
A little wine for the stomach's sake
A glass or two my dear may take

D.C.H.S. Archives

This is from Seth Daggett's account book in the Dukes County Historical Society's archives, dated 1831.

As a very young man Seth Daggett may have gone whaling for a voyage or two but for most of his life he was a pilot working out of Holmes Hole, now Vineyard Haven. Many Vineyard pilots who had taken vessels over the shoals and around Cape Cod to Boston, Lynn, and other ports in the area would walk home to Falmouth or Woods Hole and then get a lift in a small boat that was bound for the Vineyard. But Seth had evidently delayed his walk much too long to suit his wife.

The Luce and the other Daggett in the song evidently operated little schooners or sloops — coasters or packets — between the ports around Massachusetts Bay and the Vineyard.

It was Seth Daggett who piloted the French fleet from the West Indies to Chesapeake Bay and thus cut off access to the Bay to the British and thus so greatly contributed to Washington's victory at Yorktown.

MISCELLANEOUS SONGS

THE VIRTUOUS WIFE: A NEW SONG

In Rome I read a nobleman
The Emperor did offend
And for that fault he was adjudged
Unto a cruel end

That he should be in prison cast
With irons many a one
And there be famished beath
And brought to skin and bone

And more if any one was knowd
By night or yet by day
To bring him any kind of food
His hunger to allay

The Emperor swore a mighty oath
Without remorse quoth he
Thou shall sustain the cruelest death
That can devised be

This cruel sentence one pronounced
The nobleman was cast
Into a dungeon rank and deep
With irons fettered fast

Then when he had with hunger great
Remained ten days apace
And tasted neither meat nor drink
In a most woeful case

THE GAM

The tears along his aged face
Most piteously did fall
And grievously he did begin
For to lament withal

O Lord quoth he what shall I do
So hungry Lord am I
For want of bread one bit of bread
I perish starve and die

How precious one grain of wheat
Unto my hungry soul
One crust or crumb one little piece
My hunger to control

Had I this dungeon heaped with gold
I would forego it all
To by and purchase one brown loaf
Yea were it never so small

O that I had but every day
One bit of bread to eat
Tho near so moulday black or brown
My comfort would be great

Yea albeit I would take it up
Trod down in dire and mire
It would be pleasing to my taste
And sweet to my desire

Good Lord how happy is the hand
That labours all the day
That drudging mule the peasant poor
That at command do stay

They have their ordinary meals
They take no heed at all
Of those sweet crumbs or crusts that they
Do carelessly let fall

MISCELLANEOUS SONGS

How happy is that little chick
Who without fear may go
And pick up those most precious crumbs
That they away do throw

That some pretty little mouse
So much my friend would be
To bring some old forsaken crust
Unto this place to me

But oh my heart it is in vain
No succor can I have
No meat no drink no water Eke
My loathed life to save

O bring some bread for Christ his sake
Some bread some bread for me
I die I die for want of food
Naught but stone walls I see

Thus day and night he cried out
In most outrageous sort
That all the people far and near
Was grieved at his report

And tho that many friends he had
And daughters in the town
Yet none durst come to succor him
Fearing the emperors frown

Yet now behold one daughter dear
He had as I do find
Who lived in his displeasure great
For matching ganst his mind

Altho she lived in mean estate
She was a virtuous wife
And thus to help her father dear
She ventured thus her life

THE GAM

She quickly to her sisters went
And of them did entreat
That by some secret means they would
Convey their father meet

Our father dear doth starve she said
The emperors wrath is such
He dies alas for want of food
Of which we have too much

Pray sisters therefore use such means
His life for to preserve
And suffer not your father dear
In prison for to starve

Alas quoth they what shall we do
His hunger to sustain
You know tis death for any man
That would his life maintain

And tho we wish him well quoth they
We never will agree
To spoil ourselves we had as Lief
That he should die as we

And sister if you love yourself
Let this attempt alone
Tho you do need so secret work
At length it will be known

O hath our Father brought us up
And nourished us quoth she
And shall we now forsake him quite
In his extremity

Now I will venture life and limb
To do my father good
The worst that is I can but die
To fit a tyrants mood

MISCELLANEOUS SONGS

With that in haste away she hies
Unto the prison goes
But with her woeful father dear
She might not speak each knows

Except the Emperor great would grant
Her favor in that case
The keeper would admit no weight
To enter in that place

Then she unto the Emperor hies
And falling on her knees
With wringing hands and bitter cries
These words pronounced she

My hapless father souvering Lord
Offending of your grace
Is judged unto the pining death
Within a doleful place

Which I confess he hath deserved
Yet mighty Prince quoth she
Vouch safe in gracious sort to grant
One single boon to me

It chanced so I matched myself
Against my fathers mind
Whereby I do procure his wrath
As certain hath assigned

And seeing now the time is come
He must resign his breath
Vouch safe that I may speak to him
Before his hour of death

And reconcile myself to him
His favor to obtain
That when he dies I may not then
Under his curse remain

THE GAM

The Emperor granted her request
Conditionally that she
Each day unto her father come
Should thoroughly searched be

No meat nor drink she with her brot
To help him there distressed
But every day she nourished him
With milk from her own breast

Thus by her milk he was preserved
A twelve month and a day
And was as fair and fat to see
Yet no man knew which way

The Emperor musing much there at
At length did understand
How he was fed and not his laws
Was broke by any hand

He much admired at the same
And her grate virtue shone
He pardoned him and honored her
With great prefarments known

Her father ever after that
Did love her as his life
And blessed the day that she was made
A loving wedded wife

Ship *Polly* 1794

This long and very unusual ballad would seem to be quite unique in folksong. However, the theme is known in folklore and John Steinbeck used that theme in *Grapes of Wrath*. Both the title and the fact that this is broken down into stanzas seem to surely indicate that it was sung, as well as the fact that it is in a journal that contains many songs.

In *Early Vermont Broadsides*, edited by John Duffy there is a broadside of the story, not divided into stanzas, which almost certainly was not sung.

MISCELLANEOUS SONGS

There it is called "The Grecian Daughter." Duffy thinks that it was a protest against the embargo that was ruining New England's overseas trade. But it is difficult to follow his argument.

It must have been put in the ship *Polly* journal after the end of the voyage. The simple melody used here sounds very familiar; however, I think it is supplied. The song is very long, but even longer folksongs were sung. The second melody is supplied.

"Whale-oil Pete" Photograph of a man who is most likely a crew member of the *Charles W. Morgan*

Gospel Songs and Songs with a Religious Flavor

Whalemen, overall were not noted for being overly religious. Although some captains insisted on regular services, the conflicting demands of observing the Sabbath and pursuing whales whenever they were sighted tended to put a definite strain upon organized religious observance. The actions of whalemen returning to tropical islands after many months in the north Pacific also put them at odds with the clergy and missionaries. Nervertheless, hymns and gospel songs were sung.

THE GAM

THE CLEANSING FOUNTAIN

Behold the lamb whose gracious blood
Poured from his opening veins
We had best to make our peace with God
He will cleanse our deepest stains

Chorus
I do believe, I will believe
That Jesus died for me
That on the cross he shed his blood
From sin to set me free

The dying thief beheld the lamb
Expiring by his side
And knew the value of the name
Of Jesus crucified

We too, the cleansing power have known
Of that atoning blood
By grace have learned the name to own
That brings us close to God

For Him, then, let our songs ascend
Who stooped in grace so low
To Christ, the lamb, the sinner's friend
Let endless praises flow

Bark *Andrew Hicks* 1879

GOSPEL SONGS AND SONGS WITH A RELIGIOUS FLAVOR

The melody used here for "The Cleansing Fountain" is from the singing of Edward Tilton. The words in *Songs of Redemption* are very different from those in the bark *Andrew Hicks* journal but the melody is very close to Edward Tilton's.

Songs of Redemption, p. 248; *Songs of Joy and Gladness*, p. 2.

THE MARINER'S HYMN

Launch the bark mariner
Christian God speed thee
Let loose the rudder bands
Good angles lead thee
Set thy sails warily
Tempests will come
Steer thy bark steadily
Set our course home

Look to the weather bow
Breakers are round thee
Let fall the plummet now
Shallows may ground thee
Reef in the foresail there
Hold the helm fast
So let the vessel wear
There swept the blast

What of the night mariner
What of the night
Cloudy all quiet
No land yet all right

THE GAM

Be wakeful be vigilant
Danger may come
At an hour when all seemed secure to thee
Danger may come

How gains the leak so fast
Clear out the hold
Hoist out the merchandise
Heave out the gold
There let the nuggets go
Now the ship rights
Huzza the harbor's near
Lo the red lights

Slacken not sail yet
An island an island
Straight for the beacon steer
Straight for the high land
Crowd all the canvas on
Cut through the foam
Christian cast anchor now
Heaven is home

Bark Sunbeam 1860

Some of the nautical language here is interesting. The rudder bands were the beckets that held the helm steady when not in use. "Let fall the plummet" is unusual. The regular command would be "Heave the lead."

The melody is adapted from a sheet music version of the song by Oliver Ditson, Boston, n.d. The title of the song there is "Launch Thy Bark, Mariner!"

SABBATH MORNING NOV. 13TH 1852

My thoughts now return to the home I love well
I hear the sweet sound of the church going bell
I see them preparing to answer its call
May they pray for a blessing to rest on us all

GOSPEL SONGS AND SONGS WITH A RELIGIOUS FLAVOR

Now they to the church repair
Now they bow in worship there
Seeking for the promised love
Of their heavenly friend above

Now we are denied that blessing
Here (?) upon the distant sea
But the same God who looks upon them
Is here and will ever with us be

Ship Catawba 1852

This song was probably never sung and the meter is so irregular that I could not supply a melody to fit.

Perhaps on many whale ships, Sunday was just another day, but on others the captain conducted regular services and not a boat was lowered no matter how many whales were spouting in the area. For those in the crew who were not overly religious that was very painful.

REVIVE US AGAIN

We praise Thee O God for the son of thy love
For Jesus who died and is now gone above

Chorus
Hallelujah Thine the glory Hallelujah amen
Hallelujah Thine the glory revive us again

All glory and praise to the Lamb that was slain
Who has borne all our sins and has cleansed every stain

THE GAM

All glory and praise to the God of all grace
Who has bought us and sought us and guided our ways

Revive us again fill each heart with love
And may each soul be kindled with fire from above

Edward Tilton

"Revive Us Again" is another of Edward Tilton's gospel songs, and like most of his others it would not be welcomed in many churches today. It will be found in many of the older books of gospel songs. But the most beautiful thing about it is a most ungodly parody called "Hallelujah I'm a Bum." The last three references in the head notes are for the parody.

HALLELUJAH I'M A BUM

Oh why don't you work like other men do
How the hell can I work when there's no work to do

Chorus
Hallelujah I'm a bum hallelujah bum again
Hallelujah give us a handout to revive us again

I went to a house and I asked for some bread
A lady come out says the baker is dead

I went there again and I knocked on the door
The lady come out says you been here before

Gospel Hymns No. 6, p. 160; *Gospel Hymns and Sacred Songs*, No. 27; *Pentacostal Hymns*, p. 202; *Windows of Heaven*, No. 199; *Winona Hymns*, No. 181; *Songs of Service*, No. 327.

Lomax and Lomax, *American Ballads and Folk Songs*, p. 26; Robinson, *Country Songs and Ballads*, p. 43; Sandburg, *The American Songbag*, p. 184.

GOSPEL SONGS AND SONGS WITH A RELIGIOUS FLAVOR

MEN ARE LIKE SHIPS

Men are like ships upon the main
Exposed to every gale
Each passion is a fatal blast
That tears away a sail

Each pleasure is a latent rock
And life a stormy sea
But while our reason holds the helm
We ride from perils free

Yet oft alas our pilot sleeps
Or leaves his place to pride
And then the vessel drives ashore
Before the Foaming tide

Ship Condor 1832

Perhaps this is an original. However it certainly seems as though it should go with the gospel hymns. The melody is adapted from "He Healeth To-Day," No. 122 in *Pentecostal Hymns*.

THE GAM

WHEN THE ROLL IS CALLED UP YONDER

When the trumpet of the Lord shall sound and time shall be no more
And the morning breaks eternal, bright and fair
And the saved on each shall gather over on the other shore
And the roll is called up yonder I'll be there

Chorus
When the roll is called up yonder
When the roll is called up yonder
When the roll is called up yonder
When the roll is called up yonder I'll be there

On that bright and cloudless morning when the dead in Christ shall rise
And the glory of his resurrection share
When his chosen ones shall gather to their home beyond the skies
And the roll is called up yonder I'll be there

Let us labor for the Master from the dawn till set of sun
Let us talk of all his wondrous love and care
Then when all of life is over and our work on earth is done
And the roll is called up yonder I'll be there

Edward Tilton

Edward Tilton was a famous gospel singer and this was one of his favorite songs. He was known to every isolated farm on Martha's Vineyard, Nantucket and Cape Cod. On the Cape he was known as the Chilmark singer. He was welcome wherever he went because he brought the local news

GOSPEL SONGS AND SONGS WITH A RELIGIOUS FLAVOR

with him. He most certainly was not a whaleman but he had four brothers who were so it seems proper that some of his songs be included here.

Like his brother Bill Tilton the chanteyman, he had a terrific voice and on a still day one could hear him almost a mile away. He never did any work if he could help it, but more or less his brothers took care of him. Once when Mildred was a small girl (Edward was her great uncle) Emma, Mil's mother, had just made a batch of salaratus biscuits. It was not meal time but to be polite she said, "Edward, will you have a biscuit?" Edward certainly did have one. He finished the batch.

Songs of Redemption, p. 132; *Songs of Service*, No. 301.

WORK FOR JESUS

Go work in my field Christian now sayeth the Lord
Your labor with blessings he'll quickly reward
The harvest is made so you must not delay
Be quick then, oh Christian, while yet it is day

Chorus
Work work work Christian work
Go labor for Jesus while yet it is day

There are dieing souls oh will you them warn
Though roughly they treat you and sometimes with scorn
With patience press forward and tell them in love
That Jesus to save all came down from above

THE GAM

And the deal little children you constantly meet
You may lovingly teach and bring to Christ's feet
Instruct them to love the dear Lord in their youth
And learn the ways of life and of truth

When your work is finished and the days are spent
You give up to God all the talents he lent
And Jesus will greet you with a loving well done
And welcome you home to the rest you have won

Bark Andrew Hicks 1879

The journal says that the tune for this Gospel song is "Home Sweet Home." It certainly does not fit perfectly. But what we have here *almost* fits the first stanza and the chorus.

There is another Gospel song entitled "Work for Jesus" by W.J. Kirkpatrick, "teacher of piano, organ and singing" the melody of which does not fit this song at all.

WILL YOU BE FOUND AMONG THE WHEAT

If death should take you unawares
Would you be found among the tares
Or would your happy joyous feet
Be standing there amongst the wheat

Chorus

Oh sinner flee oh sinner flee
Oh flee from sin the Lord's to be
For he is waiting to receive

GOSPEL SONGS AND SONGS WITH A RELIGIOUS FLAVOR

If on his love you will believe
Confess to him your guilt and sin
He wants poor souls like yours to win

The tares will all be burnt with fire
Will you escape the flames so dire
So stand and sing your praise to him
Who died to save us all from sin

Oh pray why will you linger still
On the broad road that leads to hell
Oh come why will you longer stay
A loitering on the primrose way

Hasten sinner delay no more
Christ is knocking at your door
Come open now and let him in
He'll cleanse and make you pure within

Bark Andrew Hicks 1879

Edward Tilton sang this gospel song. The melody as we have it here is from his singing as well as I can remember it.

A SINNER SAVED

One night I was in sorrow
My heart with fear did ache
To think that on the morrow
The thread of life might break

THE GAM

But soon the savior found me
Wandering in the cold
He threw his arm around me
And took me to his fold

Each day I look for courage
To walk the narrow way
And Jesus gives sufficient
To last me all the day
So come now brothers, sisters
Let us all work tonight
To tell the world of sinners lost
His blood has washed each white

Bark *Andrew Hicks* 1879

There is a notation in the journal under the song that says it is sung to the tune of "The Sands of Time are Sinking." So that is the melody used here. Many gospel songs were sung to the same tune just as many folksongs were. The setting of the melody here is as nearly as I can remember Edward Tilton singing it.

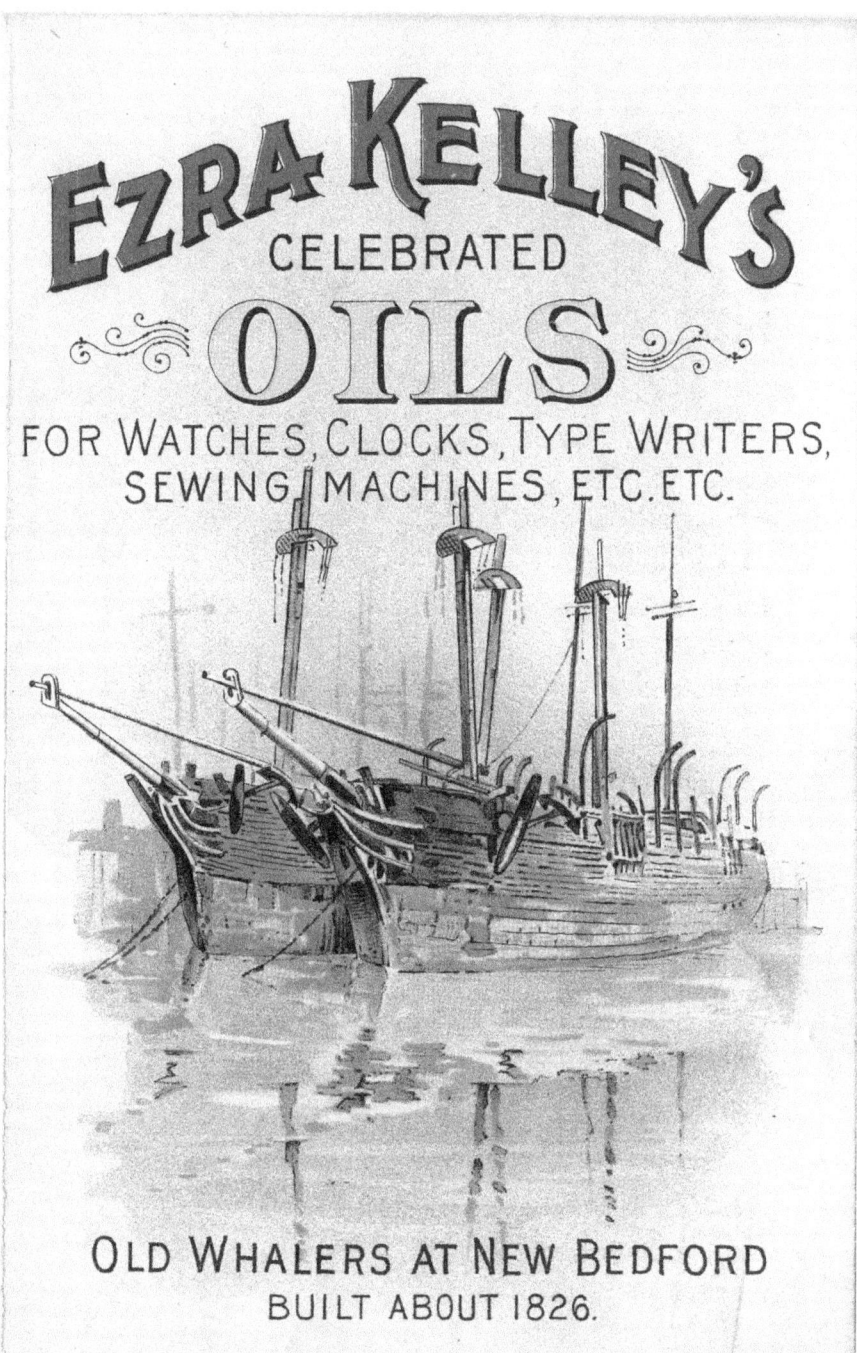

Advertising booklet, circa 1869

Two Fiddle tunes

PISCATAQUAG AND THE EDINBURGH

The fiddle was the premier seagoing musical instrument of the nineteenth century. Almost every whaleship had a fiddle player aboard and some had several. But just as in the logbooks and journals only a very few songs were found which included the musical notation of the melody to which they were sung, so these are the only fiddle tunes that were located. The chief reasons for that must be that most singers were musically illiterate, just as most fiddle players could not read nor write music.

No references for "Piscataquag" have been found.

THE GAM

The Piscataquag, or Piscataqua, is the river that flows into Portsmouth Harbor after forming the boundary between New Hampshire and the State of Maine for some eighty miles.

"The Flowers of Edinburgh" which is the proper title of "The Edinburgh" has been an exceedingly popular tune for many years. Bayard in *Hill Country Tunes*, No. 53, gives us more than twenty-two places where various settings of the tune may be found. Also, see, Paul Deville and Maurice Gould, *The Violin Player's Pastime*, p. 41; *The Musician's Omnibus*, Elias Howe with brief dance directions, p. 44; *The Robbins Collection of Jigs, Reels and Country Dances*, p. 9; Robertson, James Stewart. *The Athole Collection of the Dance Music of Scotland*, p. 146; A. Shattuck, "A Shattuck's Book," p. 79.

GLOSSARY
OF WHALING AND NAUTICAL TERMS WITH SOME DESCRIPTION

Aback. When the wind hits the sail from forward thus stopping the boat's progress. See *heave to.*

Abaft. Astern. Towards the stern.

Aft. To go towards the stern of the vessel. As *to go aft*

All Hands. Meaning all the crew needed on deck. The call that brought up the off-duty watch.

Bark. A three-masted vessel with square sails on the fore and mainmasts and fore-and-aft rig on the mizzenmast.

Barkentine. A three-masted vessel with square sails on the foremast and fore-and-aft rig on main and mizzen.

Beam. The beam of a ship is its width at the widest point as measured at the ship's nominal waterline. Also the side of the central part of the vessel, and off that part as *on the lee beam.*

Beat. To tack, to change direction of the wind on the sails, as *beat to windward*

Belay. To secure or make fast. Also to stop some activity.

Belaying Pin. A large metal pin to which a line or rope was made fast. The belaying pins were set in holes in a pin rail at the base of the mast, and also in holes in the bulwark rail.

Bend on. Sometimes a whale would run or even sound, until the line in the tub was almost exhausted. Then the line from one of the other boats would be bent on to the line fast to the whale. Then the second boat was fast to the whale. The bending on must be done very quickly. The knot usually used was a ground hitch, which doesn't slip.

Bight. A curve or loop in a line or rope. Also a curving indentation of a shoreline.

THE GAM

Binnacle. A stand forward of the wheel containing a compass on gimbals, or floating in alcohol, and a small oil lamp.

Bitts. Timbers at the heel of the bowsprit to which the fluke rope was made fast after the whale had been brought alongside.

Blackskin. A whaleman's name for a sperm whale.

Blanket Piece. A long strip of blubber as it was cut from the whale.

Block. A large, usually wooden, pulley in which there were two or more sheaves.

Blubber. The the blanket of fat with which whale was provided and from which the oil was extracted.

Boat Crew. There were six men in each boat. They were: The boatsteerer who was also the harpooner; the boatheader who was one of the mates and the four men at the oars. In the earlier days of whaling, the captain also lowered and was in command of the boat. The same crew always went in the same boat. The boat was always ready to be lowered at a moment's notice; it was the boatsteerer's responsibility to see that everthing needed in the boat was ready and in its proper place.

Boathook. A blunt pointed hook on a pole used to fend a boat off, as from the side of the vessel, or to hold the boat where it was wanted.

Boat Sail. A fore-and-aft sail used in whaleboats. In the earlier days of sailing, the lugsail was universal. The sail had a spar across its top holding it to the mast, But the lugsail was awkward to stow on the thwarts when not in use. Then came the spritsail, which had a spar extending from the foot of the mast to the peak of the sail. This was much easier to stow. Still later, the gaffsail was used on some ship's boats.

Boatsteerers. See *Boat Crew*. The boatsteerers were petty officers and received a lay between that of the mates and the foremast hands. The boatsteerer slept in the steerage, but in most vessels ate with the captain and his mates.

Bos'un (Boatswain). He was crew foreman. Whaleships seldom if ever carried a bo'sun, for with four hardfisted mates a bo'sun was not needed.

Bowsprit. A heavy spar-timber extending forward from the stem of the vessel. The jibboom extended forward from the bowsprit.

Brace. A line through a block at the end of a yard by which the sail was swung, to sail closer to, or off, the wind

Brace Up. To haul in the lee brace so that the vessel could sail closer to the wind.

Breach. As when a whale would leap out of, or almost out of the water

GLOSSARY

Brig. A two-masted vessel with square sails on both masts.

Brigantine. Like a brig but with a fore-and-aft sail on the mainmast.

Bulwarks. The side of a vessel above the deck topped with a heavy rail, or the top of the side of an open boat.

Cabin. The living quarters of the afterguard — the captain and his mates. It was furnished with a long table and with chairs. Each mate had his own small stateroom, and the master a larger one. The steward kept the cabin neat and orderly.

Capstan. A large vertical drum turned by the men pushing on the capstan bars. It was used to do very heavy work such as getting the anchor up.

Cast Away. Lost, particularly when the vessel was wrecked on shore.

Cat. To bring the anchor to the cathead to secure it.

Cathead. A heavy timber projecting from each side of the vessel to which the ring of the anchor was made fast when it was raised.

Centerboard. A broad board hinged on a pivot at its forward lower end so that it could be raised or lowered. Its purpose was to diminish leeway when it was lowered as when going into the wind. It was raised when going before the wind. Also it was raised when using oars or paddles and not sail. In the earlier days of whaling the boats had no centerboards. They were added, perhaps, sometime near the middle of the nineteenth century.

Centerboard Box. The narrow watertight box in which the centerboard was raised and lowered.

Chainplates. Narrow metal plates extending some distance down the side of the vessel to which the deadeyes were fastened to reinforce the attachment points.

Chocks. A groove in the head of a whaleboat through which the line passed as it came out of the tub. A small wooden pin kept the line from jumping out of the chocks.

Clew Garnets. The lines by which the courses were hauled up to the yards to be clewed.

Close Hauled. Sailing as close to the wind as possible.

Clue (Clew). To shorten but not furl a squaresail by hauling it loosely up to the yard.

Cooper. The craftsman who repaired and also put together the casks that held the oil.

Counter. The overhang, if any, of the vessel's stern. Most whaleships had a wide transom stern and any counter was minimal.

Courses. The lowest square sails, thus the foresail, mainsail and mizzensail of a ship and the foresail and mainsail of a bark.

Cranes. See *davits*.

Crossjack. The common name for the course or lowest square sail on the mizzenmast.

Crosstrees. The mast of a large sailing vessel as formed in three sections as *foremast, fore-topmast* and *fore-topgallant.* And the same for main and mizzen. The crosstrees were wide transverse members where the mast were joined, to the outer edge of which the shrouds for the upper masts were attached. A man on the lookout for whales would stand on the crosstrees. The top crosstree, where the main topmast and main-topgallant masts were joined, was the highest.

Cutting Stage. A large platform lowered from the starboard side of the vessel from which the blubber was stripped from the whale. Cutting was usually done by the boatsteerers.

Dart. Throw the harpoon.

Davits. A pair of cranes at the side of the vessel by which the boat was swung out from the side, lowered and brought up.

Deadeyes. Sheaveless blocks used to set up the shrouds. Much later, turnbuckles took the place of deadeyes.

Dog Watch. A two hour period, morning and night, when the watches were changed.

Drogue. Pronounced drug by the whalemen. A wooden device, something like a sea anchor, usually triangular in shape and held vertically in the water by a three-part bridle to the end on the harpoon line. Its purpose was to slow down the flight of the whale. In later whaling, the boat itself became the drogue, thus leading to the term, "a Nantucket sleighride."

Duff. A pudding made of flour, water and slush and boiled in sea water.

E Town. Edgartown.

Fish. As fish the anchor, or bring the anchor inboard.

Flake. One layer of harpoon line coiled in the tub.

Flukes. A whale's tail or the lobes of the tail.

Flurry. The spasm of a dying whale.

Fo'c'sl.e (Forecastle). The space in the fore part of the ship where the foremast hands lived and slept. It was a dismal, crowded place never overly clean and with no light except for the hatchway and an oil lamp overhead. The men's bunks were along the sides of the fo'c'sle. There was no furniture except the men's

GLOSSARY

sea chests which served both as tables and seats. It could be a terribly hot place, and also "bitterly cold." In spite of all that it was often lively with song and fiddle.

Fore-and-Aft Sail. A sail with its leading edge attached to a mast.

Galley. The cubicle on deck where the cook prepared the food.

Gally. To frighten or scare. All the whales were galled.

Gam. A visit between the crews of two or more whaleships that met in the open sea at a time when there were no whales about. A social time.

Gear carried in a whaleboat. Besides the oars, paddles, lance, spade and tub there were spare harpoons and lances, a keg of drinking water, a tinder box, matches, candles, a boathook, two or more buckets, spare tholepins, a hatchet and boat knife so that a line could be cut instantly. With all that gear it is difficult to see how there was any room for movement in the boat. But there was.

Gimbals. A double set of pivots so that a compass or lamp would remain level no matter how much the vessel heeled, pitched or rolled.

Glass. The captain's spyglass. Also the barometer.

Grease the lead. To put grease in the cup at the bottom of the lead so that sand, gravel or mud would adhere to it to show the nature of the bottom.

Greasy Luck. A whaleman's way of saying "good luck."

Grog. A mixture of rum and water. See "Ben Backstay's Warning."

Grommet. A loop of rope or a metal ring sewn into a sail so that a line may be made fast to the sail without tearing it.

Gunnel (Gunwhale). A strip of wood above the top strake of a whaleboat into which the tholepins or oarlocks were set. The upper part of the side of any open boat.

Halyards. The lines by which the vessel's sails are raised or lowered.

Hardtack. A square flat biscuit made of flour, water and suet.

Headman or *Headsman.* The boatheader, who was in command of the whaleboat.

Heave. To pull on a line or rope. To strain at any task. To throw.

Heave To. To stop the vessel's progress by backing the main topsail so that the sail was pushing the vessel astern.

Helm. The steering gear, wheel, tiller or whatever.

Helmsman. The man at the wheel.

THE GAM

Hermaphrodite Brig or *Morphodite Brig*. A two-masted vessel with only fore-and-aft sails on the mainmast but with square sails on the fore-mast. Thus neither a schooner nor a brig.

Hove To. Lying stationary.

Hulk. A vessel no longer seaworthy or one that had outlived its usefulness.

Hull. The body of a boat or vessel.

Indian Whaleman. If there was an Indian in the crew he was very like to be a boatsteerer. Many Indians rose the ladder of command to the rank of mate. None seemed to want to be master.

Iron. The harpoon was usually called the iron by whaleman.

Jib. A triangular sail set on a stay running from masthead to jibboom.

Jibboom. A stayed spar extending forward from the bowsprit.

Jibe. To change the course of a fore-and-aft rigged vessel by bringing the sails over so the wind hits them from the other side. That is, of course, when the vessel was sailing before the wind.

Keep clear of his eye. To try to approach the whale so he could not see what was attacking him.

Kippler Hump. Another whaleman's name for a sperm whale.

Lance. A very sharp knife at the end of a pole with which the boatheader would try to kill the whale after it was tired out. The lance could be thrown and retrieved with a short line, but the boatheader always tried to get as close as possible so he could thrust for the whale's heart. Killing the whale was extremely dangerous, for the whale might go into a flurry caused by its fear, pain and fury, so lancing duty fell to the boatheader, as the most experienced man.

Lanyard. A cord holding a whistle, knife or some other object. The ropes that tightened the deadeyes were also called lanyards. Any short piece of rope used to perform a particular task.

Larboard. The older term for the port, or left side of a vessel or boat.

Lay. A share in the proceeds of a whaling voyage. The men on a whaleship were never paid wages. After the vessel's share was taken out—usually forty percent—the remainder was divided among the men. The captain's share was the largest, sometimes as much as twenty percent. Then on a descending scale came the lays of officers, specialists and boatsteerers. Finally came the lays of the foremast hands which sometimes was as little as one hundred and nineteenth.

GLOSSARY

Leach. The after edge of a fore-and-aft sail, and the two outer edges of a square sail.

Lead. The plummet with which depth of the water was sounded, which, because of the grease-filled cup in its bottom also showed the nature of the ocean floor.

Lee Side. The side of the vessel away from the direction of the wind. It was always best to spit tobacco juice over the lee rail.

Leeward. Always pronounced *looward*. Away from the direction of the wind.

Leeway. Pronounced *leeway*. A lateral movement off the desired course, caused by wind and tide. A lowered centerboard helped reduce leeway. The course was corrected as much as possible to allow for leeway. A heavily laden vessel would make much less leeway caused by the wind than one that was light.

Let Fall. Lower the square sails from the yards.

Loggerhead. A short upright post in the whaleboat around which the line is passed as it leaves the tub. Its purpose was to put pressure on the line and thus slow down the flight of the sail.

Luff. To turn the vessel or boat into the wind.

Mainmast. The second mast of a sailing vessel.

Make Fast. To secure.

Mariner. A man who followed the sea no matter what his rank or position might be. A master mariner was a captain or one who held master's papers. Whalemen, merchant seamen, coasters, pilots and fishermen were all mariners.

Marlin. A tarred, loosely twisted two-stranded twine, perhaps mostly used for seizing the end of a line

Marlin Spike. A sharp pointed tool used to separate the strands of a rope or cable for splicing; also used to tear apart the strands of old rope so those strands, after more separation could be made into marlin.

Messmates. Fellow sailors.

Mill. The term used when whales swam in a tight circle.

Mizzen Gaff. The spanker was raised to the mizzen gaff, which was not raised and lowered with the sail.

Mizzenmast, The aftmost mast of a sailing vessel.

Morphadite Brig. See Hermaphrodite Brig

Nantucket Sleighride. When the whale in its flight was pulling the boat through the water.

THE GAM

Paddles. Paddle were used instead of oars when approaching the whale in very still or quiet water as they were less likely to be heard and frighten the whale than the thumping of oars. Perhaps this was a carry-over from Indian whaling.

Painter. The bowline of a boat.

Parcelling. Canvas or other cloth wrapped around a rope or cable to keep it from being damaged by chafing against a stationary object, and also to keep the stationary object from being damaged by the rope or cable.

Pawls. Short metal bars that were hinged by a pin to the lower part of the capstain and which ran around a slotted track. The purpose of the pawls was to prevent the capstan and its bars from walking back against the pushing of the men. Thus the capstain could only turn in one direction.

Peak. The upper outer corner of a fore-and-aft sail.

Peak Your Oars. The order from the boatheader to hold the oars back out of the water, but ready to be used at the command to pull, or back.

Pin Rail. A rail or rack, usually at the foot of a mast, with holes into which belaying pins fitted.

Plum Duff. A special duff to which fruit was added, as raisins, pitted prunes and sometimes cranberries.

Pod. A group or cluster of whales.

Port. The left side of a vessel or boat.

Press of Sail. Every possible sail set.

Privateer. A privateer was a privately owned ship authorized by a government by letters of marque to attack foreign vessels during wartime.

P Town. Provincetown. Most Provincetown whalers were schooners, with some brigs and sloops.

Quarter. The side of the after part of a vessel.

Quarter Deck. The afterdeck, reserved for the captain, his officers and the man at the wheel.

Reef. To shorten sail; to reduce the sail area by folding up the head of a square sail, or the foot of a fore-and-aft sail, and securing the fold with short lines called reefpoints which were sewed into the sail at their middle part.

Rig. The number of masts, sails, and types of sails of a vessel; as, ship, bark, etc.

Roundhouse. A privy on the fore deck in which there was a bucket,

Running Gear. Ropes and lines that moved, as halyards, sheets, etc.

Salt Horse. Salt beef.

GLOSSARY

Schooner. A vessel with fore-and-aft rig on all masts. Most earlier schooners were two-masted. A topsail schooner had one or more square sails on the foremast above the fore-and-aft sail.

Scuppers. Opening at the bottom of the bulwark, so that if a sea came aboard, the vessel could free itself of water.

Sea Anchor. See *Drogue.* The sea anchor kept a vessel from going too fast to leeward when hove to.

Seizing. A binding, as about the end of a rope or line to keep the strands from separating.

Shank Painters. Lashings of line or chain used to secure the shank of the anchor when taken on board.

Sheet. A line attached to the foot of a fore-and-aft sail by which the angle of the sail could be regulated. Also lines to the two outer lower edges of a square sail.

Ship (rig). A three-masted vessel with square sails on all masts.

Ship Carpenter. The ship carpenter's most important job was to keep the whaleboats in perfect condition, and to repair such as had been damaged by a fighting whale. Spare boats were always carried on a whaler as well as the materials for repairing damaged boats.

Shipkeepers. These were the cooper, carpenter, steward, cook and cabin boy, if there were one. On some vessels there might also be a blacksmith, but more often the ship's carpenter also did the blacksmithing. It was the duty of the shipkeepers to take care of the vessel while the boats were out after whales. The must keep an eye on the boats and go to one if it was in trouble and, of course, go to a boat that had killed a whale. From this it will be seen that shipkeepers also had to be seamen. The shipkeepers were often called the *specialists.*

Sheave. Always pronounced *shiv.* A grooved wheel in a block or pulley.

Shooks. The bundle of staves from which the cooper made the casks to hold the oil. When the vessel left port, only the lower tier of casks had been put together, and they were filled with fresh water. As the water was used, the casks were filled with oil. All through the voyage, the cooper was busy building casks for as one tier was filled with oil, another tier would be started.

Shrouds. The standing gear that gave lateral support to the masts. They consisted of three or more cables connected by cross members, thus they could be used as a ladder in going aloft. The shrouds were fastened to the sides of the vessel by chainplates to which the deadeyes were connected.

THE GAM

Signals. These gave information from the vessel to the boats such as where the whales were, in what direction they were travelling, and so on. The signals were communicated by means of flags and balls set in the rigging. Each whaler had its own predetermined set of signals which, it was hoped, could not be interpreted by another vessel.

Slew. To sweep around, to turn suddenly.

Sloop. A fore-and-aft rigged vessel with only one mast. Most whaling sloops had one or two squaresails above the mainsail.

Slush. Melted grease, or fat. Drippings.

Sound. To go down. Often a whale would sound instead of running when it had been struck by the harpoon. Also, *Sound* was the order to heave the lead to determine the depth of water under the vessel.

Spade. The spade was a tool resembling a garden spade with a very sharp edge by means of which a hole could be cut in the head of a dead whale. A rope was then passed through the hole so that the whale could be towed by the vessel.

Spanker. The fore-and-aft sail on a vessel's mizzenmast.

Specialist. See *Shipkeepers.*

Spout. The vapor from a whale's blow hole which arose into the air with the breath that a whale expelled after coming up from a dive. The species of whale could usually be determined by the spout.

Square Sails. Rectangular sails that were supported by horizontal spars called yards. First, and lowest were the courses. Above them were the topsails. On later vessels the topsails were divided into upper and lower topsails for easier handling. Above the topsails were the topgallant sails. Above the topgallant sails were the royals. On early whalers these were the only square sails. But on some later vessels there were skysails above the royals.

Standing Gear. Ropes or cables which held the masts and rigging in place and which did not move.

Stand Out. To sail out of a harbor.

Stand Up. The order for the boatsteerer to get ready to strike the whale. And also at that order, if the men in the thwarts had been using paddles they shipped them and took the oars to be ready to back away from the whale when he felt the harpoon.

Start the Anchor. To break it loose from the bottom.

Staunch. Usually pronounced *Stanch.* Meaning sound or shipshape.

GLOSSARY

Stays. The standing grear that gave fore and aft support to the masts. Triangular sails could be set on most of the stays.

Steerage. The space in the after part of the vessel where the rudder post came through the lower deck, and where the steering gear that connected with the wheel on deck were located. The boatsteerers lived in the steerage. It was a cramped place and noisy from the creaking and clacking of thr steering gear. But even so, it was better than the fo'c'sle.

Stem. The most forward part of the hull of a boat or vessel.

Stern. The after part of a boat or vessel's hull.

Stern All. The order for the oarsmen to push the boat astern to get out of the way of the whale after it had been struck.

Steward. The steward was in charge of the cabin and saw to the well-being of the master and his mates. He kept the place clean, set the table and brought the food from the galley. On some vessels the steward had a cabin boy to help him.

Stove. A hole or break in the hull of a boat or vessel. As *a stove boat*.

Stuns'l booms. Short yards extending from the yards to hold the stuns'ls.

Studding Sails (Stuns'ls). Small sails extending out from the regular square sails. They were used in light winds to give extra sail area.

Tack. To change the course of a vessel when beating to windward. Tacking brought the wind to the other side of a fore-and-aft sail or reversed the position of a square sail.

Tar. Tar or pitch was used on much of the rigging. Sailors were often called tars.

Tarpaulin. A tarred or waterproofed piece of canvas.

Taut. Tight or set up hard.

Thole Pins. Pins whittled from hard wood, usually white oak or ash. They were set in holes in the gunnel in pairs and were the oarlocks. They were used until the metal oarlock came into general use, perhaps about 1870.

Thwarts. Transverse seats on which rowers sat.

Topsail Schooner. A schooner with two, sometimes only one square sail set on the foremast above the foresail. Most whaling schooners were topsail schooners.

Trim. To trim the sails so that they are properly set for the course the vessel was on. Also to trim the boat so that the weight in it is properly distributed.

Tryworks. The furnace in which the blubber was tried—cooked or fried—to render, or extract the oil. It consisted of a brick platform on the foredeck and a brick firebox over which there were two huge iron kettles (trypots). The blubber was sliced or minced before it was put into the pots. The fire was started with from the cook's supply, but after it was going, it was fed with pieces of the blubber from which the oil had been extracted. The oil was bailed from the pots into large pans to cool before it was put into the casks.

Tub. A shallow tub in which the line attached to the harpoon was coiled. The coiling was done very carefully so that there was no danger of the line kinking.

Tusks. What the whalemen called the sperm whale's teeth.

Underweigh (Underway). The anchor is catted, some sails are set. And the vessel is beginning to move.

Waif. A small flag, red or black, on a short pole which was waved to let the vessel know that the whale was dead, and to come down to them. Fishermen also used a floating, anchored waif to indicate where the fish seemed to be most plentiful.

Waist. The central deck area of a vessel.

Watch. The crew was divided into two watches, one on duty, the other free.

Wear. To change the direction of the wind on the sails when going downwind. The term applies only to square-rigged vessels. Fore-and-aft rigged vessels achieved the same thing by jibing.

Weather Side. The side of the vessel facing the wind.

Weigh Anchor. To bring the anchor up.

Wet Line. The order to pour water on the line in the tub to prevent it being hurt by friction as it turned around the *loggerhead*.

Whaleboat. A graceful double-ended boat of very light lap-streak construction, about twenty-five feet long and six feet wide. Most whaleships after about 1840 carried five boats, three on the port and two on the starboard side. A brig might carry three boats, a sloop two. It was always from the whaleboats that the whales were attacked. There were five rowing oars in a whaleboat. These were: The *boatsteerer's oar;* this was the forward oar on the starboard side. When the boat header called "stand up," the boatsteerer shipped his oar and took the harpoon. *Bow oar;* this was the forward oar on the port side (really the second oar.) The *midship oar;* this was the longest rowing oar and usually pulled by the strongest man in the boat. *Tub oar;* the second oar on the port side. The *stern oar;* the third oar on the starboard side was the lightest oar and pulled by the smallest man in the boat. The *steering oar;* this oar was more than twice as long as the longest rowing oar. It was handled by

GLOSSARY

the boatheader before the whale was struck and when the whale was fast, by the boatsteerer. With that long oar the boatheader or the boatsteerer could actually swing the boat around as well as steer it.

Windlass. Used on smaller vessels to do the same work as the capstan. It had a horizontal cylinder and was turned by handspikes.

With the Sun. From left to right. A line was always coiled with the sun.

Wreckers. See "Shipwreck on Long Island Shore."

Yards. The spars from which the square sails were set.

REPOSITORIES

Where the logbooks and journals cited in this work may be found.

Ship *Abraham Barker* – 1871
John Hay Library, Brown University, Providence, RI

Bark *Andrew Hicks* – 1879. This journal probably lost.

Letter Of Marque *Brig Argus* –1813
Peabody Museum, Salem

Bark *Benjamin Cummings* – 1866
New Bedford Whaling Museum New Bedford

Ship *Brewster* – 1860
Peter Folger Museum, Nantucket

Broadsides, "Tarpaulin Jacket"
Providence Public Library

Bark *Catalpa*– 1856
Providence Public Library

Ship *Catawba*– 1852
Peter Folger Museum, Nantucket

Bark *Champion* – 1842
Houghton Library, Harvard University

Ship *Charles and Edward* – 1858
New Bedford Public Library

Ship *Citizen* – 1844
Peter Folger Museum, Nantucket

Ship *Clarkson* – 1842
Peter Folger Museum, Nantucket

REPOSITORIES

Ship *Clifford Wayne* – 1855
Peter Folger Museum, Nantucket

Ship *Condor* – 1832
New Bedford Whaling Museum

Ship *Cortes* – 1847
New Bedford Public Library

Ship *Courier* – 1842
Dukes County Historical Society, Edgartown

Ship *Dartmouth* – 1836
Providence Public Library

Sloop *Dolphin* – 1790
Peter Folger Museum, Nantucket

Ship *Edward* – 1849
Peter Folger Museum, Nantucket

Ship *Edward Carey* – 1854
Peter Folger Museum, Nantucket

Ship *Eliza Adams* – 1879
Providence Public Library

Ship *Elizabeth* – 1844
Kendall Whaling Museum, Sharon, MA

Ship *Euphrasia* – 1849
Peabody Museum, Salem

Ship *Frances Henrietta* – 1835
Barbara Johnson collection, Nantucket

Ship *Governor Carver* – 1854
Peter Folger Museum, Nantucket

Ship *Galaxy* – 1827
Peabody Museum, Salem

Ship *Hillman* – 1854
New Bedford Whaling Museum

Ship *Jasper* – 1839
Providence Public Library

THE GAM

Ship *Java* – 1854
Kendall Whaling Museum, Sharon, MA

Ship *Jireh Perry* – 1869
Dukes County Historical Society, Edgartown

Bark *John Dawson* – 1860
Houghton Library, Harvard University

Bark *Josephine* – 1891
Kendall Whaling Museum, Sharon, MA

Ship *Leonidas* – 1856
Kendall Whaling Museum, Sharon, MA

Ship *L.C. Richmond* – 1834
Essex Institute, Salem

Ship *Lexington* – 1853
Peter Folger Museum, Nantucket

Ship *Lotos* – 1833
Essex Institute, Salem

Ship *Lydia* – 1855
Kendall Whaling Museum, Sharon, MA

Bark *Mattapoisett* – 1852
Peter Folger Museum, Nantucket

Bark *Midas* – 1861
Dukes County Historical Society, Edgartown

Ship *Minerva Smythe* – 1852
Dukes County Historical Society, Edgartown

Bark *Morning Light* – 1861
Dukes County Historical Society, Edgartown

Ship *Nauticon* – 1848
Peter Folger Museum, Nantucket

Sloop *Nellie* – 1769
New Bedford Whaling Museum

Bark *Pacific* – 1870
Peter Folger Museum, Nantucket

REPOSITORIES

Bark *Paulina* – 1852
Dukes County Historical Society, Edgartown
see the Minerva Smythe journal

Brig *Pavilion* – 1858
Dukes County Historical Society, Edgartown

Ship *Pocohontas* – 1832
Peter Folger Museum, Nantucket

Ship *Polly* – 1794
Kendall Whaling Museum, Sharon, MA

Bark *Roscius* –1858
New Bedford Whaling Museum

Ship *Sharon* – 1845
New Bedford Whaling Museum

Bark *Stella* – 1860
New Bedford Whaling Museum

Bark *Sunbeam* – 1860
New Bedford Whaling Museum

Ship *Three Brothers* – 1851
International Marine Archives, Nantucket

Ship *Trident* – 1846
Providence Public Library

Ship *Uncus* – 1843
Providence Public Library

Bark *Vernon* –1854
Dukes County Historical Society, Edgartown

Ship *Virginia* – 1843
Kendall Whaling Museum, Sharon, MA

Ship *Walter Scott* — 1844
International Marine Archives, Nantucket

Ship *Young Phoenix* – 1844
New Bedford Public Library

BIBLIOGRAPHY

Abrahams, Roger D. *A Singer and Her Songs, Almeda Riddle's Book of Ballads*, Louisiana State University Press, Baton Rouge, La., 1970

Allen, Everett S. *Children of the Light, The Rise and Fall of New Bedford Whaling*, Little Brown and Company, Boston — Toronto, 1973

Anderson, Hugh. *Colonial Ballads*, F. W. Sheshire, Melbourne, Canberra, Sydney, 1955, reprint, 1962.

The Antihipnotic Songster. T. Town and S. Merritt, Philadelphia, 1818.

Arnold, Byron. *Folksongs of Alabama*, University of Alabama Press, University, Alabama, 1959.

Ashley, Clifford. *The Yankee Whaler*, Houghton Mifflin Company, Boston, 1926.

Ashton, John. *Modern Street Ballads*, Chitto & Windus, London, 1888.

Banks, Charles Edward. *The History of Martha's Vineyard*, 3 Vols. George H. Dean, Boston, 1911, reprint Dukes County Historical Society, Edgartown, 1966.

Baring-Gould, Sabine, and Gordon Hitchcock. *Folk Songs Of The West Country*, David & Charles, London, North Pomfret, Vermont, Vancouver, 1974.

Baring-Gould, S. and Cecil J. Sharp. *English Folk-Songs for Schools*, J. Curwen & Sons, London, n.d. (1906)

Baring-Gould, S. and H. Fleetwood Sheppard. *A Garland Of Country Song*, Methuen, London, 1895, reprint, Norwood Editions, Norwood, Pa., 1973,

Barrett, Wm. Alexr. *English Folk Songs*, Novello and Co., London, n.d. (1891), reprint, Norwood Editions, Darby, PA., 1973.

Barry, Phillips. *The Maine Woods Songster*, The Powell Printing Company, Cambridge, Massachusetts, 1939.

Beck, Horace P. *The Folklore of Maine*, J. B. Lippincott Company, Philadelphia and New York, 1957.

BIBLIOGRAPHY

Belden, H. M. *Ballads And Songs Collected By The Missouri Folklore Society*, The University Of Missouri Studies, Columbia, Missouri, 1940, reprint, 1955.

Bockstoce, John R. *Steam Whaling in the Western Arctic*, published at the New Bedford Whaling Museum by the Old Dartmouth Historical Society, New Bedford, Mass., 1977.

Bodfish, Captain Hartson H. and Joseph C. Allen *Chasing The Bowhead*, Harvard University Press, Cambridge, Mass., 1936.

The Book of Navy Songs, (The Trident Society) Doubleday, Doran & Company, Inc., Garden City, N.Y., 1930.

The Book of Popular Songs, G. G. Evans, Philadelphia, 1860.

Botkin, B. A. *The American Play-Party Song*, University Studies of the University of Nebraska, 1937, reprint, Frederick Ungar Publishing Co., New York, 1963.

Broadwood, Lucy E. *English Traditional Songs And Carols*, Boosey & Co., London, 1908, reprint, E.P. Publishing, Limited, East Ardsley, Eng. and Rowman and Littlefield, Totowa, N. J., 1974.

Broadwood, Lucy E. and J. A. Fuller Maitland. *English Country Songs*, J.B. Cramer and Co., London, n.d. (1910?), Press, London, 1893.

English County Songs, also The Leadenhall Press, London, 1893.

The Frank C. Brown Collection Of North Carolina Folklore, Vol. 5, Duke University Press, Durham, North Carolina, 1962.

Browne, J. Ross. *Etchings of A Whaling Cruise*, Harper Brothers, Publishers, New York, 1846.

Brunnings, Florence E. *Folk Song Index,* Garland Publishing Co., NY and London 1981

Buchan, Norman and Peter Hall. *The Scottish Folksinger*, Collins, London and Glasgow, 1973.

Buchan, Peter. *Gleanings of Scarce Old Ballads*, Peterhead, London, 1825, D. Wyllie & Son, Peternead, 1891, reprint, Norwood Editions, Norwood, Pa., 1974.

Bulletin of the Folksong Society of The Northeast, Cambridge, Massachusetts, 1931–1937, reprint, The American Folklore Society, Philadelphia, 1960.

Cazden, Norman. *The Abelard Folk Song Book*, Abelard Schuman, New York & London, 1958.

Chappell, William. *Popular Music of the Olden Time, 2 Vols.* Chappell and Co., London, 1855, reprint, Dover Publications, New York, 1965.

Cheever, Rev. Henry T. *The Whale and His Captors*, Harper and Brothers, Publishers, New York, 1850.

Child, Francis James. *The English And Scottish Popular Ballads*, 5 Vols., Houghton, Mifflin and Company, Boston, 1882–1898, reprint, Dover Publications, New York, 1965.

The Clown's Songster, Robert M. DeWitt, New York, 1871.

Coffin, Tristram. *The British Traditional Ballad in North America*, The American Folklore Society, Philadelphia, 1950, reprint, 1963.

Cohen, Mike. *101 Plus 5 Folk Songs for Camp*. Oak Publications, New York, n.d. (1974?).

Colcord, Joanna C. *Songs Of American Sailormen*, W. W. Norton & Company, Inc., New York, 1938, first printed as Roll And Go, Bobbs-Merrill Company, Indianapolis, 1924.

Cornell, E. C. *Eighty Years Ashore and Afloat*, Andrew F. Graves, Boston, 1873.

Cox, John Harrington. *Folk-Songs of the South*, Harvard University Press, Cambridge, Mass., 1925, reprint, Folklore Associates, Inc. Hatboro, PA., 1963.

Cox, John Harrington. *Traditional Ballads and Folk-Songs Mainly From West Virginia*, first published in mimeograph, 1939, reprint, The American Folklore Society, Philadelphia, 1964.

Creighton, Helen. *Folksongs from Southern New Brunswick*, National Museums of Canada, Ottawa, 1971.

Creighton, Helen. *Maritime Folk Songs*, Ryerson Press, Toronto, 1961.

Creighton, Helen. *Songs and Ballads from Nova* Scotia, J. M. Dent & Sons Limited, Toronto & Vancouver, 1933.

Creighton, Helen and Doreen H. Senior. *Traditional Songs from Nova Scotia*, The Ryerson Press, Toronto, 1950.

Davis, William. *Nimrod of the Sea*, Harper & Brothers, Publishers, New York, 1874.

Dean, Michael Cassius. Flying Cloud, Quick-print, Virginia, Minn., 1922, reprint, Norwood Editions, Norwood, Pa., 1973.

Dibdin, T. *Songs of Charles Dibdin*, Henry G. Bohn, London, 1864.

Dixon, James Henry. *Ancient Poems, Ballads and Songs Of The Peasantry of England*, The Percy Society, London, 1846, reprint, EP Publishing Limited, East Ardsley, Yorkshire, 1973.

BIBLIOGRAPHY

Doerflinger, William Main. *Shantymen and Shantyboys*, The Macmillan Company, New York, 1951.

Downs, Olin and Elie Siegmeister. *A Treasury of American Song*, Howell, Soskin & Co., New York, 1940.

Duffy, John, Ed. *Early Vermont Broadsides*, University Press of New England, Hanover, NH, 1975.

Dunston, Ralph. *Cornish Dialect and Folk Songs*, Ascherberg, Hopwood & Crew Ltd., London, 1972.

Eckstorm, Fannie Hardy and Mary Winslow Smyth. *Minstrelsy of Maine*, Houghton, Mifflin Company, Boston and New York, 1927, reprint, Gryphon Books, Ann Arbor, MI, 1971.

Eddy, Mary O. *Ballads and Songs from Ohio*, Mary O. Eddy, 1939, reprint, Folklore Associates, Hatboro, PA, 1964.

Finger, Charles J. *Sailor Chanties and Cowboy Songs*, Haldeman-Julius Company, Girard, Kansas, 1923, reprint, Norwood Editions, Norwood, Pa., 1974.

Firth, C. H. *Naval Songs and Ballads*, The Navy Records Society, London, 1908.

Flanders, Helen Hartness, Elizabeth Flanders Ballard, George Brown and Phillips Barry. *The New Green Mountain Songster*, Helen Hartness Flanders, 1939, reprint, Folklore Associates, Inc., Hatboro, PA, 1966.

Flanders, Helen Hartness & George Brown. *Vermont Folksongs & Ballads*, Helen Hartness Flanders, 1959, reprint, Folklore Associates, Hatboro, Pa., 1968.

Flanders, Helen Hartness and Marguerite Olney. *Ballads Migrant in New England*, Farrar, Straus and Young, New York, 1953.

Ford, Ira W. *Traditional Music in America*, E. P. Dutton &Co., New York, 1940, reprint, Folklore Associates, Inc., Hatboro, PA., 1965.

Ford, Robert. *Vagabond Songs and Ballads of Scotland, 2 Vols.*, Alexander Gardner, Paisley and London, 1899, 1901.

Fowke, Edith. *Traditional Singers and Songs From Ontario*, Folklore Associates, Inc., Hatboro, Pa, (and) Burns & MacEachern, Ltd., Don Mills, Ontario, 1965.

Fox, C. Milligan. *Songs of The Irish Harpers*, Bayley & Ferguson, London and Glasgow, 1910.

Fuson, Harvey H. *Ballads of the Kentucky Highlands*, The Mitre Press, London, 1931.

Gardner, Emelyn Elizabeth and Geraldine Jencks Chickering. *Ballads and Songs of Southern Michigan,* Emelyn Elizabeth Gardner, 1939, reprint, Folklore Associates, Inc., Hatboro, PA., 1967.

Gems of Irish Songs, Mozart Allan, Glasgow, n.d.

Gems of Scottish Song, Oliver Ditson Company, Boston, London, 1894.

The Golden Wreath, L. O. Emerson, Ed., Oliver Ditson And Company, Boston, 1857.

Gospel Hymns No. 6, The John Church Co., Cincinnati, OH, 1892.

Gospel Hymns and Sacred Songs, Bigelow & Main, New York and Chicago, 1875

Greenleaf, Elisabeth Bristol (and) Grace Yarrow Mansfield. *Ballads and Sea Songs of Newfoundland,* Harvard University Press, Cambridge, MA, 1933.

Greig, Gavin. *Folk-Song of the North-East*, The Buchan Observer, Peterhead, 1907–1911, reprint, Folklore Associates, Inc., Hatboro, PA, 1963.

Grigg's Southern and Western Songster, Grigg & Elliot, Philadelphia, 1835, reprint, Lippincott Grambo & Co., Philadelphia, 1850.

Grover, Carrie B. *A Heritage of Songs*, Gould Academy, Bethel, ME, n.d., reprint, Norwood Editions, Norwood, PA, 1973.

Hamer, Fred. *Garners Gay*, EFDS Publications, Ltd., London, 1967.

Harlow, Frederick Pease. *Chanteying Aboard American Ships*, Barre Gazette, Barre, MA, 1962.

Hart, Colonel W. H., *Miriam Coffin or the Whale-Fisherman, two Vols. in one*, C & C & H Carvell, Philadelphia, and Allen & Ticknor, Boston, 1834.

Healy, James N. *Ballads From the Pubs of Ireland*, The Mercier Press, Cork, 1965.

Heart Songs, The Chapple Publishing Company, Boston, 1909.

Hegarty, Reginald B. *Returns of Vessels Sailing from American Ports; A Continuation of Alexander Starbuck's History of the American Whale Fishery*, The Old Dartmouth Historical Society and Whaling Museum, New Bedford, 1959.

Hegarty, Reginald B. *Addendum to "Starbuck" and "Whaling Masters"* New Bedford Customs District, New Bedford Free Public Library, New Bedford, MA, 1964.

Henry, Mellinger Edward. *Folk-Songs from the Southern Highlands*, J. J. Augustin, New York, 1938.

Henry, Sam. *Songs of the People.* The Northern Constitution, Coleraine, Northern Ireland, 1923–1932.

BIBLIOGRAPHY

Hubbard, Lester A. *Ballads and Songs from Utah*, The University of Utah Press; Salt Lake City, Utah, 1961.

Hudson, Arthur Palmer. *Folksongs of Mississippi and Their Background*, University Of North Carolina Press, Chapel Hill, N.C., 1936.

Hugill, Stan. *Shanties from the Seven Seas*, Routledge & Kegan Paul, Ltd., London, 1961.

Hugill, Stan. *Shanties and Sailors' Songs*, Frederick A. Praeger, New York and Washington, 1969

Huntington, Gale. *Folksongs from Martha's Vineyard*, Northeast Folklore, VIII, Orono, Maine, 1966.

Huntington, Gale. *An Introduction to Martha's Vineyard*. The Dukes County Historical Society, Edgartown, 1974.

Huntington, Gale. *Songs the Whalemen Sang*, Barre Publishing Co., Barre, Mass., 1964, reprint, Dover Publications, 1970.

Ives, Burl. *The Burl Ives Song Book*, Ballantine Books, New York, 1953.

Ives, Burl. *Irish Songs*, Wayfarer Music Co., New York (?), 1955, reprint, Duell Sloan and Pearce, New York, n.d.

Ives, Burl. *Sea Songs*, Ballantine Books, New York, 1956.

Ives, Edward D. *Folksongs from Maine*, Northeast Folklore, VII, Orono, Maine, 1965.

Johnson, Helen Kendrick. *Our Familiar Songs and Those Who Made Them*, Henry Holt and Company, New York, 1881.

Johnson, James. *The Scots Musical Museum, six Vols.*, James Johnson, Edinburgh, 1839, reprint in two vols., Folklore Associates, Inc., Hatboro, PA, 1962.

Jolliffe, Maureen. *The Third Book of Irish Ballads*, The Mercier Press, Cork, 1970.

The Jovial Songster II, S. Jenks, Dedham, MA, 1806.

Joyce, P.W. *Old Irish Folk Music And Songs*, Longmans, Green and Co., New York, 1909, reprint, Cooper Square Publishers, Inc., New York, 1965.

Karpeles, Maud. *Folk Songs from Newfoundland*, Archon Books, Hamden, CT, 1970.

Kenedy, P. J. *The Universal Irish Song Book*, P. J Kenedy, New York, 1890.

Kennedy, Peter. *Folksongs of Britain and Ireland*, Schirmer Books, New York, 1975.

Kidson, Frank. *A Garland of English Folk Songs*, Ascherberg, Hopwood and Carew, (London) n.d.. (1926).

Kidson, Frank. *Traditional Tunes*, Chas. Taphouse & Son, Oxford, 1891.

Kidson, Frank and Ethel Kidson, Ed. *English Peasant Songs*, London, 1929.

Kincaid, Bradley. *My Favorite Mountain Ballads and Old-Time Songs*, Radio Station WLS, Chicago, 1928.

Kinscella, Hazel Gertrude. *Folk Songs and Fiddle Tunes of the U.S.A.*, Carl Fischer, Inc., New York, 1959.

Lahey, John. *Australian Favorite Ballads*, Oak Publications, New York, 1965.

Laws, G. Malcolm. *American Balladry from British Broadsides*, The American Folklore Society, Philadelphia, 1957.

Laws, G. Malcolm. *Native American Balladry*, The American Folklore Society, Philadelphia, 1964.

Leach, MacEdward. *Folk Ballads & Songs of the Lower Labrador Coast*, National Museum Of Canada, Ottawa, 1965.

Leavitt, John F. *The Charles W. Morgan*, The Marine Historical Association, Inc., Mystic, CT, 1973.

Leavitt, John F. *Wake of the Coasters*, The Marine Historical Association, Inc., Mystic, CT 1970.

Lomax, John A. *Cowboy Songs and Other Frontier Ballads*, The Macmillan Company, New York, 1930.

Lomax, John A. and Alan Lomax. *American Ballads and Folk Songs*, The Macmillan Company, New York, 1934.

Lomax, John A. and Alan Lomax. *Our Singing Country*, The Macmillan Company, New York 1941.

MacKenzie, W. Roy. *Ballads and Sea Songs from Nova Scotia*, Harvard College, Cambridge, MA, 1928, reprint, Folklore Associates, Inc., Hatboro, PA, 1963.

Macy, Captain W. H. *There She Blows*, Lee & Shephard, Publishers, Boston, 1877.

Manifold, J. S. *The Penguin Australian Song Book*, Penguin Books, Ltd., Hammondsworth, Baltimore, Ringwood, 1964.

Manny, Louise and James Reginald Wilson. *Songs of Miramichi*, Brunswick Press, Fredericton, NB, 1970.

Mayhew, Eleanor Ransom. *Martha's Vineyard a Short History* (and) *a Guide*, Dukes County Historical Society, Edgartown, MA, 1956, reprint, 1966.

Melville, Herman. *Moby Dick*, Richard Bentley, London, 1851. Numerous later editions.

BIBLIOGRAPHY

Meredith, John and Hugh Anderson. *Folk Songs of Australia*, Ure Smith, Sydney and London, 1967.

Miller, Pamela A. *And the Whale is Ours*, The Kendall Whaling Museum, Sharon, MA, 1979.

The Mohawk Minstrel's Magazine of Favorite Songs and Ballads, F. Day & Hunter, London, 1878.

Moore, Ethel and Chauncy O. Moore. *Ballads and Folk Songs of The Southwest*, University Of Oklahoma Press, Norman, Oklahoma, 1964.

Munch, Peter A. *The Song Tradition of Tristan da Cunha*, Indiana University Research Center, Bloomington, IN, 1970 .

O'Conor, Manus. *Irish Com-All-Ye's*, Manus O'Conor, New York, 1901.

O Lochlainn, Colm. *Irish Street Ballads*, The Three Candles, Limited, Dublin, 1939, reprint, 1962.

O Lochlainn, Colm. *More Irish Street Ballads*, The Three Candles, Dublin, 1965.

O'Shaughnessy, Patrick. *Twenty-One Lincolnshire Songs*, London, 1968.

Owens, William A. *Texas Folk Songs*, The Texas Folklore Society, Unversity Press In Dallas, Dallas, TX, 1950.

Palmet, Roy. *Songs of the Midlands*, EP Publishing Limited. East Ardsley, Yorkshire, 1972.

Palmer, Roy. *The Valiant Sailor*, Cambridge University Press, Cambridge, 1973.

Peacock, Kenneth. *Songs of the Newfoundland Outports*, National Museum Of Canada, Ottawa, 1965

Pentecostal Hymns, Hope Publishing Co., Chicago, 1898.

Peters, Harry B. *Folk Songs out of Wisconsin*, The State Historical Society of Wisconsin, Madison, Wisconsin, 1977.

Purslow, Frank. *The Constant Lovers, More English Folksongs from The Hammond & Gardiner Mss.*, E.F.D.S. Publications, Ltd., London 1972

Purslow, Frank. *The Foggy Dew, More English Folk Songs from The Hammond & Gardiner Mss.*, E.F.D.S. Publications, Ltd., London, 1974.

Purslow, Frank. *Marrow Bones, English Folk Songs from The Hammond & Gardiner Mss.*, E.F.D.S. Publications, Ltd., London, 1965.

Purslow, Frank. *The Wanton Seed, More English Folk Songs from The Hammond And Gardiner Mss.*, E.F.D.S. Publications, Ltd., London, 1968.

Ramsey, Allan. *The Tea-Table Miscellany, 15th Edition*, Robert Duncan, Glasgow, 1768.

Ranson, Joseph. *Songs of the Wexford Coast*, Richmond Bros., Enniscorthy, 1948, reprint, Norwood Editions, Norwood, Pa., 1973.

Reddall, Henry Frederick. *Songs That Never Die*, Joseph McDonough, Albany, 1894.

Reeves, James. *The Everlasting Circle, from the mss. of S. Baring-Gould*, H.E.D., "Hammond and George B. Gardiner, Heinmann, London. Melbourne, Toronto, 1960.

Reeves, James. *The Idiom of the People*, James Reeves, London (?) 1958, reprint, W. W. Norton & Company, New York, 1965.

Reynolds Leaflet, Reynolds Publishing Co., New Bedford, MA, n.d., c.1920 (?)

Richardson, Ethel Park. *American Mountain Songs*, Greenburg Publisher, New York, 1927, reprint, 1955.

Rickaby, Franz. *Ballads and Songs of The Shanty-Boy*, Harvard University Press, Cambridge, MA, 1926.

Ricketson, Daniel. *The History of New Bedford*, B. Lindsey, Printer, New Bedford, MA, 1858.

Robinson, Carson J. *Country Songs*, Triangle Music Co., NY, 1928.

St. John, Hector (de Creveceur). *Letters from An American Farmer*, Thomas Davies, London, 1783. Numerous later editions,

Sandburg, Carl. *The American Songbag*, Harcourt Brace & Company, New York, 1927.

Scarborough, Dorothy. *A Song Catcher in the Southern Mountains*, Columbia University Press, New York, 1937, reprint, AMS Press, Inc., New York, 1966.

The Scottish Students' Song Book, Bayley & Ferguson, London and Glasgow, 1891.

Sharp, Cecil J. *English County Folk Songs, in five Vols.*, 1908–1912, .in one Vol., 1961, Novello and Company Limited, London, 1961.

Sharp, Cecil J. *English Folk Songs, 2 Vols.*, Novello and Company Limited, London, 1920, reprint in one Vol., 1959.

Sharp, Cecil J. in two Vols., London, 1960. *English Folk Songs from the Southern Appalachians*, 1917, two Vols. in one, Oxford University Press, London, 1960.

Sharp, Cecil J. *One Hundred English Folksongs*, Oliver Ditson Company, Philadelphia, 1916.

Shay, Frank. *Barroom Ballads*, The Macaulay Company, New York (?), 1927; reprint, Dover Publications, New York, 1961.

BIBLIOGRAPHY

Shay, Frank. *Drawn From the Wood*, The Macaulay Company, New York, 1929.

Shay, Frank. *Iron Men & Wooden Ships*, Doubleday, Page & Company, Garden City, NY, 1924.

Sherman, Stuart C. *The Voice of the Whaleman*, Providence Public Library, Providence, RI, 1965.

Shoemaker, Henry W. *Mountain Minstrelsy of Pennsylvania*, Newman F. McGirr, Philadelphia, PA, 1931.

The Silver Chord. Oliver Ditson & Company, Boston, 1862.

Smith, C. Fox. *A Book of Shanties*, Methuen & Co., Ltd., London, 1927.

Smith, Laura Alexandrine. *The Music of the Waters*, Kegan Paul, Trench & Co., London, 1888, reprint, Singing Tree Press, Detroit, 1969.

Songs for Service. The Rodeheaver Gospel Music Co., Philadelphia, PA, n.d.

Songs of Joy and Gladness, Donald Gill & Co., Boston, n.d. (c. 1885).

Songs of Redemption, The Christian Witness Co., Boston, Mass., 1899.

Songs that Lincoln Loved, John Lair, Ed., Duell Sloan And Pearce, New York, and Little, Brown and Company, Boston, MA, 1954.

Spaeth, Sigmund. *A History of Popular Music in America*, Random House, New York, 1948.

Spaeth, Sigmund. *Read 'Em and Weep*, Doubleday, Page & Company, Garden City, NY, 1927.

Spaeth, Sigmund. *Weep Some More My Lady*, Doubleday, Page & Company Garden City, NY, 1927.

Sparling, H. Halliday. *Irish Minstrelsy*, Walter Scott, London, 1888.

Stackpole, Edouard. *The Sea Hunters*, J. B. Lippincott Company, Philadelphia, PA, 1953.

Starbuck, Alexander. *History of the American Whale Fishery*, Self Published, Waltham, MA 1878.

Stone, Christopher. *Sea Songs and Ballads*, The Clarendon Press, Oxford, 1906.

Stubbs, Ken. *The Life of Man*, EFDS Publications, Ltd., London, 1970.

Thompson, Harold W. *Body, Boots & Britches*, J. B. Lippincott Company, New York, 1939, reprint, Dover Publications, Inc., New York, 1962.

Thompson, Harold W. *A Pioneer Songster*, Cornell University Press, Ithaca, N.Y., 1958.

Tilton, Captain George Fred. *Cap'n George Fred*, Doubleday, Doran and Company, Garden City, NY, 1927, reprint, Dukes County Historical Society, Edgartown, MA, 1969.

Tom Thumb A Sheaf of Songs, Samuel Booth, New York, 1874.

Vincent, Elmore. *Lumberjack Songs*, M.M. Cole Pub. Co., Chicago, 1932.

Walton's 132 Best Irish Songs and Ballads, Walton's Musical Instrument Galleries, Ltd., Dublin, n.d.

Walton's New Treasury of Irish Songs and Ballads, two parts, Walton's Musical Instrument Galleries, Duplin, 1966, 1968.

Wells, Evelyn Kendrick. *The Ballad Tree*, The Ronald Press Company, New York, 1950.

West, Captain Ellsworth Luce, as told to Eleanor Ransom Mayhew, *Captain's Papers*, Barre Publishers, Barre, Mass. 1965.

Wetmore, Susannah and Marshall Bartholomew. *Mountain Songs of North Carolina*, G. Schirmer, Inc., New York, 1926.

Whall, W. B. *Sea Songs and Shanties*, 5th edition, James Brown & Son, Glasgow, 19?6.

Whiting, Emma Mayhew and Henry Beetle Hough. *Whaling Wives*, Houghton, Mifflin Company, Cambridge, MA, 1953, reprint, Dukes County Historical Society, Edgartown, MA., 1965.

Wier, Albert E. *The Book of a Thousand Songs*, Mumil Publishing Co., New York, 1918.

Wier, Albert E. *Songs of the Sunny South*, D. Appleton and Company, New York, 1929.

Williams, Alfred. *Folk Songs of the Upper Thames*, Duckworth & Co., London, 1923.

Williams, Alfred M., *Studies in Folk-Song and Popular Poetry*, Houghton, Mifflin and Company, Boston and New York, 1894.

Williams, R. Vaughan and A. L. Lloyd, *The Penguin Book of English Folk Songs*, Penguin Books, Limited, Hammondsworth, Middlesex, 1959.

Windows of Heaven, Hall Mack Co., Philadelphia, PA, 1900.

Winn, Cyril. *Some Less Known Folk-Songs, 2 Vols.*, Novello and Company, London, n.d. (1930).

Winona Hymns, The Westminster Press, Philadelphia, PA, 1906.

Woodgate, Leslie. *The Penguin Song Book*, Hammondsworth, 1951, reprint, 1958.

BIBLIOGRAPHY

Wyld, Lionel D. *Low Bridge—Folklore and the Erie Canal*, Syracuse University Press, Syracuse, N.Y., 1962, reprint, 1977.

Wyman, Loraine. *Lonesome Tunes*, The H. W. Gray Company, New York, 1916

Wyman, Loraine. Twenty Kentucky Mountain Songs, Oliver Ditson Co., Boston, 1920.

The following references are for the Fiddle Tunes:

Bayard, Samuel Preston. *Hill Country Tunes*, American Folklore Society, Philadelphia, PA, 1944.

Deville, Paul and Maurice Gould. *The Violin Player's Pastime*, Carl Fisher, New York, n.d. (c. 1900).

Howe's Musicians' Omnibus, Elias Howe, Boston, 1863.

Robbins Collection of Jigs, Reels and Country Dances, Robbins Music Corp., New York, 1933.

Robertson, James Stewart. *The Athol Collection of the Dance Music Of Scotland*, Robertson, Edinburgh, 1884.

Shattuck, A., *A. Shattuck's Book*, a manuscript collection of fiddle tunes in the Library of Congress, Washington, D.C., 1801.

INDEX OF SONG TITLES

A Brand Fire New Whaling Song	2
Across The Fields of Barley	228
All's Well	288
Annie of the Vale	300
Answer to Ben Bolt, The	272
Bark Roscius Outward Bound	65
Barney Buntline	105
Barque Ohio Outward Bound 1850	64
Belle of Baltimore, The	306
Belle of the Mohawk Vale, The	309
Ben Backstay's Warning	111
Ben Bolt	272
Bering Sea	113
Bill Grimes	228
Black-Eyed Susan	165
Blow Ye Winds	24
Boatswain's Call, The	108
Bold Privateer, The	123
Bold William Taylor	156
Bonnie Annie Laurie	263
Brave Boys	18
Brennan on the Moor	202
Bruce's Address to His Army	268
Buccaneer's Bride, The	133
Bury the Dead	118
Butcher Boy, The	230
Calm	55
Captain Bunker	27
Captain Calls All Hands, The	162
Caroline and Young Sailor Bold	159

INDEX OF SONG TITLES

Chicago	336
Chile Girls, The	163
City of Columbus, The	98
Cleansing Fountain, The	354
Columbia the Gem of the Ocean	310
Come All That Sail From Edgartown	40
Constant Lovers	184
Cruiskeen Lawn	227
Darling Nellie Gray	303
Dashing Through the Snow	277
Deep Deep Sea, The	126
Diego's Bold Shores	20
Do They Miss Me At Home	294
Drinking Gin	343
Drownded Miner, The	128
Drunken Fool, The	195
Eastbound Train, The	256
Ella Rhee	302
Ellen the Fair	218
Female Cabin Boy, The	174
Female Sailor, The	176
Fisherman's Girl, A	241
Floating Home, A	146
Flower Girl, The	244
Flying Dutchman, The	180
Free Thinkers Reasons for Refusing to Preach	317
Gentle Annie	301
Golden Slippers	255
Good Old Jeff	305
Grave of Ben Bolt, The	273
Green Beds	170
Hallelujah I'm a Bum	358
Hardtack and A Half, A	56
Heave Away	44
Her Bright Smile Haunts Me Still	290
High Germany	192
Highland Mary	262
Highwayman, The	225
Home Again	289

Hurrah For the Rover and His Beautiful Lass	132
I'll Taste No More the Poisonous Cup	338
Ill-Fated Steamer, The	97
Jessie the Flower of Dunblane	266
Jingle Bells	276
Kathleen Mavourneen	252
Lady Franklin's Lament for her Husband	178
Lady's Answer, A	258
Lament of the Irish Emigrant, The	250
Lass of Maui, The	48
Letter Edged In Black, The	260
Lily Dale	291
Lily of Lake Champlain, The	328
Lily of the West, The	219
Lines to Delia	312
Little Brown Jug	212
Little Nell of Narragansett Bay	253
Lone Starry Flower, The	278
Long Long Ago	293
Lord Lovel	236
Loss of the Albion, The	91
Maggy By My Side	282
Maid of Erin, The	238
Mariner's Grave, The	127
Mariner's Hymn, The	355
Mariner's Life, The	150
Marm Haucket's Garden	151
Mary on the Wild Moor	239
Meet Me by Moonlight	296
Men Are Like Ships	359
Murphy Delany	334
My Highland Home	265
My Love	280
My Willie's on the Dark Blue Sea	173
Nantucket Skipper, The	151
Nassau Homeward Bound, The	47
Nautical Philosophy	106
Nauticle Filosophy	105
Ned Bolton	139

INDEX OF SONG TITLES

Nellie	287
Never Change the Old Love for the New	224
New Song	216
New Song Maide, A	94
Nightingale, The	233
Noble Ship *Catalpa*, The	341
Norah O'Neal	248
Ocean King, The	103
Oh Captain, Captain Tell Me True	172
Old Bog Hole, The	249
Old Oaken Bucket, The	71
Old Song, An	235
On the Green Mossy Banks of the Lea	221
Our Goodman	195
Outward Bound	69
Parody on Ben Bolt	274
Pirate Lover, The	136
Pirate of the Isle, The	138
Piscataquag and The Edinburgh	367
Pity the Poor Seaman	131
Poor Little Joe	243
Pretty Maid of Mohe, The	51
Pretty Polly	168
Psalm of Life, A	315
Raging Canal, The	214
Revive Us Again	357
Rob Roy McGregor-O	264
Rolling Down To Old Maui	53
Rolling Home	134
Rose That All are Praising, The	279
Sabbath Morning Nov. 13th 1852	356
Sailing Home from England	135
Sailor Boy, The	172
Sailor, The	110
Sailor's Farewell, The	125
Sailor's Grave, The	121
Sailor's Return, The	170
Sea Girt Isle, The	75
Serenade Song	132

THE GAM

Ships In the Ocean	115
Shipwreck Near Gay Head, January 14, 1782	87
Shipwreck on Long Island Shore	101
Silk Merchant's Daughter, The	184
Sinner Saved, A	363
Song Concerning Love, A	162
Song for a Wedding, A	323
Song of Love, A	192
Song of Old	330
Song of the Nantucket Mariner	32
Song of the Ship Vineyard	62
Song of Whaling, A	33
Song to Captain S.D. Oliver	67
Soon Thy Bark Must Leave Our Harbor	31
Spanish Ladies	144
Speaking Flower, The	333
Sperm Whale Song, The	21
Stepmother, The	246
Stove Boat, A	36
Suffolk Miracle, The	198
Sweet America	28
Sweet Nellie Brown	285
Sweet William	182
Tarpaulin Jacket	148
Tarry Trousers, The	168
Ten Thousand Miles Away	194
The Greenland Whale	18
The Sperm Whaling Song	23
There She Blows	45
Tin Swankey Pot, The	43
Uncle Sam and Johnny Bull	205
Under Way	142
Unmooring....	108
Up Anchor For Home Boys	117
Vacant Chair, The	308
Virgin Nineteen Years Old, The	318
Virtuous Wife: A New Song, The	345
Voyage On New Holland, A	76
Watcher, The	299

INDEX OF SONG TITLES

Water Lue	340
We Met 'Twas in a Crowd	207
Weaver, The	210
Wedlock	325
Whaler's Song	30
Whaling Song, A	15
Whaling Voyage, The	58
When the Roll is Called up Yonder	360
When the Roses Were in Bloom	297
White Squall, The	120
Why Art Thou Not Here	284
Will You Be Found Among the Wheat	362
William and Nancy	182
William Taylor	153
Willie Brennan	202
Wind of the Winter's Night	286
Winds That Blew 'Cross the Wild Moor, The	239
Woman's Rights I	320
Woman's Rights II	321
Wonderful Whalers, The	72
Work for Jesus	361
Wounded Whale, The	21
Wreck of the City of Columbus I, The	96
Wreck of the City of Columbus II, The	97
Wreck of the City of Columbus III, The	98

www.ingramcontent.com/pod-product-compliance
Lightning Source LLC
Chambersburg PA
CBHW060229240426
43671CB00016B/2890